A Postcolonial Theology of Life

A Postcolonial Theology of Life

Planetarity East and West

Jea Sophia Oh

Sopher Press
Upland, California

© 2011 Sopher Press
Please direct inquiries to info@sopherpress.com.
ISBN 978-1-935946-01-4

To Catherine Keller, my teacher,

guide to living through wisdom and beauty

CONTENTS

Foreword by Jay McDaniel ix
Acknowledgements xi

I. Introduction 1
    A Call for a Postcolonial Ecofeminist Theology of *Salim*
    Ecological Concerns in Process Theology
    Ecological Hope in Postcolonialism
    Salim and *Donghak*
    Argument of the Book
    Mapping This Book

II. *Salim* as the Korean Metaphor of Life:
    Kim Ji-Ha's Meditation on Life 17
    Salim [enlivening] not *Jugim* [killing]
    Salim and Women
    Becoming the Other: Body Without Organ of Man

III. Decolonizing Life: A Postcolonial Reading of *Salim* 51
    Donghak as a Decolonizing Movement, a Religious Hybrid
    Nature as a New Subaltern
    The Hybridity of *Salim*: Spatiality of Planetarity

IV. A Process Ecotheological Reading of *Salim* 95
    Su-Un's *Si-cheon-ju* [侍天主] and John Cobb's Life as G*d
    Hae-Weol's *Gyeong-mool* [敬物] and McDaniel's Reverence for Life
    Bab [rice] is *Hanul* [the divine]

V. *Salim* for All: Toward a Postcolonial Ecofeminist Theology 147
    Salim as *Shalom*: *Jo-hwa-jeong* [造化定: Creative Transformation]
    Salim Eschatology: *Hu-cheon-gae-byeok* [後天開闢, a New Creation]

Glossary of Korean Terms 175
Bibliography 179
Notes 195

Foreword

Jea Sophia Oh knows that we are enlivened and divided by religion and politics. She shows, however, that deeper than this division is the fact that we are alive: creatures of the flesh who share our lives with one another and other forms of life, sometimes willingly and sometimes against our will.

Is there hope for us on this small but gorgeous planet? Yes, she says, if we give ourselves to a process of creative transformation – found everywhere in life on earth – and if we trust that this process is itself alive with divinity, with *Hanul*. She speaks with a voice wisened by postcolonial theology, process theology, and ecofeminist theology. She shows how a nineteenth century Korean tradition – *Donghak* – brings these traditions together into a living whole. *Donghak* comes from the future not only the past. It is our better hope, wherever we are on the journey called Earth. Letting go *into* life…that's the hope into which we are inspired by her planet-sensitive theology.

Of course many of us are already planet-sensitive in one way or another. We have enjoyed a sense of wonder at being present under the night sky, knowing that we and other creatures are small but included in a greater whole. Or we have gazed into the eyes of an animal and realized that we are kin to other creatures of the flesh, sharing with them the pleasures and pains of mortality. We carry within our own psyches a knowledge of planetarity; we do not really need theology to validate those intuitions. But we do need to theology to help us build upon these intuitions, weaving them into a way of thinking where respect for life and environment comes to us, not as an afterthought, but as first thought.

When theology points us toward respect for life and environment, it becomes post-colonial. After all, in modernity the very concept of life was colonized by the assumption that "thinking about life" and "thinking about divinity" were different activities. According to colonial thinking, if we think about life in its particularity – about a woman in Korea boiling rice over a stove, for example -- we are not thinking about divinity. And if we think about divinity, we are no longer thinking about the grandmother. There is a competition for attention, and one of them must win the battle. In truth, says Jea Sophia Oh, there need be no battle, because two ways of thinking ought never to have been separated. There's divinity in the act of boiling rice, and there's rice in divinity. What can this fresh way of thinking be called? How about a Postcolonial Theology of Life.

> Jay McDaniel, author of *With Roots and Wings: Christianity in an Age of Ecology and Dialogue*

Acknowledgements

This book is the fruit of my academic journey in the United States of America that began over a decade ago with an F1 foreign student visa and finished with a U.S. citizenship. The process of my hybrid life of being/becoming an Asian American theologian resulted in this book. I have devoted myself to theology with a special regard to 'Life.' My *salim* project took a long time to birth. I visited Korea in 2004 where I happened to encounter Kim Ji-Ha's works and *Donghak*. I have chosen *salim* as the *kōan* [question] of my life. When I returned to America, the books of Kim Ji-Ha and *Donghak* filled my new luggage and directed me on a new course in my theological journey.

I have to confess that I feel deeply grateful to G*d for letting me study process theology and postcolonial theory with Catherine Keller. She is the true one who has gone forth [先生, *seonsaeng*], embracing all the best living as a scholar, mentor, teacher, sister, colleague, and much more. She has guided me to wholesome living through "wisdom and beauty [智娥, *Jea*]." I send her my *salim* energy with my gratitude, admiration, and respect from "the deep" in my heart. Without her endless support and advice, I would never have been able to complete my *salim* project. I would like to give very special thanks to Jay McDaniel and our web-magazine, *Jesus, Jazz, and Buddhism*, for inspiring me to pursue East-West dialogue. My deep appreciation is also extended to Melodie M. Toby, my colleague at Kean who became my best friend, mentor, big sister, fairy godmother, wisdom tree, and so much more. I thank Lee Hyo-Dong, Stephen Moore, Laurel Kearns and Whitney Bauman for their mentorship and scholarly challenges. I offer my appreciation to my former teachers, Letty M. Russell, Cynthia Rigby, David Kwang-Sun Suh, Park Soon-Kyung, Lee Kyung-Sook, Chang Sang, and Chung Hyun-Kyung. They have become the soil of my theology.

I would like to thank my editors, Katherine Brown, Lynne Darden, and Joseph Duggan. I offer my appreciation to the publisher Jon Berquist at Sopher Press for his efforts and patience in the publication of this book. I send my appreciation and love to my family, my mother Jung Sun-Nim, my late father Oh Sung-Suk, Jea-

Eun, Jea-Young, Mi-Young, Gibbeum, David, Gilhan, Harim, and Ben for their love, trust, patience, and prayer. This project is the sum of my theological journey to date and my response to G*d's call as a theologian. *Salim* is my meditation on *Life*.

CHAPTER I

INTRODUCTION

A Call for a Postcolonial Ecofeminist Theology of Life
Since ecological crises have arisen in every part of human life, the awareness of "symbiosis"—the term that signifies that an individual is not separated from other living things but interconnected and interdependent--has become urgent for the life of creation. In the theological arena, ecotheology argues that a relationship exists among human/religious/spiritual worldviews and the degradation of nature. It explores the interaction between ecological values, such as sustainability, and the traditional Christian assumption of human dominion over nature. In terms of ecological concerns, a shift in worldview from an anthropocentric worldview to an eco-centric, life-centered one has begun to take shape.

In this book, further discussion of "life" as a theological concept reflects the ecological crisis as suggested and discussed by process thinkers. One can rethink the term, "life," by connecting a Whiteheadian vision of "Life"[1] to a Korean metaphor of life, *salim*,[2] which implies "enlivening" life in practical ways. *Salim* [살림], in a narrow sense, and traditional, refers to women's tasks such as cooking, gathering wood, cleaning and washing, raising children, cultivating gardens, and managing household affairs. *Salim* can also include all the diverse activities that make things alive and keep things living. In the process of becoming, the creative power of *salim* functions as a key to an Asian postcolonial ecotheological perspective that can be read through the bi-focal lens of postcolonial thought and process ecotheology.

Postcolonial thought criticizes the modern versions of a dualistic hierarchy,[3] deconstructing various oppositional differences, while opening a new space of hybridity for the colonized other. When one defines nonhuman nature as "the other" that has been colonized by the human species in the anthropocentric worldview, it becomes clear that the decolonization of nature is necessary in our era. As Gayatri Spivak suggests, today's subaltern must be rethought.[4] She has emphasized women's global subalternity along with economic subalterns. Elaborating on Spivak's suggestion, I consider nature as a new subaltern in the anthropocentric world. By analyzing Spivak's notion of subalternity and Bhabha's hybridity, I bring an ecological attention to postcolonial studies by considering earth as a new subaltern and conceptualizing the hybridity of life.

Since postcolonial theory helps to find the otherness of nature as a new subaltern, one can say that nature is not simply a projection of the human mind that can be exploited by human needs but something that suffers as well as becomes abundant in which human beings are a part as living organisms. In order to rethink the intrinsic value of nature, this book proposes an interstitial dialogue between the life-centered *Donghak* of nineteenth-century Korea and ecocentric process theology. *Donghak* is a Korean modern religious experience as well as the first indigenous religion in Korea. *Dong* [東: 동] means "the East" and *Hak* [學: 학] means "learning." Therefore, *Donghak* can be translated, literally, "Eastern Learning." In the middle of the nineteenth century, in the midst of colonization and westernization by Japanese and Christian imperialism, Su-Un initiated a national religion of Korea, called *Donghak* which was influenced by other Asian philosophies, i.e. Confucianism, Buddhism, and Daoism as well as Christianity which Su-Un called *seo-hak* [西學, western learning]. Three Asian religions were Koreanized and syncretized in *Donghak*. One can say that at its inception *Donghak* was inter-religious, inter-cultural, inter-ideological, and inter-traditional.

Therefore, *Donghak* was already an holistically inclusive tradition as a philosophical and religious hybrid.[5] The notion of life in *Donghak* is comparable to that of the Whiteheadians in their understandings of G*d[6] and life, their non-dualistic understanding of spirit and body, of the organic and inorganic.[7] Therefore, for interpreting the Korean metaphor of life, *salim*, this book borrows conceptual tools from process theology, especially its life-centered worldview and eco-theological perspective.

Among Whiteheadian ecotheologians, the key conversation partners of this book are John B. Cobb Jr. and Jay McDaniel. In *Donghak*, Su-Un's notion of *si-cheon-ju* [侍天主, G*d's indwelling in life] can be juxtaposed with Cobb's understanding of Life as G*d while Hae-Weol's notion of reverence toward bodies including G*d, human beings, animals, plants, and even non-organic bodies can be viewed in relation to Jay McDaniel's ecological theology. Su-Un was the initiator of *Donghak* and Hae-Weol was the follower of Su-Un as well as the second leader of *Donghak*. Su-Un discerns *Hanulnim* [the divine, G*d] not as a static ontological being but as one who keeps working in an incomplete sense, therefore, becoming.[8] In his notion of *si-cheon-ju* [embracing *hanul*] every body, including inorganic bodies, is *Hanulim*'s indwelling place. Su-Un's understanding of *si-cheon-ju* is similar to Cobb's notion of "Life" as G*d. Cobb distinguishes "Life" from "life" as an abstract noun or collective reference to all living things and indicates that "Life" is the central religious symbol hence he uses a capital "L."[9] In this understanding of life, the boundary of life is broadened even toward inorganic bodies.

Following Su-Un's understanding of *si-cheon-ju* [embracing *hanul*], Hae-Weol emphasizes "reverence [敬, *gyeong*]" toward every body as *hanul* because "*hanul* is embodied everywhere [*si-cheon-ju*]." Hae-Weol's notion of reverence [敬, *gyeong*] is firstly directed toward heaven [敬天, *gyeong-cheon*], human beings [敬人, *gyeong-in*] and reaches everything [敬物, *gyeong-mool*] on the earth including not only organic bodies but also non-organic things. The anthropocentrism of western theology can be challenged by Hae-Weol's *gyeong-mool* theory which is life-centered and biocentric, and is comparable to Jay McDaniel's notion of openness toward G*d and reverence toward life. McDaniel expresses deep ecological concerns in his theology of life. For him, reverence is not just an act of thinking but an act of feeling the presence of the surrounding world with respect and appreciation. His suggestion of reverence toward gods, people, animals, and the earth, including both organic and non-organic beings from his ecological sensitivity, provides a strategy with which to interpret the notion of life in *Donghak*, theologically. By engaging in such comparative eco-theological discourse, this book has the potential to develop an alternative to the Enlightenment legacy of western perspectives that dichotomizes the world under androcentric and anthropocentric assumptions.

Ecological Concerns in Process Theology

In confronting the ecological crisis, western postmodern philosophies and theologies have responded by suggesting alternative theories and better ways of life. The issue of "Life," symbiotic living, is the most distinctive concern in the beginning of the twentieth century. Whiteheadian cosmology played a significant role in explicating the ecological issues and providing the alternatives. John Cobb shaped the meaning of process theology from the ideas of process thought of Alfred North Whitehead (1861-1947). Cobb's ecological concern was originally actualized in *Is It Too Late? A Theology of Ecology* (1972), the first ecotheological text in process theology as well as in theological studies. It was also one of the very first theological responses to the ecological crisis. In the face of mounting social problems, Cobb suggests that the relation of ecological issues to justice is a theological theme, a Christian duty. The ecological commitment of a new Christianity, he argues, can be an inclusive creative process, which is also the ground for believing it is not too late to save life.

With his ecological concerns, Cobb moved toward a kind of interdisciplinary project which bore fruits with the publication of *The Liberation of Life: From the Cell to the Community* (1982) with

Charles Birch, which was based on Cobb's conviction that "no problem could be more critical than that of a decent survival of a humanity that threatened to destroy itself by exhausting and polluting its natural context." *The Liberation of Life* argues that all forms of life should be liberated from any kind of oppressive power combined with the mechanistic and dualistic world-views, claiming the cooperation of biology with ecological thinking and the reshaping of religious thoughts and political policies by the idea of liberation of life.

In his ecological responsibility in Christian theology, Cobb has constantly focused on the interrelationships of religion and nature in the light of ecological concerns and endeavored to learn life-centered cosmologies from other religions through interreligious dialogues. His openness toward the worldviews of Asian traditions provides wisdom for our bio-spiritual life, suggesting a new Christianity that must substitute the biotic pyramid for the absoluteness of humanity.

Following Cobb's ecological thinking, in *Earth, Sky, Gods & Mortals* and *Of God and Pelicans* (1989), Jay McDaniel suggests an ecological Christianity and paves a path toward a new context for an ecological spirituality. Similar to Cobb he invokes G*d, a Life-centered G*d in *Of God and Pelicans*.[10] He speaks not only about Life as G*d, but also concerns about nonhuman nature. Much like John Cobb's ecological concerns and openness toward other world religions, McDaniel brings together insights from the natural sciences, Christian theology, and interreligious dialogue in his study, *With Roots and Wings* (1995), breaking new ground in the search for a life-centered theology. His interdisciplinary and interreligious approaches can support a comparison of *Donghak* and the process school in their common and shared ecotheological concerns for life.

With her vision of theology of becoming, a process ecofeminist theologian, Catherine Keller, proposes a theology without an end of the world by suggesting a counter-apocalyptic eco-eschatology in her book, *Apocalypse Now and Then* (1996). In addition, she calls attention to creation as a whole in our weblike world, and our interconnectedness as subjects with others and nature in *From the Broken Web* (1986) and reads Genesis through a process perspective of *creatio ex profundis* (creation out of the deep) in *Face of the Deep* (2003). In her effort to bridge Revelation and *Genesis* in terms of *chaos* theory, her ecological feminist concern attempts to deal with a postcolonial term, hybridity, comparing it with the process notion of *chaos*. Keller suggests that Christianity has to confront imperial globalism with "a counterimperial ecology of love" for colonized nature.[11] The multiplicity and hybridity in her theology hopes for an interdisciplinary dialogue between postcolonialism and process theology and helps to construct a postcolonial ecotheology, bringing an ecological concern together with her passion toward creation.

An Ecological Hope in Postcolonialism

The field of postcolonial studies gained prominence in the 1970s through the scholarly work of Edward Said with the publication of *Orientalism* (1978). Through this text, Said is widely acknowledged as breaking ground for postcolonial criticism. Following Foucault, Said grasps the dynamic structure of knowledge in terms of power and applies this dynamism to the notion of Orientalism. Said's *Orientalism* has opened a space through which to challenge the west from and within, by demystifying its formative cultural representations of the Orient in the colonial period.

In *The Location of Culture* (1994), Homi K. Bhabha challenges the unfortunate and perhaps false opposition of theory and politics that some critics have framed in order to question the elitism and Eurocentrism of prevailing postcolonial debates. By means of a complicated repertoire of Lacanian psychoanalysis, postmodern notions of mimicry and performance, and Derridian deconstruction, Bhabha has encouraged a rigorous rethinking of nationalism, representation, and resistance that, above all, stresses "hybridity."

Since the 1999 annual meeting of the AAR hybridity has become a controversial theme in the area of theology. At that conference, Kwok Pui-lan presented "Jesus the Hybrid: What Do You Say That I Am?" Discovering the images of hybridity in the historical Jesus, Kwok reconceptualized the meaning of Christ from the perspective of the Third World which can be helpful in deconstructing the imperialistic Christ featured in the western tradition.[12] In her essay, "Hybridity and *Chaos*: Theology on the Face of the Deep," Catherine Keller gives new theological meaning to the term hybridity by applying *chaos* theory to a postcolonial biblical hermeneutics. Keller sees that hybridity can be construed as the cultural opening where "the ocean of heteroglossia" has already leaked into the system.[13] In a similar way, postcolonial concepts of hybridity, especially as they have developed theological resonance, can be relevant in analyzing the Korean concept of *salim* [enlivening] in its meaning, function, and movements theoretically from an ecotheological perspective.

In her major book, *A Critique of Postcolonial Reason* (1990), Gayatri Spivak challenges fellow postcolonial theorists by unexpectedly proposing a powerful ecological move. She suggests a global movement for "non-Eurocentric ecological justice" beyond the European Economic Community.[14] Confronted with the profound ecological loss of forests and rivers as foundation of life, the European Economic Community cannot be a role model. She suggests that we embrace human *dharma* [responsibility] for nature from *Rg-Veda*[15] rather than from Eurocentric Christianity.[16] As a scholar of postcolonialism, she articulates the bodily connections of justice, gender, and the global ecology suggested by several ecofeminists.[17] In her view, it could be a hopeful message and a suggestion to go beyond a theoretical investigation toward a practical and ethical demand which can be both postcolonial and ecological. She opens an important new possibility for an ecological application in postcolonial studies. Her signification of women's "subalternity" can be applied to nature as the subaltern which has been alienated from an anthropocentric world.

Hence postcolonialism in its beginning had been focused on the conflicts between humans and human structures, Spivak made a transition from the anthropocentric postcolonialism to "planetary love" by suggesting the term "planetary" instead of globe in *Death of A Discipline* (2003). According to Spivak, the planetary stands in opposition to the globe. While the globe is an abstract notion of the whole in the way that maps are abstract, the planetary is fully embodied and as such cannot be charted:

> The globe is on our computer. No one lives there. It allows us to think that we can aim to control it. The planet is in the species of alterity, belonging to another system; and yet we inhabit it, on loan. It is not really amenable to a neat contrast with the globe....When I invoke the planet, I think of the effort required to figure the (im)possibility of this underived intuition.[18]

At the seventh Drew Transdisciplinary Theological Colloquium (TTC7) 2007, theologians and biblical scholars opened a table to discuss Spivak's "planetarity" and "planetary love" for constructing postcolonial theologies. As a fruit of TTC7, Stephen D. Moore and Mayra Rivera edited a collection of essays, *Planetary Loves: Spivak, Postcoloniality, and Theology* (2011). Spivak's notion of planetary provides fertile ground for theologians to probe and engage in dialogue and allows postcolonialism to move beyond anthropocentric discourses of nation, gender, class, culture, and colonialism toward ecological concerns.[19] Spivak's reflections on the concept of "planetarity" raise urgent questions about the possibility of collectivity and the challenges of responsible engagement with subaltern constituencies. Spivak's notion of "planetary love" is nonsentimental. For her, love is an effort, *dharma*, therefore, practice. Spivak's earthly vision demands attentive effort to practice what I call "*eco-dharma*," ever-arriving politics of becoming together, conviviality. Spivak's planetarity and planetary love provide many insights for a theological revisioning of creation.

Although there is not yet a full version of a postcolonial ecotheology, there have been recent and more sustained attempts to bring postcolonialism and ecology into dialogue outside of the theological field that shape a "postcolonial ecocriticism" or "green postcolonialism." However, critics have also highlighted fundamental differences of perspective between the two fields. Postcolonialists tend to envision human identity through human history while ecocriticists invest in the authenticity of nature and emphasize the conflicts of humans with other species more than those of humans with humans defined as radically other. In his essay "Environmentalism and Postcolonialism, " Rob Nixon argued that ecocriticism has tended to value ideas of purity with regard to ecosystems and places, while postcolonialists have primarily focused on hybridization and border crossing.[20]

Despite the different perspectives, in terms of justice and sustainability, ecocriticism and postcolonialism must be understood as a parallel project. For this purpose, Bonnie Roos and Alex Hunt edited a collection of essays which attempt to bridge postcolonialism and ecocriticism, *Postcolonial Green: Environmental Politics and World Narratives* (2010). The essays elaborate the Bhabhan concept of hybridity which refers to a coming together of many identities that produce a critical challenge to hegemonic authority in a relatively inclusive methodological framework, so-called, "a postcolonial green perspective."[21] Postcolonial ecocriticism promises to make new contributions to the analysis of how imperialism, colonialism, neocolonialism, and postcolonialism not only create basic conditions of inequality between colonizer and colonized, but also give rise to complex material and symbolic transactions between different classes, nations, genders, which determine each other unevenly.[22]

As such, in *Postcolonial Ecocriticiam: Literature, Animal, Environment* (2010), Graham Huggan and Helen Tiffin examine relationships between humans, animals and the environment in postcolonial literary texts. Huggan and Tiffin construct a historical narrative of European/ western global colonialism and contemporary neocolonialism in which human and environmental implications are thoroughly enmeshed. The most recent publication in this new area of "postcolonial ecocritisism" is *Postcolonial Ecologies: Literatures of the Environment* (Oxford: Oxford University Press, 2011), edited by Elizabeth DeLoughrey and George B. Handley. This collection attempts to bring ecocritical studies into a necessary dialogue with postcolonial literature to explore the relationship between humans and nonhuman nature around the planet, drawing from texts from Africa, the Caribbean, the Pacific Islands, and South Asia.

It seems useful to turn to contributions from non-western environmental scholars, as well as to case studies from other parts of the world that explore the intersections between postcolonial and ecological concerns. As Robert Young points out, non-western ecofeminism significantly pre-dates the emergence of North American ecocriticism, showing the way for western practitioner's ongoing self-examination of their own motives and laying the basis for their own internal gendered/racialized critiques.[23] For instance, the sociologist Ramachandra Guha's historical account of the Chipko (Himalayan peasant antideforestation) movement in the 1970s, and the ecofeminist-activist Vandana Shiva's analysis of the disastrous consequences of the Green Revolution for subsistence-farming communities in late-twentieth-century Punjab.

Spivak calls the western-elitist construction of the Third World, the "overworlding"[24] of the Third World as a locus of "anti-imperialist resistance," the overpowering rhetoric that risks silencing the very masses on whose behalf it claims to speak. Like "worlding," "subalternization" is a process related to the general psycho-social mechanism of "othering."[25] Elaborating on the Spivakian notion of subaltern, we should rethink postcolonial/colonial subalternization of nature as similar to the subaltern woman as the 'othered subject,' nature (nonhuman/more than human) is the 'othered subject' in the subalternization of nature as objects of discursive management and control.

> In the colonial mind, nature was 'out there,' never 'in here,' and the possibility of knowing human engagement with nature was rarely considered. White men feared nature in the form of disease and the dark forest, and did their best to overcome it. They venerated nature in the shape of formalized hunting rituals and wilderness preservation; but always the

distance between human and non-human was maintained, an apartheid at special level.[26]

Eastern religions had intrigued Europeans for several centuries like the oral cultures of the Pacific Islands and Africa had provoked interest and admiration in many westerners.[27] Likewise, the *Donghak* tradition in Korea illustrates the Spivakian notion of subalternity and provides an Asian context for internalizing insights from postcolonial thought.

Salim [enlivening] and *Donghak* [Eastern Learning]

The unique understanding of *salim* and the awareness of life have been strongly emphasized in *Donghak*. *Donghak* was initiated by Su-Un (1824~1864) and spread by his follower, Hae-Weol (1827~1898). The philosophy of *Donghak* was influenced by three major East Asian philosophies -- Confucianism, Buddhism, and Daoism -- as well as by Christianity to some extent, along with the unique Korean cultural life-centered cosmology, standing for reverence toward life and creation.

Influenced by the philosophy of life in *Donghak*, Kim Ji-Ha inspired the Korean ecological movement, "the *Salim* Movement," in the 1980s, after he was released from prison. Kim Ji-Ha is a *minjung* poet in Korea who resisted dictatorship in order to gain a *minjung* government in Korea in the 1970s. Kim recognizes *salim* as a new paradigm for the future of the world and the very content of a new consciousness. In his remarkable book, *Bab* [Rice] (1984), he writes that the key of liberation is "life." *Bab* is a daily meal for the Korean people and, therefore, a source of living. According to Kim's description, *bab* is G*d. Kim elaborates his theory of *salim* in his book, *Salim* (1987). Since the Korean civilian government was established in 1993, Korean people's movements have been changed to advocate not only for human rights but also for a symbiotic life for all things. On the waves of ecological concerns, the so-called "*Salim* Movement" has become broadly diffused. Kim's recent books, *The*

Theory of Life (2003) and *The Way of Life and Peace* (2005) have greatly influenced Korean people's ecological thinking and understanding.

Korean eco-activist Chung Hyun Kyung names a Korean eco-feminist or anyone who wants to share the vision of a Korean eco-feminist, *salimist* in her (Korean) book, *Miraeeseo On Pyeonji*: *Goddess-spell According to Hyun Kyung* [A Letter from the Future] (2001). *Salimist* means a person who is doing *salim*, which means making things alive. It is a Korean-English word that combines *salim* and the English suffix, -ist, for a person who is "doing" something such as an idealist, a novelist, or a specialist.[28] This word has become a term in Korean language. The *Salim* movement has been embraced most enthusiastically by Korean women who are called "*salimists*" and has spread throughout the whole nation to improve the well-being of every life.

Argument of the Book

As a Korean-American, eco-feminist who has studied process theology and postcolonialism, and who seeks to address the urgent ecological crisis of the earth, I offer the term, *salim* [enlivening] as encoding a saving message for life in my own cultural background and articulate it through a transcultural and interdisciplinary method I have lived through. This *salim* project is my commitment to my own living as a cultural religious and academic hybrid responding to the ecological problems at hand. It deploys "Life" as its key theological term. It comprises three foci: cultural analysis, postcolonial theory, and a comparative ecotheological analysis, weaving *Donghak* and process theology, as a new hybrid from which an 'Asian postcolonial ecofeminist theology' of *salim* can be developed.

To accomplish the above, a comparative discussion of *salim* and the philosophy of life in *Donghak*, as a root of the theory of *salim*, is undertaken through a cultural analysis to discern the unique Korean concept of *salim* in its etymological meanings and practical applications in Korean people's daily life. Its closest meaning can be expressed as enlivening, that is, referring to all kinds of activities for 'letting things live.' One can especially understand the deep ecological meanings of *salim* in the philosophy of life cultivated in *Donghak*.

As previously mentioned, in postcolonial studies, life as an ecological issue has not been explored in depth, nor are the original theorists in any sense theologians. However, by reading Spivak's suggestion of the non-Eurocentric global movement for ecological justice which Keller interprets as "a counterimperial ecology of love,"[29] there is potential to explore and develop a 'postcolonial ecotheology.' Spivak's subaltern study is important for making an ecological transition from postcolonial studies in terms of life so as to create a postcolonial move from ecothology.

For a comparative study of Korean *Donghak* and process theology, I attempt to take a position of "complementary pluralism"[30] which considers that the insights of the many religions are different but complementary, such that no religion contains all truth even as all contain some truth. Throughout this process, I define ecotheological meanings of *salim* by the practice of folding and unfolding an Asian metaphor together with western theologies.

Process ecotheology and postcolonialism have challenged the androcentric anthropocentric Christian theologies and contributed to the construction of a new cosmological paradigm. To take the notion of life as a theological theme, this book introduces the contextual and cultural term of Korea, *salim*, for theological praxis. Thus, the methodological significance of this book is the interreligious (comparative theological) and transcultural dialogue between *Donghak* and process theology that engages with the interdisciplinary work of 'postcolonialism and ecotheology.'

Through this interdisciplinary and transcultural research, this book brings diverse traditions religions into dialogue by which the rule of patriarchy is replaced by the guidance of 'Life' as understood in process theology, postcolonial theory, and *Donghak*. But, still more deeply, it points toward a way of living available to many in our world, as adapted to concrete situations in Korea. This book offers an alternative way to talk about 'Life' in an Asian postcolonial ecofeminist perspective that not only challenges western modernity, but also brings a new hybrid voice to both 'ecotheology and postcolonialism' as the first full version of 'Asian/Asian American postcolonial eco/ecofeminist theology.'

Mapping This Book

My *salim* project is an interdisciplinary and comparative research based on Kim Ji-Ha's works and *Donghak* thought. Key leading scholars from areas of process eco-theology, poststructural theory, and postcolonial studies are the principal sources and voices that serve as tools of criticism and interpretation for my discussions.

Chapter II is written for understanding the meaning of *salim* by analyzing the work of Kim Ji-Ha and comparing it with process, postcolonial and poststructural works on "life." The first section defines *salim* [enlivening] as "becoming together as part-whole" not *jugim* [killing, distorting, demolishing, disguising, lying, torturing which goes against the way of nature]. Using the dual structure of *salim* and *jugim,* this chapter indicates that death is not contrary to *salim* but *jugim* is. To validate the meaning of *salim* as *becoming together* as a symbiotic part-whole, the Whiteheadian and Deleuzian concepts of becoming are applied. The second section focuses on Kim's connection of *salim* and women in which Kim recognizes women as the subjects of *salim*. Kim's notion of *koja* [the castrated] is compared with the poststructural understandings of the Freudian Oedipus complex as understood by Catherine Keller, Gilles Deleuze, and Luce Irigaray. Kim's essentialistic suggestion of feminine culture (*yin*-culture) as a new paradigm can be defined as "a strategic essentialism" through a postcolonial analysis of the works of Gayatri Spivak and Trinh Minh-ha. This chapter is designed to find an ecological clue in *salim* that can change a conventional paradigm of the world from one that is anthropocentric and andocentric toward one that is ecocentric and cosmocentric.

Chapter III examines the Korean concept of life according to postcolonial theory. The first section acknowledges *Donghak* as a decolonizing movement and a religious hybrid. Through the contextual and historical analysis of the *Donghak* movement, the movement can also be understood as a *minjung* movement as well as a *salim* movement. Philosophically, *Donghak* can be understood as a cultural and religious hybrid that was influenced by Buddhism, Confucianism, Daoism, and Christianity. In the second section of this chapter, Hae-Weol's notion of women as *hanul* [the divine] is compared with Spivak's women as the new gendered subaltern. To answer her famous question, "Can the subaltern speak?" Homi Bhabha's and Kwok Pui-lan's notions of subaltern are applied. Taking it one step further, nature can be called as a new subaltern. To do so, this section analyzes the Deleuzian notion of becoming the Other and the Foucauldian notion of "bio-power" which can be understood as the power of *salim*. The complexity and multiplicity that the term "hybridity" attempts to convey is similarly attributable to *salim*. I compare Bhabha's notion of hybridity and third space (interstitial space) with Kim's notion of *teum* [gap] in the last part of chapter III, Spatiality of Palnetarity. Kim's definition of *teum* as *chaosmos* is elaborated by analyzing the Whiteheadian and Deleuzian notions of *chaos+cosmos* and in which Catherine Keller forms a bridge between postcolonial hybridity and the process *tehom* [the deep] in which everything is becoming.

In chapter IV, I propose the interstitial dialogue between life-centered *Donghak* and ecocentric process theology by comparing Su-Un's *si-cheon-ju* [侍天主, embracing *hanul* in life] and Cobb's Life as G*d. The notion of life in *Donghak* is comparable to one of the Whiteheadian school in their understandings of G*d and life, their non-dualistic understanding of spirit and body, of organic and inorganic. Su-Un's notion of *hanul* as the cosmic life, a symbiotic part-whole can be understood as both pantheism and panentheism in some ways, and, therefore, cannot be classified in the western classification of pantheism or panentheism.

The second section of this chapter provides a comparison between Hae-Weol's notion of reverence [敬, *Gyeong*] and Jay McDaniel's deep ecological process in his notion of openness toward G*d and reverence toward life. I analyze Hae-Weol's triad structure of reverence toward heaven, humans, and more than humans as *hanul* employing the Spivak and Deleuzian notions of becoming the Other. The hybridization of life is processing through eating and sharing foods together. This process of sharing can be referred to as "*bab* [rice, also meaning food in general] hybridity." Hae-Weol's *Gyeong* theology becomes deepened in his notion of *bab* as *hanul* as for Kim Ji-Ha (food is G*d). In the last part of chapter IV, Hae-Weol's notion of *bab* as *hanul* is compared to Jesus as the bread of life and finds the Eucharistic meaning in *hanul*.

    The conclusion of this book provides a constructive move to articulate a postcolonial ecofeminist theology of *salim*. The first section of chapter V discusses the content of *salim* as the process of life which is and should be a quality life, a life of *shalom*. *Salim* as the process of life can be found in Su-Un's notion of *Jo-hwa-jeong* [造化定, creative transformation with peace and harmony] which I describe *salim* as *shalom*. Through the comparison between the Whiteheadian notion of *creatio continua* [G*d's continuing creative activity throughout the history of the universe] and *Donghak*'s *Jo-hwa-jeong* as the creation through non-doing,[31] and *mu-wi-i-hwa* [無爲而化, becoming through non-doing], chapter V invites us to envision a new heaven and a new earth which *Donghak* suggests through Su-Un's eschatological message of *hu-cheon-gae-byeok* [後天開闢, opening a New Heaven and a New Earth]. I rename *hu-cheon-gae-byeok* "*salim* eschatology" and find a connection with Catherine Keller's *eco-eschatology* in the last part of this study. Su-Un's *gae-byeok* [beginning] and Keller's "recycling eschatology" are discussed through the postcolonial notion of strategic catachresis of Spivak and Stephen Moore. *Salim* eschatology requires an ethical responsibility and dimension to deal with our endangered ecosystem as the cosmic organic body as part-whole, *hanul*. Through *Salim, the Process of Life*, we are hybridizing, decolonizing (or liberating), reconciling, enlivening, healing, mending, feeding, sharing, caring, saving, and, therefore, *becoming together*.

Chapter II

Salim as the Korean Metaphor of Life

On March 15, 2010, the Korean Religious Leaders Association of Buddhism and Christianity opened an environmental symposium and decided to have a united prayer meeting for the "river of life [*salim*]." Korean people worry that building the Grand Canal of four rivers threatens the eco-system which can be defined as "environmental disruption [*jugim*]." We have to repent for this human violence against the ecosystem and build a world which respects life. Myeong Gae-Whan, the President of the Religious Environmental Activists Association said, "the river is a living organism. It is a process of destroying [*jugim*] the circle of life by blocking the streams of the rivers artificially. The Religious Eco-activists should fight against the Grand Canal Project."[1] (translation mine)

This is one of the resistance movements against the Grand Canal Project which was one of the presidential manifestos of the presidential election by Lee Myung-Bak, the President of South Korea.² Many ecological movement groups and individuals resist against this *jugim* [killing] project which will eventually break the rhythm of the eco-system and destroy the multiple life forms, including trees and fishes unless the government retracts the project. It is an irony that in the midst of active *salim* movements generated by ordinary Korean people, there is a *jugim* [killing] project from the central power against life. For the Korean people in the twenty-first century, one of the greatest concerns is the ecological crisis. *Salim* has become a *kōan* [公案, topic in the time] for the Korean people who have pursued the well-being of life and have attempted to solve ecological problems on our endangered planet since the late 1980s. For Koreans, the 1970s and the early 1980s were the periods of the *minjung* movement, a Korean liberation movement, while the late 1980s through the present represents the period of the "*salim* movement," the Korean ecological movement.

Kim Ji-Ha is a well-known *minjung* poet/activist in Korea who had struggled against the military government in the 1970s and 1980s. He transformed his poetic world into *salim* as life in symbiosis from the *minjung* movement after he was released from prison in the mid-1980s. His transformation in becoming a *salim* activist (*salim-kun* in Korean) challenged Korean people to have an awareness of the ecological crisis and inspired them to transform the *minjung* movement into a *salim* movement, in accordance with people's needs of the times.

This chapter analyzes Kim's works in order to discover the meaning and function of *salim* in Korean culture, in both its most narrow as well as its broader meanings. Kim's meditation on *salim* has great potential for developing the postcolonial ecofeminist theology of life that I pursue in this book. Kim is not a theologian, yet his theory of *salim* and *bab* [food] are explored theologically in this chapter through a hermeneutical reading of his poetic writings via my translation work of specific Korean texts into English.³ His notion of *salim* is deeply rooted in *Donghak* which was an ecocentric and cosmocentered philosophy in Korea even before the emergence of the ecological treatment of process theology (or "eco-process theology") which has resonance for our times.[4] By discerning the salvific and liberative meaning of *salim* in Korean culture, through analyzing the notion of life in Kim Ji-Ha and *Donghak*, this chapter takes a bold step toward engaging the transformation of the notion of *jugim* culture into one of *salim* culture. Kim's suggestion of *salim* culture as a new model of living is actually an outgrowth of his unique understanding of women in relation to *salim*. His essentialistic understanding of women and *salim* are analyzed through the Irigarayan and Deleuzian anti-phallogocentric (or anti-Oedipus) idea of becoming.

Salim not *Jugim*

One spring day, through the bars of the window in my cell a bunch of shiny white remnants of dandelions blew in and scattered. That was so beautiful. I saw a tiny seed set on a chink between the bars. Then I saw that it was budding between the bars and growing, sucking rain and sunlight. The day I discovered it suddenly, I cried silently for a long while. There was no serious reason. Only the word, "Life" freshly and radiantly penetrated into my heart. That overwhelmed me into endless trembling and mysterious ecstasy.[5]

This textual fragment is Kim Ji-Ha's meditation on life while he was in prison in the mid-1970s. One day he was shocked by the reality of life as endless, powerful, and boundless, when he witnessed a weed budding in between the bars of the window of his prison cell. Nothing could block its growth and extension. For a hundred days, he meditated on life and realized that life is symbiotic and interconnected with the whole cosmos. He saw that life embraces death. Therefore, despite the fact that a body dies, the whole of life never dies. For him, the problem is not death but intentional killing, murder, "*jugim*." "Is death contrary to *salim*?"[6]

Death is not the opposite of life because it is a part of life and always and already exists as a necessary aspect of the process of life. The opposite of life, he realized, is *jugim* which means all the activities of an anti-life, a package of social pathology. Killing [violence] as a phenomenon of culture is broadly customized in our daily life and systematically pursued. Death is an inevitable reality that humankind cannot avoid. Nevertheless, killing, the intentional destruction of reality, is distinguished from death because it is preventable.

Life reflects the full cycle of birth, growth, death, and transformation (or change) into different forms. Life is not contrary to death. Rather, life always contains death as part of a very necessary process. Therefore, life does not stand against natural death but counters artificial killing. According to Kim Ji-Ha, *salim* is a counter-concept to *jugim*, including all the destructive activities such as oppression, exploitation, coercion, contamination, destruction, marginalization, killing, etc.[7] In this sense, I understand *jugim* as contrary to *salim*, not only as an expression of annihilation but also as a term reflecting different forms of violence, in general, which disturbs all the intentional and spontaneous movements of *salim*. In Kim's view, in order to counter intentional killing and to restore life as it returns to nature, the *salim* movement should be intentional, conscious, and constructive.[8] In other words, *Salim* must become intentional and active much like *jugim*. Therefore, they both have power and an effect, yet, *salim* is countering *jugim*. *Jugim* is not natural but exists contrary to nature and the unnatural activity of life engages violence. *Salim* represents all diverse activities of life that include intentional efforts to overcome *jugim* and thus restore life and all its spontaneous changes and natural growth.

In December 1980, Kim Ji-Ha was released from prison after seven years of incarceration. During his incarceration, he had dramatically converted his perspective from the *minjung* movement to the *salim* movement. During his very difficult time in prison, he realized the strength and endurance of life, itself, regardless of the context and situation.

Kim sees both the intentionality and spontaneity of *salim*. While *salim* as a social movement should reflect an intentional effort, *salim* as the process of life happens spontaneously by nature.

> Ah! Life is omnipresent! Life transcends the prison bars, the high walls, and the guards! In the midst of distraction life buds, blooms radiantly! Even I as a human have no reason to be disappointed in front of the prison wall, if I realize the endurance and expansion of life tangibly through my body and spirit, there will no longer be prison for me. Nothing could ever imprison life.[9]

As Kim discovered the spontaneity and omnipresence of life in his prison cell, as we see weeds grow in between cement blocks of sidewalks which barely contain soil, life is everywhere in everything. Life extends and grows in quantity and evolves and seeks to be better, that is, abundant and happy, in quality. Unless there is a disruption of living, *jugim*, life just tends to grow and become beautiful and fruitful, if possible, which is part of the natural cycle of life, the omnipresence of life which is the power of life, the power of *salim*. *Salim* refers to all these intentional efforts against *jugim* and the spontaneous and natural changes that make life abundant and happy in terms of quality. Therefore, *salim* reflects the qualitative evolution of life.

In this sense, *salim* reflects the very practical tasks and notions of life that can also be used as an abstract word. Kim's notion of life is very practical and real. Therefore, for Kim, *salim*, as an expression of life can be described as follows: "*Donghak* teaches life as *salim* which means the activities and movements for living; it is not an abstract noun. In this sense, *Donghak* is not a religion or a philosophy but is related to a *salim* movement."[10]

Kim sees life and death together as the whole process of living as a circulation of convergence and diffusion of living energy [氣, *ki*].

> Every form of life in the whole universe, including
> human life, never dies, regardless of death. Natural
> death is just a transformation of a life form and a
> change of self-realization. Death and life are actually
> one from the birth to death, becoming together
> asymmetrically. Living is a convergence of *ki* [氣,
> *chi*, spiritual energy][11] yet, dying is a diffusion of *ki*.[12]

For Kim, these two activities are actually one movement of *ki*. Thus, death is a total dissolution of an organism in the process of diffusion. In this sense, one can say that life and death are one in this endless creative evolution of life. Nevertheless, *jugim* violates this process of becoming life. According to Kim, *jugim* does not only infer to the destruction of living organisms but also all the attitudes that are contrary to the natural process of becoming life.[13] Then, what we call violence, in many different expressions and forms, can be recognized as *jugim* which harms the symbiotic living for all.

Kim recognizes life in a symbiotic structure of organic bodies in which a form of life cannot be separated completely from the whole web of life, just as a microcosm is connected to a macrocosm. In other words, the whole universe is not only comprised of inorganic matter but is a massive organic body. Although Kim does not use the ancient Greek schema of seeing the *cosmos* on both a large scale and a small scale as one unity, using the words, *macrocosm* and *microcosm* to explain the living unity of the world as an organic body, it seems to me that those terms help one to interpret his notion of life as a symbiotic web:

> In my body, the endless cosmic life is living. Even if
> I become an old, ugly, and immoral human, the
> cosmic life lives endlessly without a beginning and an
> end in my body. My life is connected to the cosmic
> life in the whole universe with all my neighbors,
> animals, plants, and nonorganic matter as one life

which will never cease even after I become sick and die.[14]

We can notice from the passage above that Kim sees the universe as a living organism, regardless of self and others, animals and plants, the organic and nonorganic. As Kim notes, in this symbiotic organic structure, everything is interconnected with and interdependent on everything. "*Salim* is a very condensed metaphor and *kōan* [question] for creative movements. Our daily living in our community is *salim*. Therefore, *salim* is a living practice in reality."[15] Likewise, whatever activities happen in this organic unity, beyond myself, will affect me eventually as well. It is not a structure of chronological orders but an interdependent and interconnected relationship. Because the community and individual are interconnected and interdependent as one organic body, social change and individual transformation should occur simultaneously. Then, the starting point of the *salim* movement is from the restoration of one's own life, which should be extended throughout the whole community.

I elaborate on Kim's observation of life as being endless, without a beginning or an end, regardless of individual life in terms of symbiotic living of the whole organism of the universe. The continuity of life is eternal in many different forms through the endless process of death and birth. Life has continued in this process of "immortal mortality" and "eternal temporality." Life can be embodied in an organic form temporarily during the process of life. However, life never disappears through the process of birth, growth, maturation, and death. Thus, life is a symbiotic living organism in which individual life can be understood in terms of the whole process of life as a microcosm of the macrocosm. Even in an individual life form, life does not stay in a static form. Yet, it is constantly changing and moving, becoming. Life is not a substantial form but one of becoming. Therefore, life continues when an organism dies.

As I elaborate on Kim's notion of life as a complex whole which includes death and living as well as an individual and the whole community in the process of becoming, Whitehead reconstructs substantial forms as "macrocosmic repetition" of patterns in a series of events described as the development of a formal structure of temporal societies.[16] The Whiteheadian notion of life is an "entirely living nexus." Such a nexus cannot be defined as form but as "living vitality." Then, the individual living is an intensification process of events in a complex organism that shapes itself into a historical unity, similar to Roland Faber's definition of human personal life as "a highly creative integration of intensity."[17] In the Whiteheadian notion of life, one may refer to *salim* as a symbiotic becoming, a becoming together.

Deleuze points to the Whiteheadian process of life as an endless folding and unfolding of life. Nevertheless, Deleuze describes repetition differently by emphasizing the difference of a singularity. That is, for Deleuze, there is no repetition but only a genuine unrepeatable reactivation of pure immanence of virtual becoming. In this sense, Deleuze defines "mimicry as a very bad concept"[18] since it relies on binary logic to describe phenomena of an entirely different nature:

> The Pink Panther imitates nothing, it reproduces nothing, it paints the world its color, pink on pink; this is its becoming-world, carried out in such a way that it becomes imperceptible itself, asignifying, makes its rupture, its own line of flight, follows its aparallel evolution through to the end.[19]

Yet, creation always invokes a multiplicity. The earth generates difference and is a source of becoming. Deleuze formulates a nonfinalistic evolutionism according to which the immanent world is characterized by constant change, which grows from within a diversity of milieu, connected in various complex ways. He comments, "It is not a multiple derived from the One, or to which One is added (n+1). It is composed not of units but of dimensions, or rather directions in motion. It has neither beginning nor end, but always a middle (*milieu*) from which it grows and which it overspills."[20] For the Deleuzian notion of life, organism and *milieu*, thus, develop, grow, and change together within the continuous processes of becoming.

One can grasp Deleuze's process of life when he explains, "When an organism dies, it does not really vanish, but folds in upon itself, abruptly involuting into the again newly dormant seed by skipping all intermediate stages. The simplest way of stating the point is by saying that to unfold is to increase, to grow; whereas to fold is to diminish, to reduce, to withdraw into the recesses of a world."[21] The Deleuzian process of life can be understood as a circulation of folding and unfolding: in his view, even after the death of an organic body, life continues to make endless and countless movements. Death is actually a process of life or a living process as a form of change. In this aspect, death is in this infinite process of life as a folding form of recess: "The living organism by virtue of preformation has an internal destiny that makes it move from fold to fold, or that makes machines from machines all the way to infinite."[22]

Accordingly, one of the aspects of nature is elusive change. Whitehead points out that nature has to face two facts: change and endurance. In reading Shelley's poem, *The Cloud*,[23] Whitehead says that the verse, "I change but I cannot die," shows the aspects of nature as elusive change and eternal endurance. Regarding this passage, Whitehead interprets that Shelley places his emphasis on the change of what cannot die. Whitehead beautifully explains the "eternality" of nature by observing its endurance: "The mountain endures. But when after the ages it has been worn away, it has gone. If a replica arises, it is yet a new mountain. A color is eternal. It haunts time like a spirit. It comes and it goes. But where it comes, it is the same color. It neither survives nor does it live. It appears when it is wanted."[24] As Whitehead explains about nature, he discusses the endless, elusive change of things. The reality of life is in its endless change. It is inaccurate to say that life is a static noun but the process of becoming. Life as *salim* is a form of movement, the process of life. Therefore, *salim* is the whole movement of life in which all the organic systems and human life are interwoven as one organic body, the macrocosm.

Kim Ji-Ha's observation of the world as one organic unity of microcosm [*sowooju*] and macrocosm [*daewooju*] can be comparable with the Christian sense of "*oikoumene*," the whole inhabited world, seeing the world as a whole organic unity of humankind. The term, ecology, is derived from the Greek, *oikos* (οἴκος), [household]; and *logos* (λόγος), [knowledge]. The roots of ecology, economics, and ecumenism are all found in *oikos*. Thus, ecology is defined as a study of the household of organisms. However, *oikoumene* has been used to refer to the human inhabited world of the cosmos in an anthropocentric sense.

When a model of the human household is suggested in a broad sense, we cannot avoid the conventional patriarchal structure in which the father is almost always the head of the household. I suggested earlier that all life in the cosmic body, including inorganic things, not only human beings, should be considered as family members, if one uses the analogy of *oikoumene* to explain the interconnectedness and interdependency of every singularity of the earth and the whole universe as microcosm and macrocosm. The key points of this analogy, then, is to overcome the anthropocentric and patriarchal culture and to transform them into cosmocentric and ecocentric one. If one is to include everything in this household as family members who live, and of course, die together, as a community of communities, the things in the world are not simply decoration or furniture in our planet-home but are considered active participants.

The Christian ecofeminist theologian, Sallie McFague, sees that at the heart of an alternative Christian good life is the imagination of the whole earth as G*d's household, G*d's *oikos*. The earth is *oikos*, the household, in which we are all called to live.[25] Her household concept of G*d is based on her body concept of G*d. For her, all creatures are, in a holistic sense, the world as the body of G*d. She writes:

> A different kind of economy is the *oikos*, the
> household. To discover who we are (what the world

> is) we see ourselves within God in Christ. We are the body of God. We are God spread out, we are God incarnate. We (the universe) come from God and return to God. We all together make up the body of God — God going out, God enfleshed, *God becomes matter*.[26]

For McFague, the word, "we," does not mean humankind only but the earth and universe as a whole organic unity, the body of G*d: "We are all in this together. We are, indeed, flesh of its flesh, bone of its bone."[27] McFague emphasizes, everything is coherently connected to every other thing. The author of *Dark Green Religion* (2010), Bron Taylor also uses the home as metaphor for the earth: "Earth is our home and home to all living beings. Earth itself is alive. We are a part of an evolving universe. Human beings are members of an interdependent community of life with a magnificent diversity of life forms and cultures."[28] Thus, *oikos* as the image of home has two crucial aspects: first is a dwelling space, shelter; the second aspect of *oikos* is connections (interconnectedness). I would also emphasize our bodily connection to all things in the whole universe as one living body, that is, as "a homelike organism." A living subject cannot completely distance itself from the other living subjects as well as from non-organic things. In this endless organic communication of the micro and macro level of life, we live together and die together as well as create and become together, becoming multiple and multiply becoming.

In terms of an interconnected symbiosis, Kim prefers to refer to the natural world as "life" rather than as environment. For example, Kim points out that it is improper to refer to nonhuman nature as "environment" rather than to "life."[29] From the perspective of Kim's preference to change the name of "nature" to life, when we see nature as environment, the ecological crisis becomes a problem among many problems of the world. When we refer to this natural world as environment, it becomes anthropocentric because the word "environment" means surroundings and conditions of humans, existing for human beings.

Nevertheless, nature as "a whole" is an organic body, *daewooju* [macrocosm], and human beings are a part of that nature as *sowooju* [microcosm]. They are never separated but are interconnected within a greater whole. The whole planet is then understood as one vast ecosystem or bio-system. In this symbiotic system like a web, everyone's life is involved with others, affecting each other. Everything is interfused into every other thing. This natural world is basically life, the full movements of *salim*. Kim notes that participating in the full movements of *salim*, "the human body is not just a miniature of the whole cosmos, but the endless movements of this gigantic cosmos."[30] This assumption deconstructs the dualism of the anthropocentric idea.

Kim Ji-Ha does not use the term, "process," when he defines life. Nonetheless, in his symbiotic view of life as an organic unity resembling home, he replaces the word, being, with the term, life. He then refers to life as becoming. He distinguishes our living as 'becoming' [*saengseong*, 生成] distinct from the understanding of static 'being' [*jonjae*, 存在].[31] Kim emphasizes that "life means living which is changing, creative evolutions of actions."[32] From the process view, life is not being but becoming. Yet, life can be recognized as being temporally and conditionally in the process of becoming as Kim chose the word, becoming [*saengseong*, 生成], rather than being [*jonjae*, 存在] to define life as *salim*.

Kim Ji-Ha's observation of life as endless movements, therefore, becoming, bears a surprising resemblance to the Whiteheadian notion of becoming. The Whiteheadian being as discussed in *Process and Reality* reflects being of actual entities. For Whitehead, being or existing, is acting. The Whiteheadian being is equally becoming in its aspect of acting. The Whiteheadian being is not the Aristotelian *ousia* but the being of its becoming, its becoming actual:

> The nature of a being is a potential for every becoming. The being of a *res vera* [actual entity] is constituted by its becoming. The way in which one actual entity is qualified by other actual entities is the experience of the actual world enjoyed by that actual entity, as subject. *Process is the becoming of experience.* Apart from the experiences of subjects there is nothing, nothing, nothing, bare nothingness.[33]

Therefore, for Whitehead, being is equally becoming, the becoming of experience. I recognize both the Kim and Whiteheadian understanding of 'life as becoming' in its mobility and continuity of living as *salim*, since *salim* is life in movement.

Both Kim and Whitehead see life in the process of movement, not in the static essence. For Whitehead, life is actually "process." Whitehead sees the universe as in rhythmical pulsation in which there is an endless process of actualization of potentiality, from potentiality to actuality, and from actuality to potentiality, from the many to one, and from the one to the many.[34] For Whitehead, the term, "one," is not the integral number one but the indefinite article "a" or "an," and the definite article "the," since it stands for the singularity of an entity. Therefore, the term "many" presupposes the term, "one," and *vice versa*. "The many become one, and are increased by one."[35] In the Whiteheadian cosmology, in terms of creativity one and many are interconnected in "the category of the ultimate;" its function is irreducible, coherent interconnection between unity, multiplicity, and creativity.[36] Thus, for Whitehead, being means becoming, more accurately, "becoming together." For one actual occasion, all diverse entities coherently enter into complex unity together. This process, by which one actual entity involves the other actual entities among its components, is called "concrescence."[37] The Whiteheadian notion of being is not a given but a "moving whole" that constitutes itself within a perpetual creative transition from multiplicity to unity.[38] It is the process whereby a plurality of entities becomes a creative novelty of experience.

Likewise, Kim writes, "life is a process of convergence and dissemination in which one becomes many and many become one endlessly."[39] Kim uses the "dandelion seeds" metaphor to explain the *salim* movement as the process of convergence and dissemination that should emerge through both the centrifugal force and the centripetal force.[40] In my understanding of Kim, the *salim* movement should start from both the whole as the multiple and the individual. In this process 'the obvious solidarity of the world' receives its explanation as Whitehead requires. This process shows the Whiteheadian process of the ultimate that "the many become one, and are increased by one."

Nonetheless, Kim's dandelion seeds metaphor for *salim* does not seem like a vertical movement or a top-down structure but a horizontal one, a rhizomatical movement in the Deleuzian language. Dandelion seeds blow rhizomatically without a program or a plan and create multiplicities. Deleuze and Guattari assert that multiplicities are rhizomatic and expose arborescent pseudo-multiplicities for what they are.[41] They present "rhizome" as a nomadic and fluid movement that rejects a pivotal center but a horizontal becoming. Through this figure of the "rhizome," they envision structure-free-movements that spread towards the multiple exteriors and become unpredictably permutated by coming into contact with whatever lies in their exterior. The rhizome is an achronological system where non-categorizable singularities and multiplicities traverse the fixed boundaries without being arranged and schematized by the central order.[42]

Kim, however, asserts to build a "grassroot-democracy" through the "dandelion seed-movement."[43] I would say that both "dandelion seeds" and "grass roots" are good examples of Deleuzian rhizomatic movements that there are neither points nor positions but only lines in a rhizome such as those found in a structure of "tree or root."[44] Any point within a rhizome can be connected to any other point. Thus, a rhizome has no definitive beginning or ending. Rhizomes are converging lines of movement. There are no hierarchies of rhizomes but only horizontal connections: "From the cosmological to the microscopic, but also from the microscopic to the macroscopic."[45] A dandelion flower blooms by a seed among thousands of seeds and creates numerous seeds that again blow away through the continual process of convergence and dissemination. A singularity creates a multiplicity; a multiplicity is a source of transformation composed of configurations of fuzzy, flexible, and vibrating lines with indeterminable trajectories. In other words, a multiplicity is necessary for regeneration, becoming new. As Kim suggested above, *via* the dandelion seed and grassroot analogies, the *salim* movement must not be dictatorial from a pivotal order but should be multiple and horizontal through the interconnectedness of "the cosmic way of life."[46]

Kim briefly mentioned Deleuze to explain his notion of *salim*: "Deleuzian *chaosmos* is an empty space from which life springs out as becoming."[47] It is surprising that Kim quoted Deleuze though he did not develop it any further discussions. Also, Whitehead strikingly claims that life is characteristic of "empty space."[48] Though Kim does not mention Whitehead, he explains "*chaosmos* as empty space" which is a space of freedom, and a primal condition of *salim*. Whiteheadian empty space is a space of freedom that keeps living occasions (re)producing novelties. Through analyzing Kim Ji-Ha's observation of life, I understand that *salim* is the actual movement of life, therefore, life as becoming, reflects the process of life. *Salim* is the movement in the process of becoming through which potentiality becomes actuality not "once and for all," but constantly and endlessly. Therefore, life is neither a substance nor an essence, defined in terms of a changeless entity much like the Platonic form [*eidios*] or Aristotle's essence [*ousia*]. Thus, life as becoming is not ontological sense of part whole but a living (moving) organism as a whole that I call "the ecosystem." The ecosystem and the body together constitute the complexly ordered matrix, which is woven from both inorganic and organic bodies, can sustain the threads of living occasions as Whitehead calls "entirely living nexus"[49] and Deleuze calls "Body Without Organ." For Deleuze, the BwO can be a place, a plane, and a collectivity such as assembling elements, thing, plants, animals, tools, people, powers, and fragments of all of these. Both Whiteheadian living nexus and Deleuzian BwO constitute a novel space of betweenness that gives rise to new becomings.[50] *Salim*, life as becoming, somehow embraces (or bridges, or even goes beyond) both Whiteheadian and Deleuzian notions of becoming(s). This complex spatiality allows living occasions to access the ecosystem as a whole organic body (or BwO), and they are constructively integrated into a novelty of becoming(s). Nothing else can absolutely stay in a static form of being in the endless movements of perishing and becoming. If they do, then that is an empty appearance. *Salim* is neither an abstract concept nor an ontological being but the very movement of actualization, therefore, becoming. That is, becoming or concrescence is a self-creative act, which carries the responsibility for how and what it becomes. Therefore, I assert that *salim* is not just a movement but also 'a self-creating movement' as life in the process of becoming, reflecting the very nature of life.

Kim Ji-Ha notes that the principle of *salim* which Su-Un taught under the Daoist influence was "action through non-doing."[51] Non-doing means not doing intentionally but doing spontaneously in its natural way. Change and spontaneity reflect the nature of life. When one follows its own nature, it does not need forceful interaction such as that which occurs when birds fly and snakes crawl. Non-doing [*wuwei*, 無爲], therefore, refers to "doing non-doing" which proceeds freely and spontaneously from one's own nature. A bird's non-doing is to fly. Attempting to crawl would be a forced action for a bird.[52] For a cow, eating grass is natural; it is its non-doing. When people artificially engage in their diet and distort their natural way by feeding cows, cow meat and bones, it may result in problems such as mad cow disease. Mad cow disease is a manifestation of human's *jugim* culture. Instead of grazing and eating grass as the animals do naturally, they are fed diets that include products made from their own species. We have turned vegetarian animals into carnivores and cannibals, a gross violation of the order of nature. Therefore, *jugim* includes systemic violence against the way of nature.

The expression of *wuwei* is negative but the meaning is positive. However, Su-Un's Daoist notion of non-doing could be understood as a passive attitude toward life. If so, how can our intentional effort of *salim* be justified? According to Kim's interpretation of Su-Un, acting through non-action is the primary worldview of symbiosis that is self-realization of life.[53] Thus, non-doing does not mean mere passive immobility but rather an active practice of the way of life.

Kim calls the process of self-realization of life through non-action, "*ecocracy*."[54] Kim's suggestion of *ecocracy* offers a key to transferring the passivity of non-action to the active movement of life, *salim*. For Kim, "action through non-action means *ecocracy* by which all individual entities satisfy and realize the rules of nature without coercion but by spontaneous movements."[55] As Kim recognizes non-action as a new living system of *ecocracy*, beyond the anthropocentric worldview to the *ecocentric* worldview, I would suggest that we need to move from a democracy with its focus on the people to an *ecocracy* in which a process of decision-making where the interest of nonhuman species, local and global ecosystems, and future generations are taken into account, because their interest is our interest. The planet is a whole organic body of which we are a part and the earth is our home in which all things are biologically connected. Therefore, claiming *ecocracy* instead of democracy is a paradigmatic shift from a human-centered view to a cosmo-centric one.

As democracy suggests people's rule, *ecocracy* suggests nature's rule which is based upon non-doing principles. As a principle of *ecocracy*, non-doing is a kind of paradoxical concept. Actually, Su-Un's notion of non-doing is "doing non-doing." Even though it sounds paradoxical, it suggests the active passivity by negation of violence against life's spontaneity. Therefore, it is negation of negation, double negation, because doing non-doing is the negation of violence which is negation of life. Thus, I see non-doing a positive negativity and an active passivity rather than a mere lazy attitude toward life. When life is interrupted by destructive forces such as *jugim*, life resists *jugim*. It is nonviolent resistance, uttering a sacred "No!" to *jugim* and a sacred "Yes!" to *salim*. *Salim*, therefore, can be said to be a way of non-doing for life. *Salim* is an intentional effort that engages doing non-doing against *jugim* as well as being a spontaneous self-creating movement by nature.

Su-Un's notion of "doing non-doing" as active passivity, the negation of negation was concretized by his follower, Hae-Weol, who is the second leader of *Donghak* in his *Sip-Moo-Cheon* [十毋天, the ten negativities for *hanul* as the sacred]. The expression is negative but there is a positive motive of *salim*. Doing non-doing negatively restrains evil things for life. The declaration starts from the word, "do not" rather than "do" something.

> Do not deceive *hanul*.
> Do not ignore *hanul*.
> Do not hurt *hanul*.
> Do not disturb *hanul*.
> Do not kill *hanul*.
> Do not contaminate *hanul*.
> Do not starve *hanul*.
> Do not destroy *hanul*.
> Do not hate *hanul*.
> Do not defeat *hanul*.[56] (translation mine)

Hae-Weol's *Sip-Moo-Cheon* [十毋天, the ten negativities for *hanul*] does not accidentally echo the Ten Commandments from the Hebrew scripture in its negative conveyance, "Thou shall not...."[57] The Ten Commandments are actually a negative golden rule similar in meaning to *Sip-Moo-Cheon* in its non-hurting principles. Both suggest that one not harm others just as one would not want to be harmed. Thus, the negative conditions of *Sip-moo-cheon* are actually based upon the notion of "doing non-doing."

While the Ten Commandments are focused on two relationships – that between G*d and human beings and that between humans in a theocentric anthropocentric view, Hae-Weol's *Sip-Moo-Cheon* broadened its boundary to nonhuman nature and includes non-organic things beyond G*d and human beings. Thus, the important categories are *hanul* [the sacred] that includes *cheon* [天, heaven], *saram* [人, human], and *mool* [物, everything that includes organic and non-organic]. Through *Sip-Moo-Cheon*, Hae-Weol teaches us how we can practice the points of non-hurting *hanul* which include everything organic and non-organic. In all diverse living styles, not every form of living implies *salim*. There are destructive life forms, which are against the principle of *salim* within the aspects of *Sip-Moo-Cheon*: abandonment, betrayal, murder, rape, violence, deceit, discrimination, destroy, etc. and which do not represent life as *salim* but rather, life as *jugim*. Therefore, *salim* is a way of life which should be chosen intentionally in order to overcome the culture of *jugim*. Therefore, *salim* is an intentional effort to overcome *jugim* so as to enliven life following the movement of nature's spontaneity. The *salim* movement comes out of the practice of "doing non-doing," confronting *jugim*, living through the way of life.

Salim and Women

Kim Ji-Ha emphasizes that the privileged human subjects of the *salim* movement are women. The *salim* movement practiced widely by Korean people especially by Korean women. Kim established *Han-Salim* (One Ecological Organization for *Salim*) along with other ecological activists in 1989 declared "The Seven Principles *Han-Salim*"[58] which was based on his notion of *salim* movement. The *Han-Salim* organization has dealt with many ecological issues in Korean such as promoting eco-friendly organic farming, encouraging recycling, resisting against importing beef which may cause mad cow disease, etc. As a *salim* activist [*salim-kun*],[59] Kim Ji-Ha traveled to many areas throughout Korea to deliver his speech in support of the *salim* movement, concurrently giving theoretical support for dealing with many ecological issues.

Since the civilian government was established in 1993, the Korean people's movements have developed such that they not only advocate in support of human rights but also endorse symbiotic life for all life, in conjunction with the well-being of people. The Korean people have thus become more and more concerned with the ecological problems at hand. Korean people have started to bring ecological issues to the forefront of society and the people's movements [*minjung* movements] have become ecological movements. The "life saving" campaign of the *salim* movement has spread throughout the whole country.

The ecological movement in Korea started with a recycling campaign in 1990, and from that, the treatment of waste, especially, became a popular social issue. Today recycling is mandatory by the government and this is an ecological practice which is performed by most Korean women who, in the care of their homes, gather milk packs, make recycled soaps, avoid plastic bags and engaging in other socially responsible tasks. The *salim* Movement in Korea was not only an ecological movement but also became an economic (recovery) movement from 1997 on. When the International Monetary Fund (IMF) and South Korea negotiated the largest IMF rescue package ever in early December 1997, of approximately US$ 57 billion, it came as a shock to Koreans. Indeed, the situation became popularly known as the "IMF Crisis." Confronting the "IMF crisis," Korean women started the "*Ah-na-ba-da* Movement" as one of the *salim* movements to recover the Korean economy. *Ah-na-ba-da*[60] means saving [*"ah"kyuseoda*], sharing [*"na"nuoseoda*], exchanging [*"ba"kuauseoda*], reusing [*"da"siseoda*] which is, indeed, a recycling movement. The *Ahnabada* Movement is closely related to both the economy and ecology. Korean people practically have come to know the integral relationship between economic practices and ecology by working to recover from the IMF crisis (which had been caused by poor economic practices) through sound ecological practices. In capitalistic societies, people tend to think dualistically, matters related to the economy are public values while issues of ecology, related to life, are private ones. This dualistic profit-oriented capitalism has caused ecological problems as well as economic problems, leading to crises, throughout the world. By contrast, the *salim* movement functions as an ecological movement for saving the economy, connecting the economy and ecology in terms of *oikos*, our living organism, the household. There should not be a separation of concerns of ecology and economy in the household because everything we eat as well as the resulting waste products should be investigated through both economic and ecological aspects of living.

Following Kim-Ji-Ha, the Korean ecofeminist activist and theologian, Chung Hyun-Kyung, proclaimed the "*Salimist* Manifesto" (2002) in which she refers to Korean women who participate in the *salim* movement, "*salimists*" and remarks that her notion of *salim* and *salimist* are greatly indebted to Kim.[61]

> A *salimist* makes things alive, especially dying things like the earth. 2) A *salimist* touches everything like a magician, a revolutionary to smile and grow. 3) A *salimist* recycles everything: papers, milk, cartons, glass bottles, politicians and leadership positions, gods, and life. 4) A *salimist* is an activist who promotes peace, reconciliation and harmony. 5) A *salimist* loves women, nature, earth, and goddess, everything feminine and feminist. 6) If womanist is to feminist as purple, *salimist* is to feminist as dark green.[62]

According to Chung's "*Salimist* Manifesto," her audiences are apparently Korean women who are dealing with practical issues for the household and daily life. For Chung, *salimist* is actually a word for a Korean ecofeminist woman. She writes, "*Salimist* is a woman warrior who protects and enlivens the earth. She is a goddess within herself who loves and respects herself."[63] Her contribution of coining a new word for a Korean ecofeminist -- *salimist*, risks the problem of essentialism despite the shared distaste for the mystification of "woman" in feminism. Chung's identification of *salimist* with Korean ecofeminists creates difficulty for men to engage in *salim* or *salim* movements, as it implies the work is for women only. Thus, I suggest using the term, *salim-kun* [*anyone* who engage in *salim*] which does not exclude men, since men such as Kim Ji-Ha calls himself, *salim-kun*. *Kun* means both an expert or a master in a certain area in Korean. Therefore, *salim-kun* does not have to be a gender-specific word. Nonetheless, Chung's notion of *salimist* has inspired many Korean women to participate in the *salim* movement and academically influenced some Korean scholars such as Kim Seong Hee[64] and myself.

Kim Ji-Ha observes women as the forerunners of the *salim* movement, the subjects of the *salim* movement.[65] Kim's recognition of women as the subjects of the *salim* movement is both revolutionary and provocative in Korean culture. Women and *salim*, in terms of work in the home as being the function of women have been devalued in traditional Korean society. Kim emphasizes that we have to revalue and recognize women as mothers and household managers which are really important functions of life.[66] Kim asserts that women's motherhood and work in the house should not be romanticized but must be revalued scientifically, objectively, and socially. He recognizes women as subjects who give birth, nurture, care, educate, and provide comfort.[67] The value of life and the value of women are proportional because women's role as mother is inseparable from life.

In order to maintain life, the daily meal of Korean people is *bab* [밥, rice] a word that literally means rice, indicating the daily meal. The word, *bab*, is often used to indicate food in general. In Korea, *bab* has traditionally been served by women to their families. Cooking *bab* is also called *salim* but in a narrow sense, that is, of feeding. Unlike the traditional degradation of housework, Kim recognizes cooking and serving *bab* as the holy sacrament for enlivening. Kim Ji-Ha follows Hae-Weol's understanding of *bab*; "In a bowl of rice, the truth of heaven and earth exist. Serving *bab*, sharing *bab*, eating *bab* are the most sacramental rituals of all for life."[68] Kim's notion of *bab* is from Hae-Weol's *gyeong-mool* [??, reverence toward life including organic and nonorganic matter] principle.[69] The degradation of work in the home and women were popular aspects of nineteenth-century living in his days. Especially, working in the kitchen was the lowest form of housework compared to teaching children, sewing, cleaning, etc. At the time, women were ignored because they were considered as the people who take care of an unimportant part of human activities.

Thus, *bab* and women have been degraded as inferior and low (or the lowest). Nevertheless, Kim Ji-Ha recognizes *bab* as both sacred and divine, as life, following Hae-Weol's notion of life. Kim declares that the key to liberation is life: "*Bab* is a daily meal for Korean *minjung*, therefore, a source of living, *salim*. Therefore, *bab* is G*d, Jesus is *bab*, and *bab* is life."[70] This is Kim's interpretation of John 6:35. That is, Jesus said, "I am the bread of life. Whoever comes to me will never be hungry."[71] The reason for offering *bab* is to feed life. For Koreans, bread is *bab*, the daily meal. When we value *bab* as life, women who serve *bab* can be exulted as the subjects of life. Kim Ji-Ha's notion of *bab* breaks down the dualistic hierarchy of the sacred and secular. For him, serving *bab* is serving people. People are *hanul* [the sacred, G*d] as well as *bab*. Therefore, serving *bab* is serving G*d by means of G*d. When we eat *bab*, life eats life, life feeds life symbiotically. Kim exults women's role of cooking *bab* to a sacred place while it had been recognized as one of the secular tasks for which there was no compensation for work without any public value: "Those who work in the kitchen, mostly women, are, therefore, the holy priests. Serving *bab* is a holy ritual for life, *salim*, a holy work of G*d, *missio Dei*."[72] If I follow Kim's notion of *bab* as sacred not just material and the women's role or serving *bab* as the work of a holy priest, and not only in their inferior gender role, but also the food they served is sanctified and exulted. Nonetheless, the word, *salim*, in a narrow sense has been used as a replacement for cooking *bab* which is the women's task according to the traditional gender role.[73]

Then, if we are to refer to women as the subjects of *salim*, how can we avoid this essentialist romanticization of a "woman" as one who works in the kitchen? Kim's essentialist approach to define "women as life" challenges the traditional anthropocentric degradation of women and their traditional gender roles though it cannot avoid the danger of essentialism and generalization. The narrow meaning of *salim* is actually "household work," reflecting the women's stereotyped gender role. Even though that is very important for maintaining life as Kim observes, cooking food for feeding the family has been traditionally considered a private value rather than public work and, therefore, inferior to working outside of the household and making money. Though it is important to recognize women as the subjects of *salim* as Kim suggests, there is also the danger of limiting the women's gender role. Indeed, it could somehow justify the traditional gender role. Thus, in order to recognize women as the subjects of *salim*, two things should go together -- recognizing the importance of the narrow meaning of *salim* as the core part of life and broadening the meaning of *salim* as enlivening life which should be shared by everything as the subject of *salim*, not only for women but also for men, animals, plants, and nonorganic things, so that we can move beyond accepting the traditional gender role.

Kim Ji-Ha's solutions to solving this human despair in this ecological crisis in the *jugim* [killing] culture is that only femininity will save this world which is plunged into confusion. Furthermore, Kim declares that a woman is a symbol of the earth, reproduction, and the creation of culture that supports and maintains human life. Therefore, "woman and life are synonyms."[74] Kim suggests a new culture which will be created by the maternity of the earth, eros, paradoxical *chaos*, and the deep organic spirit that will save us from rupture and darkness.[75] For Kim Ji-Ha, "Culture is expression of the maternal spirit that comforts, heals the wounds, and invites becoming through endurance. Culture is like a warm-spirited woman. We need 80% of the femininity and 20% of the masculinity of our culture to solve this ecological crisis."[76] Here, Kim suggests the realization of femininity through an egalitarian vision by pointing out another unbalanced strategy in which femininity should be greater than masculinity.

Then, does Kim Ji-Ha mean that we should pursue a matriarchy after the deconstruction of patriarchy? Such thinking would suggest the danger of falling into a new dualistic structure that is the subversion of the oppressive structure of patriarchy. Not only that but also it may limit the image of woman as mother and housewife which has been the symbolic role of a woman for thousands of years emphasizing the importance of the reproduction of life. Traditionally, women have been charged with childbirth and nurturing that have blocked women from taking on other important positions in the society. Kim's efforts, however, are directed to making the unbalanced world balanced. There is no balance between *yin* [female principle] and *yang* [male principle] which are supposed to circulate rather than one oppressing the other. Actually, *yin-yang* is a complementary concept within constant change. The reason I put a hyphen between *yin* and *yang*, for it to read as "*yin-yang*," rather than as two separated characters -- "*yin and yang*" -- is because *yin-yang*, is like two sides of one coin that functions as one organic body. The *yin-yang* principle points out a world in balance and harmony in which one cannot oppress the other but both support each other and transform one another together in interconnectedness and interdependency. Nevertheless, in the anthropocentric androcentric worldview, in the so-called patriarchy, the balance of *yin-yang* has been unbalanced as Trinh T. Minh-ha, an Asian postcolonial feminist, criticizes when making reference to the *yang*-oriented world:

> Imagine a world of *yang* and *yang* instead of *yin* [the female principle] and *yang* [the male principle], and you will have the inhuman man-constructed world of Frankenstein. Nature, in such a container, will undoubtedly remain his nature, a culturalized man-made product, which one may refer to as Father Nature. The supposedly universal tension between Nature and Culture is 'a non-universal man dis-ease.'[77]

At this point, Minh-ha effectively points out the problem of an androcentric world which lost its natural balance of *yin-yang* as *yang* conquered both culture and nature as his own property and product as

Father Culture and Father Nature, *yang-yang* not *yin-yang*. In this unbalanced structure, there are two problems, one is the dualistic structure of culture versus nature by identifying man as culture and woman as nature. The other problem is that this dualistic structure, itself, is male-constructed as Minh-ha points out that the patriarchal world does not have both "Father Culture and Mother Nature" because Mother becomes a male-fashioned Mother exiled from culture, but only "Father Culture versus Father Nature."[78] This means that there is no place for women, in the patriarchal notion of nature.

By the same token Kim Ji-Ha explains why we need a feminine culture:

> Balancing *yin-yang* is living by nature, therefore, men and women are supposed to be equal. However, for thousands of years, the history has been occupied by *yang* and controlled by men. *Yin* has been oppressed for thousands of years, therefore, we have to exult *yin* with all our strength. Even if we lift *yin* highly up, *yang* will not be oppressed but be balanced at last because *yang* has been too high. It does not mean that we make *yang* a servant of *yin* yet even yin-yang as equal eventually.[79]

Nevertheless, Kim's thinking presents the danger of falling into essentialism by suggesting a reversal of the dualistic structure, though it could be understood as a "strategic essentialism"[80] as Gayatri Spivak suggests. That is, for Spivak, women today may have to take "the risk of essence" in order to think really differently.[81] According to Spivak, strategic essentialism has to look at where the group is situated, when one makes claims for or against essentialism.[82] However, Spivak reminds the reader that the reality of deconstruction is neither essentialist nor antiessentialist as she writes, "It invites us to think through the counterintuitive position that there might be essences and there might not be essences."[83] Therefore, only as a matter of strategy, as a feminist postcolonial scholar, she may become an essentialist. Then, the problem of Kim's essentialism is that Kim still depends on the traditional dualistic structure of femininity and masculinity. Therefore, there is the danger of generalization and reductionism in defining a woman as a singular noun and vice versa. In order to avoid this danger, we should discover that the power of *salim* is not of women, originally or essentially, but in everything, of course, including men as well.

> **Becoming the Other: Body Without Organ of Man**
> Becoming-woman is not imitating this entity or even transforming oneself into it. We are not, however, overlooking the importance of imitation, or moments of imitation, among certain homosexual males, much less the prodigious attempt at a real transformation on the part of certain transvestities. ... Becoming-woman must first be understood as a function of something else: not imitating or assuming the female form, but emitting particles that enter the relation of movement and rest, or the zone of proximity, of a microfemininity, in other words, that produce in us a molecular woman, create the molecular woman. [84]

For discovering the femininity in men, Kim Ji-Ha makes the startling and radical suggestion of "*koja*," a man with underdeveloped genital organs, as an ideal human. *Koja* [the castrated] was an official position for serving kings during the *Goryeo* (918~1392) and *Joseon* (1392~1910) dynasties. Their principal function was mainly to be responsible for the miscellaneous chores in the royal palace. They were the men who served the royalty. All women in the royal palace were considered the King's women. In order to prevent love affairs between the *koja* and the women in waiting in the palace, the *koja*'s genitals were castrated. *Koja* can be translated as eunuch (ευνούχος) in English. He is a person born male who is often castrated, typically early in his life for this change to have major hormonal consequences.

Eunuch literally means "a guardian of the bedroom." Castration was typically carried out on the soon-to-be eunuch without his consent in order that he might perform a special social function. This was common in many societies such as Persia, Greece, Rome, India, Turkey, Egypt, Ethiopia, China, Korea and Vietnam. In Korea, there were two types of *koja*: by accident (cf. castrated by dog bite) and by performed castration (tying his penis until necrotized by embolization).

They were the outcaste low class *minjung* (subaltern in the Spivakian term) in the society. *Koja* were the men of abjection, feminized body without organ of man. They were the people who existed only for one royal man from the imperialistic perspective. *Koja* is not a real man in that society for two reasons: first, because he has no man's organ; second, because their principal function was actually that of being the king's servant. Therefore, it was considered a woman's job. Thus, women's social position was disregarded, this feminized man with no male genitalia who took on women's tasks was not recognized as an ideal man and was oppressed as a lackey.

Unlike the traditional role of *koja*, Kim considers *koja* as a chosen human being by heaven because within *koja*, both *yin* and *yang*, femininity and masculinity, exist. Kim notes that "*koja* is a man who has been called by G*d, a celibate, a mutation, and a holy deformity."[85] It is interesting that Kim links *koja* to someone who responds to G*d's calling just as the Gospel tradition sees Jesus as a eunuch for the sake of the Kingdom of G*d (Matthew 9:12): "For there are eunuchs who have been so from birth, and there are eunuchs who have been made eunuchs by others, and there are eunuchs who have made themselves eunuchs for the sake of the kingdom of heaven. Let anyone accept this who can." As Jesus is recognized as an ideal human being in the Gospel tradition, even though *koja* is an example of one who has been made a eunuch by others, Kim considers *koja* a symbolic human being who has femininity in a man's body, a sexual hybrid. For Kim, "*Koja* does not take on traditional masculine attributes that are opposite to the feminine. He is a man who is fulfilled with love and beauty. His nurturing nature feeds and enlivens nature."[86]

Kim's suggestion of *koja* [a castrated male] as an ideal male who contains femininity in his male body is profoundly anti-phallogocentric and radically against the Freudian notion of the Oedipus complex. In the Freudian notion of the Oedipus complex, women are undeveloped males or castrated males much like little boys who have a small penis, similar to the female genitalia. Freud understood women's clitoris as a castrated penis that is a small sex organ or no sex organ at all. Thus, little boys have castration anxiety while women have penis envy. For Freud, a little girl is, therefore, a little boy with no penis. Thus, women have been recognized as being defective or lacking something essential. The Freudian phallocentric notion views women as little boys with disregard for women's differences from those of men. In this homogenizing and reductionist aspect, this world is occupied by two kinds of men only, "men and little boys," who want to recover their lost penis and who are afraid of castration, not women. Thus, as Lacan writes in *Écrits*, Freud unveiled the imaginary function of the phallus as the pivotal point in the symbolic process that completes, "in both sexes," the calling into question of one's sex by the castration complex.[87] According to Luce Irigaray's critique of Freud, "the feminine is always described in terms of deficiency or atrophy, as the other side of the sex that alone holds a monopoly on value: the male sex."[88] Her analysis of sameness in Freudian theory was particularly important because she used it to criticize his theory of female sexuality. In his view, Freud defines sexual difference by giving *a priori* value to sameness, shoring up his demonstration with time-honored devices, such as analogy, comparison, symmetry, dichotomous oppositions, and so on.[89] In the Freudian phallocentric worldview, there is no place for a mother as Catherine Keller writes, "For the Freudian patricide itself presupposes a prior, still more deeply repressed, matricide—a matricide reenacted at the level of theory when Freud privileges the father."[90]

Castration for Freud has an asymmetrical structure as two different series in girls and boys. According to Deleuze, castration for Freud is the common lot, "the transcendental phallus," which is presented in girls as desire and in boys as fear of losing it.[91] In this asymmetrical structure, nothing is in common in terms of the sexual organ between the two sexes where each subject communicates with "one sex or the other in another subject."[92] For females, this is the point of transition in which the daughter must shift from her original mother-love to father-love in the normal course of heterosexual development. Keller links the girl's desire and the boy's fear to "power." Keller interprets desire for the father as not only a desire for love but also for his social power: "Anger at her mother's importance may lead her into an alliance with the father, idealized in his distance and social power. But becoming aware of the lack of a penis in women aroused in him the terror of his own vulnerability of she lost it, so could he."[93] A penis means "power" in patriarchy. To be born as a boy means being privileged in a male-oriented society. Castration means being detached from power, becoming a minor, becoming a subaltern. For Freud women are castrated. "In Freud's theory of female castration and penis envy, ... , precisely the same structure is recapitulated: females are defined by a deforming lack."[94]

I recognize the importance of the Freudian analysis that identifies woman as a castrated male who has been ignored as a defect by the Law of the Father. For Freud, women are equivalent to castration, perhaps being cursed, because they are not quite male yet, having lost the symbol to be the ideal human -- the phallus. As the castrated, women have been alienated from the symbolic structure of the traditional Christian image of G*d. The symbolic is the realm of society and subjectivity that has been governed by the Law of the Father. Christian Religious symbolic is traditionally configured as masculine. Christianity is usually complicit with matricide and the occlusion of the feminine in so much as the Father G*d of monotheism and the homosexuated Trinity serves to affect the exclusive emergence of the male into the semiotic representation and cultural production. The castration anxiety which Freud found in the civilized male psyche exists in phallogocentric Christianity, not allowing for the mother. Applying Keller's analogy of the Freudian matricide to the phallogocentric Trinity, I would say that the traditional Christian Trinity is lacking femininity, 'the matricide Trinity.'

Kim's radical approach to idealizing a castrated male challenges the male divine image in the phallogocentric Christianity. Kim's suggestion of *koja* as an ideal human being who has femininity and masculinity in one body might be a radical feminist view that rejects the traditional image of the male in the same way that Elizabeth Johnson sees Jesus' likeness of G*d, not in his maleness but in self-giving love which is similar to women, mother. "The crucified Jesus embodies the opposite of the patriarchal ideal of the powerful man. Jesus' maleness is prophecy announcing the end of patriarchy divinely ordained. Jesus was a man but that more men are not like Jesus."[95] Thus, Johnson's notion of Trinity invites femininity in Sophia's Trinity, Spirit-Sophia, Jesus-Sophia, and Mother-Sophia.

Similarly, Luce Irigaray points out that "The life of Christ cannot be reduced to the pathein of the Father's will. It would open the way for the transcendence of the other that has always been covered over by the Father-Son paradigm."[96] According to Irigaray, it is only the female divinity that can provide the imaginary, the symbolic order, whereby women can attain subjectivities, not equal to men but different from them.[97]

> The god[98] comes. And darkness covers the earth.
> Thick shadow blots out the sky. The ocean is
> unleashed. The earth shakes. Birth of the eternal
> feminine. Women enter into mime when the power of
> the man-god is at hand. The power of the mother and
> the goddess of love give way to the nurses and female
> servants of the phallic cult.[99]

Irigaray notes, "To go beyond, to read, in it, the fruit of the covenant between word and nature, between *logos* and *cosmos*. The spirit? Not, this time, the product of the love between the Father and Son, but the universe already made flesh or capable of becoming flesh, and remaining in excess to the existing world."[100] Irigaray's approach challenges the androcentric culture and the phallogocentric Christianity and tries to deconstruct the dyadic structure of culture versus nature as man versus woman, thus, connecting *logos* and *cosmos*, word and nature.

Irigaray's declaration of the birth of a feminine G*d reminds me of Kim Ji-Ha's prediction of the coming of the feminine world (the *yin* world). According to Kim, a new creation ends the period of *yang* and brings a harmonized world with *yin-yang* in which femininity leads masculinity. Kim asserts that the *salim* movement does not suggest a subversion of a gendered hierarchy to make men and women enemies but rather, suggests that it should embrace all efforts equally including those of *yin* and *yang*, following the nature of life. Thus, the new epoch of creation is not *yang*-centered but *yin*-centered. In order to find the balance and harmony of *yin-yang*, *yin* needs to gain its subjectivity from her other-ness because this world has been traditionally *yang*-centered.[101] Kim recognizes culture as one of the most feminine aspects rather than the masculine. His notion of culture as feminine contradicts the traditional dualistic notion of culture which has been recognized and almost identified as male while nature has been identified as female. Kim's move from the dualistic distinction of culture versus nature, as man versus woman, defining woman as culture, gives hope for taking a further step. Kim shifts the androcentric notion of culture to a culture of *salim,* which is feminine in his view. I would say that Kim's notion of culture is a future-oriented one, a culture of life and spirituality, therefore, a *salim* culture.

Wonhee Anne Joh, a postcolonial theologian, writes that Kim's later works move away from a gender dichotomizing tendency to a wholistic understanding of relationality and diversity of 'life.' His image of the revolutionary is "the caring mother." However, Joh warns the danger of celebrating biological essentialism as a feminist and places her position in the interstitial space between both sites.[102] As such, I want to move beyond and take a further step from his essentialist notion of culture as feminine. The most important function of *salim* as enlivening is that of reproducing. If we limit reproduction as being only a women's task, then it can be a serious problem. When we observe all different forms of life, we can find that reproduction cannot be limited only to females. Men are producing sperm and all bodies are generating cells. Not only women but also men and not only organic beings but also non-organic beings constantly and endlessly reproduce new things and become new entities. In this sense, I can say that 'everything is feminine' and able to be feminine, if we understand the term, feminine, birthing, in the traditional gender stereotype. It gives a clue to the blurring of traditional gender roles, decolonizing both women and men from their respective oppressions.

In a certain sense, everything in this world in its molecular level is producing and reproducing. All beings are becoming new beings every second. It is the same as childbirth and nurturing which cannot be limited only to females. If we emphasize only femininity, it can be dangerous and problematic to see a woman only through the lens of her biological function rather than by appreciating the diverse aspects of personality, and the range of possibilities for her besides that of being a mother. Such thinking also can limit one from seeing the reproductive functions of men and other things. Rather, this is the time to find femininity in men as well as fertility in non-organic things in order to transform the androcentric and anthropocentric views into life-centered views. The fecundity cannot be limited to women, especially to fertile women but can be applied to this whole ecosystem. Fecundity is a movement of becoming, a creative oscillation, and dynamic vibration. This creative becoming of life can be called *salim*, that is, that from which all aspects of whole creation are born and into which every life function as the matrix of becoming, interdependently, as one organic body. We can symbolically discover the power of *salim* which can transform masculine culture into *salim* culture, liberating women from their biological and social functions of only being mothers and discovering the femininity and fecundity in men, even in all non-organic things.

Twenty-first century culture can be defined as the culture of capitalism which can be another name of masculine culture. Human beings and non-human nature are affected and controlled by the capitalist 'economy system' that has threatened the 'ecosystem,' manipulating the lifestyle of the people and distorting human environment, so-called "nature." Deleuze and Guattari claim, "Capital is indeed the body without organs of the capitalist, or rather of the capitalist being." [103] For interpreting Deleuze and Guattari's body without organ, Spivak suggests that the opposite pole of capital is nature, the limit of human being, the "Realm of Freedom," "Nature is the great body without organ of man." [104] Beyond the dichotomy of masculine feminine without the organ of man, everything is endlessly causing and creating every other thing in the process of becoming. In this sense, I would refer to every body, both at the micro and macro levels, as a maternal body: birthing, dying, and renewing itself. We must recognize that the power of *salim* exists not only in women and men but also in everything-living and non-living aspects of creation.

Chapter III

Decolonizing Life: A Postcolonial Reading of *Salim*

The Korean *salim* movement is actually rooted in the notion of life in *Donghak* and its corresponding movement. The *Donghak* movement can also be understood as a *salim* movement as well as relevant to a decolonizing movement. In its formation and philosophical backgrounds, *Donghak* can also be understood as a cultural and religious hybrid that was influenced by Buddhism, Confucianism, Daoism and Christianity. Thus, I would like to frame this chapter with an understanding of the postcolonial task in terms of 'hybridity' and the 'subaltern' to develop my argument of *salim* as a decolonizing movement of life.

Interestingly, one can say that nature as life is not only the object of decolonization but also is, in fact, the decolonizing subject. This chapter develops the concept of *minjung* in Korean *minjung* theology in relation to nature as the subaltern, reading *salim* through Spivak's postcolonial notion of subalternity by employing her initial hint toward an ecofeminist postcolonialism. The subjectivity of the subaltern, that is, the subaltern consciousness, is analyzed through the Foucauldian notion of bio-power which can also be called survival power, or *salim* power. The unfolding of *salim* is discussed in the last section of this chapter, The Spatiality of Planetarity, in which the hybridity of *salim* is compared to the Deleuzian *chaosmos* and Catherine Keller's process notion of *tehom* [the deep] through my analysis of Kim Ji-Ha's *teum* [interstitial space].

Donghak **as a Decolonizing Movement, a Religious Hybrid**

> Songweoldang: Do you study Buddhism?
> Su-Un: I like Buddhism.
> Songweoldang: Why did you not become a monk?
> Su-Un: Understanding the Buddhist principles without having to become a monk would be better.
> Songweoldang: Then, are you Confucian?
> Su-Un: I like Confucianism, but I am not Confucian.
> Songweoldang: Well, then, are you Daoist?
> Su-Un: I like Daoism, but I am not Daoist.
> At this point, the Buddhist monk, Songweoldang, is puzzled, becoming more anxious to get into the mind of Su-Un:
> Songweoldang: What do you mean exactly? What do you like best among those?
> Su-Un: You have two hands. Do you have to like one more than the other?
> Songweoldang: Now, I understand. You mean you like the whole body, don't you?
> Su-Un: I am neither Buddhist nor Confucian, nor Daoist still. I love all of the principles, for there is no place where *Cheondo* [天道, Heavenly Way] does not reach.[1]

The unique understanding of *salim* and the awareness of life have been strongly emphasized in *Donghak*. At the time that Su-Un initiated *Donghak* (1860), there were various religious and philosophical traditions such as Confucianism, Daoism, Buddhism, and Christianity, the latter being the most recently introduced to Koreans and which had been introduced as *seo-hak* [western learning].² The philosophy of *Donghak* was influenced by three major East Asian philosophies: Confucianism, Buddhism, and Daoism along with Christianity, syncretized with Korean culture. As one can observe from the conversation above, Su-Un distinguished *Donghak* from other major Asian religions and Christianity, yet, collectively, he embraced aspects of them which he viewed as constructive, and syncretized them with a Korean cultural understanding of life as a hybrid.

To what extent can one say that *Donghak* is a religious hybrid? *Donghak* is a life-centered cosmology, standing for reverence toward life and creation. The notion of life in Su-Un and Hae-Weol was familiar and thus enabled Korean people to embrace it with ease because it creatively combined Confucianism, Buddhism, Daoism, and Christianity with the traditional life-centered consciousness of the Korean people. In this sense, Kim Ji-Ha argues that "Korean people from diverse religious backgrounds could easily accept the cosmological practice of self and the praxis of social transformation of *Donghak*."³

Ahn Sang Jin, a *Donghak* scholar, notes that *Donghak* dialectics is a combination of the nonduality [不二] of Buddhism, and the *yin-yang* [陰陽] of Confucianism, as well as the Korean traditional concept of *han* [한, one or great].⁴ One can also observe that the holistic non-duality in *Donghak* was influenced by the Korean non-dualistic Mahayana Buddhism, the notion of reverence from Confucianism, and the practice of doing non-doing as being actually Daoistic. Moreover, Su-Un's concept of G*d [*hanul*] as a personal G*d as an engaged relationship with the embodied through *si-cheon-ju* [embracing *hanul*] shows the influence of Christianity.

Scholars agree that *Donghak* can be viewed as a religious and cultural hybrid. However, it is erroneous to evaluate and simplify the aspects of other Asian religions to find similarities in *Donghak* and thus conclude that *Donghak* is a combination of all of the other religions of that era. According to Shin Il-Cheol, a *Donghak* scholar, the similarities that can be found between *Donghak* philosophy and the conventional religions and philosophies are a result of Su-Un's unique hermeneutics of the traditional concepts, not just a simple appropriation or combination of those traditions.[5] Su-Un's religious experience and theology were related to his historical situatedness. There is no such thing as a pure culture. Every culture is hybrid.

Even though one cannot deny the influences of the conventional Korean religious and philosophical traditions, including Christianity, Su-Un did not confine himself to any of those traditions. Su-Un strongly differentiated *Donghak* from any other religion as noted in the dialogue with Songweoldang. That is, Su-Un noted that "My *do* [道, way] is a new teaching and philosophy which never have been heard and can never be comparable to other ways."[6] Su-Un realized that the conventional Asian religions did not give any hope for the people at the time because the *ki* [energy, spirit] was exhausted: "This is a time when such old traditions as Buddhism or Confucianism cannot lead people on. What we need to do now is grasp the limitless energy that could induce a living spirit out of the dead bodies and open a new heaven, new earth, and new human beings."[7] Su-Un pioneered a new way or *do* [道] that would change the conventional corrupt culture to a new culture, thus bringing a new heaven and a new earth for which the conventional religions and Christianity had no solution.

When Su-Un was born (1824), Korea was embroiled in dire social and political turmoil, both internally and externally. The lower classes were most affected by government corruption. The corrupt officials oppressed peasants who did not own their land under systemic and ongoing poverty. Thousands died of hunger and many were forced to abandon their villages in search of work or food.[8] Externally, Korea was threatened by colonial Japan[9] and the imperial west.[10] Su-Un described imperial western power which seemed invincible in conjunction to the dire situation of Korea in his *Podeokmun* [Book of Virtues]: "The westerners are always victorious in battle. There is nothing they cannot accomplish. I could not but be concerned that if the whole (Eastern) world was conquered, Korea would fall as well. How shall we find a way to protect the nation and secure peace?"[11]

Then, how can we characterize *Donghak* as a movement? I would like to call attention to three aspects of the *Donghak* movement: first, the *minjung* movement; second, the *salim* movement, and third, the decolonizing movement. The *Donghak* Movement was originally known as the *Donghak* Peasant Revolution.[12] According to Kim Yong-Ok, a professor of Asian Philosophy in Korea, it is erroneous to refer to the *Donghak* movement as a Peasant Revolution. The subjects of the movement were not only peasants but a cross-range of people who resisted Korean social structures and the foreign powers, regardless of their social positions. Kim points out that the name of the movement was coined by the scholars in North Korea. Kim asserts that the reason the North Korean scholars called the *Donghak* movement a Peasant Revolution is to justify communist revolution.[13] Thus, it limits the *Donghak* movement to a revolution of ideology. The participants of the movements were mostly the oppressed, the *minjung*, therefore, it could also be referred to as "the *Donghak Minjung* Movement" instead of the Peasant Revolution.[14] I agree that one can refer to the *Donghak* movement as a *minjung* movement because the *Donghak* movement not only emerged from one social class, the peasant class, but there was representation from a variety of people who believed and agreed with a new worldview of *Donghak* to find a better way of living within their own circumstances. If one considers the people of the *Donghak* movement as peasants, it could easily be viewed as being similar to the Marxist revolution by the labor class, the *proletariat*. Even though *proletariat* suggests the industrial labor class, the farmers before industrialization were also members of the working class in Korea. Nonetheless, it is important to note that *Donghak* was not an ideology which only attempted to eradicate feudalism but was a movement to honor and dignify 'life.' Therefore, people who practice *Donghak* do not say in the Korean language, "I believe in *Donghak*" but affirm, "I do *Donghak*."

Kim Yong-Ok clarifies that "*Donghak* is not a belief but a practice that does not imply a one-time revolution but a continual practice in the process of life."[15] Kim Yong-Ok evaluates the

Donghak movement as a suggestion of a new worldview which *minjung* are the subjects not the imperial monarchy. Thus, Kim Yong-Ok rejects the term, *gae-hyeok* [改革, modernization] when speaking of the *Donghak* movement. Rather, he calls it a process toward the objective of *gae-byeok* [開闢, opening a new world].[16] In this sense, the *Donghak* movement cannot be explained with the modern understanding of a class revolution, but as a *minjung* movement, understood as an event of the gradual and continual process of transformation which, according to Su-Un's teaching, is known as *gae-byeok* [opening a new world].

Secondly, one can understand the *Donghak* movement as *salim* movement. Kim Ji-Ha refers to the *Donghak* movement as the creative movement or "the restoration of life" [*salim*] and subjectivity.[17] He wrote, "The *Donghak* movement was the collective *praxis* of *salim* which resisted against the complex and all-pervasive killing, degradation, demolition of life [*jugim*] by the feudal government and Japanese imperialism."[18] In this aspect, one can see the *Donghak* movement as a movement for life, therefore, a *salim* movement, which resisted oppression against life and pursued the restoration of life.

Kim Ji-Ha remarks that his transformation toward life movement from the liberation movement was a consequence of his meditation on *Donghak*. By the influences of the philosophy of life in *Donghak*, Kim inspired "the *salim* movement" in 1980s, after he was released from prison. However, it is hard to say that Kim started the *salim* movement because the *salim* movement had already been practiced by Korean people, especially Korean women by their recycling and protecting nonhuman nature. Therefore, the ecological movement in Korea is called the *salim* movement. Kim recognizes *salim* as a new paradigm for the future of the world and the very content of a new consciousness. The core message of *Donghak* is in its notion of life. *Donghak* is a life-centered cosmology, focusing on reverence toward life and creation. Kim recognizes that the roots of the *salim* movement are in *Donghak* and the *Donghak* movement.

Lastly, I recognize the *Donghak* movement as decolonizing

movement. From this perspective, *Donghak* is a postcolonial hybrid of Asian philosophies and religions through the perspective of the colonized against the colonization of Japanese invasion and western imperialism. Even though Su-Un collected constructive elements from the conventional religions and *seo-hak* [western learning], he did not include *Donghak* in either of them. Rather, he created a unique message of life out of the colonial situation as a hybrid. According to Homi K. Bhabha, hybridity is a sign of the presence and engagement of colonial power. "The effect of colonial power is seen to be production of hybridization rather than the noisy command of colonialist authority or the silent repression of native traditions, then an important change of perspective occurs."[19]

Su-Un recognized Christianity as a powerful and destructive force of colonization. In his *Podeokmoon*, Su-Un observed the following:

> In 1860 I heard that people from the west were attacking and seizing the world, and were building churches and spreading their religion, proclaiming the will of the western god. They did not seek wealth and honor. Their only desire was to convert the world. I asked myself how could this be, how could such things happen?[20]

In spite of his recognition of western power as colonial and imperial which can be identified with Christianity, he considered the source of western power to be their spirituality which actually was identified with the western G*d of heaven. Consequently, Su-Un's attitude toward Christianity was ambivalent. Su-Un, himself, recognized that the similarities of his teaching with Christianity, at the same time, were distinct.

> The forms of our truth may be similar to those of the west, but the doctrines are very different. Our way emphasizes accomplishing everything through natural

predilection. If believers cultivate their heart, rectify their vital force, receive the divine teaching and put it into practice, transformation comes naturally. But the westerners have neither order in their words nor logic in their writing. They are ignorant of the spirituality of the vital force and lack the concept of the lord of heaven. They act as if they are praying, but they have no Sacred Incantation. Their way is vain and their doctrine does not commune with the Lord of heaven. How can one say then that their Way and our Way are the same?[21]

The similarity between the Lord of heaven in western learning and Su-Un's understanding of the Lord of heaven as *cheonju* [*hanul*] is that Su-Un accepted *cheonju* as a personal G*d who can communicate and be embodied, as he embraces *hanul* in him.[22] However, as we read through Su-Un's *Podeokmoon* above, *hanul* is also recognized as 'the process of becoming' through embodiment, rectification, and transformation by the believer as the *hanul*-embodied subject. Therefore, *hanul* is not an object of worship but the becoming subject through the endless practice of 'doing *hanul*.'

Su-Un's reaction to the west and other religions was neither rejection nor acceptance but one of creating a new value by transforming the constructive ideas from other religions through his cultural influences and historical situatedness of the internal and external turmoil of Korea. Susan Stanford Friedman, a postcolonial feminist, recognizes hybridity as both a geographical and historical term. In her view, as a geographical term, hybridity, represents a production of travel, migration, global flows, border crossing, etc. while as a historical term, hybridity, can be produced over time or under particular historical conditions.[23] In the process of transculturation, *Donghak* resulted in a historical form of hybridity as Friedman sees historical hybridity as the result of a particular set of conditions at a specific moment in history.[24]

Wonhee Anne Joh, a Korean-American postcolonial

Decolonizing Life 59

theologian, summarizes the politics of hybridity according to three basic trajectories: Her first trajectory views hybridity as the product of oppression. The second trajectory sees that hybridity undermines authority and displaces the binary thinking on which its power is based. The third trajectory, which Joh accentuates, suggests that hybridity is not an effect of inevitable political mixing but is a "thick description" of historical and geographical situations.[25] Joh emphasizes the multidimensional direction of power in the third trajectory of hybridity by suggesting the mutual agencies of all sides.[26]

Applying this mutual power of hybridity to the colonial situation, I understand Su-Un's ambivalence to the Other (other religions or power) as a double-edged mimicry. Mimicry results a resemblance which, at the same time, can be considered a menace. Bhabha articulates mimicry in two ways:

> Mimicry is a complex strategy of reform, regulation and discipline, which appropriates the Other as it visualizes power; Mimicry is also the sign of the inappropriate a difference or recalcitrance which coheres the dominant strategic function of colonial power, intensifies surveillance, and poses an immanent threat to both 'normalized' knowledge's and disciplinary powers.[27]

Donghak philosophy embraces the ambivalence of mimicry. As Su-Un differentiated *Donghak* from other religions, he emphasized the significance of the Way of *Donghak*. Even if one finds similarities in *Donghak* to other religions, *Donghak* cannot be associated with the dominant discourses at the time because *Donghak* as a religious, cultural, and historical hybrid through the process of mimicry produced a way of thinking which could also be considered as "not-quite sameness." Joh states, "The consequence is very different from the intention of the colonizer in that mimicry produces subjects whose 'not-quite sameness' acts like a distorting mirror that fractures the identity of the colonizing subject."²⁸ Thus, it is always dangerous and problematic to simplify *Donghak* as a mere combination or appropriation of the conventional religions of the era.

As one studies the influences of other religions in *Donghak*, one must also acknowledge that *Donghak* represented the Korean people's unique understanding of life in which Confucianism, Buddhism, Daoism, and Christianity were unified from the *minjung* perspective. Based upon the life-centered worldview of *Donghak*, the *minjung* recognized their own subjectivity and value and participated in the *Donghak* movement to restore their life and well-being. *Donghak* as a hybrid process of mimicry, thus problematized both the internal corruption and the external colonization in Korea, resisting both powers of authority. Similarly, Bhabha sees "the ambivalence of mimicry as a problematic of colonial subjection"²⁹ by which one can characterize *Donghak* as 'a decolonizing movement.'

Consequently, I would like to refer to *Donghak* as a *minjung*-centered, life-oriented, decolonizing movement, and therefore, 'a *salim* movement.' The term, *salim*, already refers to 'life as becoming' (a quality evolution) in which restoration and reconciliation of all different entities are included, restoration of the sick body, the poor economy, the polluted ecosystem, the wounded heart, *jugim* culture, broken relationship, imperialistic Christianity and theology, etc. Restoration (mending) is a way of recycling because it is a transformation through the conventional traces of life. The *Donghak* notion of life teaches that life is supposed to be *salim* not *jugim*. Against all of the *jugim* powers: the colonial Japanese invasion, the feudal caste system, the corrupted officials, the imperial west and Christianity, *Donghak* emerged as a hybrid through which people resisted the status quo for survival and more than survival, a quality of life, *salim*, which can also be viewed as the decolonizing power of life.

Then, what is the *salim* movement? *Salim* comprises all of the diverse movements for life as discussed above, reconciliation, restoration (including recycling), and re-creation. *Salim* is reconciliation for those who have opposed each other. Thus, *Salim* reflects and indicates the sanctification of all broken relationships which have been distorted, denied, exploited, oppressed, violated, tortured, and killed under the power of *jugim*. Life as *salim* tends to decolonize imperial power and, moreover, pursues evolution in terms of value and truth. Life as becoming, living, and *salim* in terms of expansion and transformation, finds a better way of living which is the power of life as Catherine Keller states, "Only with the holy source of all living things does hope stay alive, renewed in the power of life to renew itself, no matter what."[30]

Nature as a New Subaltern
Honor your parents, (*hyo*, 孝, filial piety)[31]
Respect your husband, (*gyeong*, 敬, reverence)
Love your daughter-in-law,
Treat your servants as your children,
Care for your cattle,
Don't cut a new branch of the trees,
Smile at your angry parents,
Neither hit your children nor make them cry.
Hitting children is hitting *hanul* [heaven, the divine]
because they have *hanul* in them, ...
Don't spit and blow your nose on the ground
For that is the face of *Hanul*.[32] (translation mine)

Hanul means heaven in Korean. Heaven is the sacred place. *Hanul* is a name for G*d in Korean as *hanulim*. *Hanulim* is a way to refer to *hanul* with a great deal of respect by the ending "*nim*." To illustrate the notion of *hanul*, the following story is told. One day Hae-Weol stayed at the house of his student, Seo Tak-Seon, on the way to *Cheongju*.[33] He was listening to the sound of cloth being woven. So he asked Seo, "Who is weaving the cloth?" Seo answered, "My daughter-in-law." Hae-Weol asked again, "Is the person weaving cloth really your daughter-in-law?" Because of the repetitive questions, Seo hesitated to answer, then, Hae-Weol replied, "The one who is weaving the cloth now is *hanul* [the divine], not your daughter-in-law. There is not even one little thing which is not *hanul* in the world."[34]

In recognizing the value of human labor as participating in G*d's creating actions at a time when human labor was ignored as the work of the low classes, the narrative of this episode elevates human labor and the working human as that of sacred work and the divine by saying *"hanul* is working." In Korean, the narrow meaning of the term, *salim*, traditionally related to household tasks such as weaving cloth, is mainly a task of women. In Korean society, at the time when women and the tasks related to female gender roles were disregarded for the most part, Hae-Weol recognized *salim*, women's housework, as G*d's creative action and women, the subject of *salim*, as *hanul*, or, that which is sacred. Thus, for Hae-Weol, G*d is labor,[35] the subject of *salim*, who keeps working for life. All forms of life, even non-organic matter, already have embodied *hanul* [the divine], while they are involved in specific movements. Therefore, everything can be considered *hanul*. When Hae-Weol called the weaving woman, *hanul*, he offered an extraordinary emancipatory praxis, a liberating message. His notion of reverence [敬, *gyeong*] is one in which there will be no discrimination of the poor under the rich, women under men, servants under masters, non-human nature and non-organic matter under human beings, since together, they are revered as *hanul*, one organic body. The life practice of Su-Un, the first leader of *Donghak*, was consistent with this vision: he freed his household servants and adopted them as his daughters and educated them after his enlightenment.[36] At the time, educating women was prohibited in the society. In that patriarchal and hierarchal aristocracy, a servant woman who was multiply oppressed by many because of her social status and gender might be referred to as the *minjung* of *minjung*.[37]

Minjung has many parallels with the term, "subaltern," adopted by Antonio Gramsci to refer to those groups of inferior rank in a society who are subject to the hegemony of the ruling class.[38] As *minjung* refers to the powerless people in society politically, economically, and sexually, according to Gramsci who focused on the historiography of the subaltern, the subaltern classes may include

Decolonizing Life

peasants, workers, and other groups denied access to hegemonic power. In order to learn about the subaltern, Gramsci noted that six points need to be considered:

> (1) their objective formation; (2) their active or passive affiliation to the dominant political formations; (3) the birth of new parties and dominant groups; (4) the formations that the subaltern groups produce to press their claims; (5) new formations within the old framework that assert the autonomy of the subaltern classes; (6) and other points referring to trade unions and political parties.[39]

The term, subaltern, was used by Antonio Gramsci in a Marxist sense, similar to the *proletariat* which is used for the working class by Karl Marx. For Marx, the *proletariat* is the low class of a capitalist society that does not have ownership of the means of production but can only sell their labor. According to Marx, capitalism is a system which is based on the exploitation of the *proletariat* by the *bourgeoisie*.[40] Similarly, for Antonio Gramsci, the term, subaltern, was primarily used to describe class dynamics, since the notion of gender had not yet been incorporated into his analysis.

Following Gramsci's notion of the subaltern, Homi Bhabha emphasizes the importance of social power relations in his working definition of 'subaltern' groups as the oppressed, "minority groups whose presence was crucial to the self-definition of the majority group: subaltern social groups were also in a position to subvert the authority of those who had hegemonic power."[41] Bhabha elaborates on Gramsci's term, subaltern, in a sense broader than simply that of class. He attempts to expand the meaning of the term, so that it refers to any group marginalized by hegemony. In his view, "The subaltern are the marginalized or minority communities who are struggling against various hegemonic oppressions of race, class, gender, generation, etc."[42] In the subaltern studies group in postcolonial studies, the subaltern refers to the general attribute of subordination in terms of class, caste, age, gender, politics, or in other ways. Ashcroft writes, "despite the great diversity of the subaltern groups, the one invariant feature was a notion of resistance to elite domination."[43]

From a postcolonial perspective, it is problematic to recognize the subaltern as well as the *minjung* in terms of class because it is difficult to find a clear borderline to classify the oppressed and the oppressor in the complex flux of society in which all diverse power distinctions in terms of gender, class, politics, age, religion, etc., interplay. By the same token, Wonhee Anne Joh asks the following: "What constitutes authentic subalternity? What epistemological criteria do we use when we continue to refer to the bifurcation of colonized and colonizer?"[44] As much as the classification of the oppressed and the oppressor is unclear and the authenticity of the subaltern is ambiguous, there may be more possibilities for elaborating the term and to expand the term, *minjung*, in a broader sense beyond the dichotomous modern understanding. If the subaltern is not a class word, then subaltern can be a more flexible term that can never be defined through ontological fixity.

Veena Das elaborates on the Gramscian historiography of the subaltern in her essay, 'Subaltern as Perspective (1989).' Das demands a historiography of the subaltern that displaces the paradigm of social action as defined primarily by rational action. She seeks a form of discourse where affective and iterative writing develops its own language. According to Das, "History as a writing that constructs the moment of defiance emerges in the magma of significations, for the representational closure which presents itself when we encounter thought in objectified forms is now ripped open. Instead, we see this order interrogated."[45] Das locates the moment of transgression in the splitting of the discursive present where greater attention is required to locate transgressive agency in "the splitting of the various types of speech produced into statements of referential truth in the indicative present."[46] In terms of speech and silence, speech can be understood as the male dominion and silence as the female in the patriarchal structure which excludes women from discourse. Nonetheless, Das' observation of speech in all diverse types through her careful consideration of transgressive agency may help to discover the invisible power and the silenced speech of the colonized.

According to Bhabha's observation of the historiography of the subaltern, "The invisible power that is invested in the dehistoricized figure of Man is gained at the cost of those 'others'—women, natives, the colonized, the indentured and enslaved – who, at the same time, but in other spaces, were becoming the peoples without a history."[47] I would like to relate Bhabha's historiography of the dehistoricization of the subaltern and Gayatri Spivak's claim that the subaltern is, by definition, speechless. Is it possible to hear the voice of the subaltern--since they have been dehistoricized, denuded of a social context in which their speech could register?

The notion of the subaltern became an issue in postcolonial studies when Spivak critiqued the assumptions of the subaltern studies group in her essay, 'Can the Subaltern Speak?' Spivak elaborates the problem of the category of the "subaltern" by looking at the situation of gendered subjects and of Indian women, in particular, both as objects of colonialist historiography and as subjects of insurgency, the ideological construction of gender that keeps the male dominant.[48] She applies the term, subaltern, to postcolonial studies, noting the following:

> In postcolonial terms, everything that has limited or no access to the cultural imperialism is subaltern -- a space of difference. Now who would say that's just the oppressed? The working class is oppressed. It's not subaltern. They are the least interesting and the most dangerous. I mean, just by being a discriminated-against minority on the university campus, they don't need the word 'subaltern'... They're within the hegemonic discourse wanting a piece of the pie and not being allowed, so let them speak, use the hegemonic discourse. They should not call themselves subaltern.[49]

For Spivak, people who represent the subaltern and can speak out on their behalf are not the true subalterns because subalterns cannot actually speak. Spivak asserts, the subaltern woman remain mute because she herself "cannot know or speak the text of female exploitation."[50] Spivak suggests that the subaltern is denied access to both mimetic and political forms of representation. The problem is that the subject's itinerary has not been abled to be traced so as to offer an object of seduction to the representing intellectual. This is Spivak's rhetorical way of saying that her (subaltern woman) indigenous language is incomprehensible to intellectuals or that she cannot produce texts because she is illiterate. Then, with what voice-consciousness can the subaltern speak?[51]

Spivak further specifies the category of the subaltern by recognizing Indian women as the gendered subaltern both as objects of colonialist historiography and as subjects of insurgency, the ideological construction of gender that keeps the male dominant. If, in the context of colonial production, the subaltern has no history and cannot speak, the subaltern as female is even more deeply hidden in the shadows.[52] Therefore, Bhabha's notion of dehistoricization for Spivak is the voiceless subaltern. When Spivak talks about the speechless subaltern, one should distinguish speech from mere talk. Unlike speech, talk requires no great amount of intelligence or cognitive skill. Her point is that there is no act or resistance that occurs on behalf of the subaltern that is entirely separated from the dominant discourse. Therefore, the subaltern cannot speak from a colonial perspective. Actually, regarding her own question, "Can the Subaltern Speak?," her answer is an emphatic no! "The subaltern cannot speak. There is no virtue in global laundry lists with a woman as a pious item. Representation has not withered away. The female intellectual as intellectual has a circumscribed task which she must not disown with a flourish."[53]

Just as Spivak sees women as the gendered subaltern, the word *minjung*, as well, is not necessarily just a class-oriented word. Insofar as *minjung* can be defined as people who are oppressed by a whole range of hardships, Korean women might then be defined as the *minjung* of *minjung*. As the *minjung* of *minjung*, can Korean women speak? In order to be able to hear Korean women's voices in the context of a Confucian society, it is very important to define *minjung* as both victims of society and the subjects of history. I would like to assert two points regarding Korean women as the *minjung* of *minjung*. First, Korean women in Korean Confucian society were the agents of history and, secondly, their role in doing *salim* (household tasks in a narrow meaning) sustained household living, despite their lack of recognition by an androcentric society. In this way, recognizing Korean women as historical agents does not necessarily contradict their status as the *minjung* of *minjung*. Insofar as *minjung* theology asserts that *minjung* are the subject of history, not victims of history, might we call *minjung* of *minjung* the subject of the subject.[54] Even though within a Confucian society, women have had less power than men, politically and economically, it is problematic to see women in Korean Confucian society as mere victims. In Korean Confucian households, women have taken on the key roles as providers of food, managers of the household finances, and the educators of their children. Therefore, they are the subjects of all the activities related to maintaining the household and sustaining the well-being of the family, in other words, of ensuring an environment of *"salim"* in the household.

Some have claimed that homes for Korean women in Confucian society are like prisons, in which they are enslaved and dehumanized. In this regard, Choi Hee-An writes in her book, *Korean Women and God*, that in Confucian Korea, "there was no room for women to be equal with men. Women's entire lives were designed to follow male orders and provide male genealogies. In Korean Confucian society, a woman's life goal was to produce a son."[55] It is possible to interpret the Korean women's role as one that produces male offspring for their patriarchal households since the society was obviously male-oriented. However, though women in Korean Confucian society could not really play active roles in public in comparison to men because of the patriarchal nature of the community values, women were not mere victims of the society.

It is very important for both *minjung* theology and postcolonial studies to reconsider the role of Korean women not as victims but as historical agents. For *minjung* theology, *minjung* is supposed to be the subject of history. When one talks about subjectivity, there can be no fixed, transcendent "I" as the subject but always the interchangeable flexible subjectivity in which we can call the Other who has been excluded from the main discourse (history) as the subject and agent. A postcolonial feminist theologian, Kwok Pui-lan, asserts that, "we can speak of women of subjectivity and of agency on the implications of these concepts for the struggle against injustice."[56] In this sense, women who struggle for surviving the unjust social structure can be considered the agents of history.

For postcolonial studies, the subaltern should be the core consciousness of the people as a historical perspective. The subaltern consciousness can challenge us to problematize the limitation and the boundaries of a given text, including the written history, instead of assuming the text to be fixed and given. From the perspective of the people who have been ahistoricized, hidden, and silenced, history should be re-viewed, reinterpreted, reiterated, and retold.

Women's subjectivity in the male-oriented and male-dominant world can be understood as "subaltern agency" as Bhabha suggests. Bhabha retells "the *chapati* tale"[57] as a major instance of the transmission of insurgency. *Chapati* is unleavened flatbread in India. Seeing almost every culture has a version of flatbread,[58] Bhabha points out the circulation of the flatbread that initiates a politics of agency negotiated in the antagonisms of colonial cultural difference.[59] Bhabha recognizes *chapati* not from its ontological cultural origins as such a perspective may be the result of a cultural binarism but as an internal transformation, hybridization, of which he finds "subaltern agency."[60]

> It is the indeterminacy of meaning, unleashed by the contingent *chapati* that becomes the totem meal. ...

They bite the greased bullet and circulate the myth of the *chapatti*. In so doing, they pass on the contagion of rumor and panic into their own serial, sensible narratives that very act of repetition.[61]

Bhabha comments, "everywhere far and near the army under some maddening impulse are looking out with strained expectation for something, some unseen, invisible agency has caused one common electric thrill to run through all."[62] The transmission and transformation of flatbread in all different communities is the process of hybridization in which the recipes were transmitted with rumors and stories through sharing bread. In my childhood, I enjoyed watching my mother while she was cooking and remembering how she made it. My mother usually let me taste what she cooked first and asked how it was. When I became a teenager, my mother and I worked together in the kitchen. I really liked the time with my mother in the kitchen. I would listen to my mother's stories as well as those related to the recipes she was using which was so educational that it helped me to recognize who I was in terms of our family history. One of our favorite recipes was *boochimgae* (Korean flat pancake mixed with lots of vegetables and flour). I have now transmitted a little bit of that hybridized recipe of *boochimgae* from my mother to my daughter along with the storytelling of our family history while teaching her Korean culture. My daughter also created a hybrid recipe that contains all the transmitted stories with her own feeling as a Korean American.

From generation to generation, the recipes have been transformed into all different styles of flatbread, carrying the stories of mothers. Not only the difference between my mother's recipe and mine but also, each time I produce a slightly different version of *boochimgae* according to what I have in my refrigerator and how I feel on that day, even though I engage a kind of repetitive action. I understand these differences of repetition in a paradoxical manner because I repeat the "unrepeatable," much like the notion of Deleuze regarding repetition and difference:

> To repeat is to behave in a certain manner, but in relation to something unique or singular which has no equal or equivalent. And perhaps this repetition at the level of external conduct echoes, for its own part, a more secret vibration which animates it, a more profound, internal repetition within the singular. This is the apparent paradox of festivals: they repeat an unrepeatable. They do not add a second and a third time to the first, but carry the first time to the 'nth' power. With respect to this power repetition interiorizes and thereby reverses itself.[63]

I repeat. Therefore, I create a hybrid. In the process of repetition, I mimic the one I have learned at the same time revise the given.

I sometimes bring *boochimgae* to my advisor's monthly advisee meeting (*Keller-collective*) for a potluck dinner. When we share all different foods on one hybrid plate, they are all hybridized with our dialogues in which the multiplicity of culture and people are being touched through a joyful border crossing. This contingent and borderline experience creates a newness which Bhabha calls "the margin of hybridity," where cultural differences converge both contingent and amidst conflict touch, at times experiencing a moment of panic which can reveal a borderline experience.[64] In such instances, it resists the binary opposition of racial and cultural groups as homogeneous polarized political consciousness.

One piece of flatbread is a cultural hybridity where subaltern agency can be found as the subject of oral transmission. From village to village, generation to generation, secret recipes have been transmitted in the shape of those flat breads made from flour and water, forming the common bread for the people *(bab)*, carrying stories behind the history as Bhabha writes, "But whatsoever the real history of the movement, it had doubtless the effect of keeping alive much popular excitement in the districts through which the cakes were transmitted."[65] Through the process of transmitting, cooking, sharing of the common bread, a mysterious recipe of the flatbread is engendered, reexamined, re-articulated, and retold.

Then, if we were to ask Bhabha Spivak's question, can the subaltern speak? Bhabha's answer quite likely would be "Yes!" For Bhabha, not only the colonizer but also the colonized has subjectivity as subaltern agency. In his view, colonization is not merely a dead time for the colonized as victims. Rather, it is a moment of hybridity which Bhabha describes as the "inside-out movement when the colonizer and the colonized are two sites of the subject in the same moment of historical agency."[66] From a subaltern perspective through a postcolonial lens, beside the meta-narrative (or history), subaltern agency has played its subjective role even in colonization. Even though their stories were unspoken through history (ahistoricized) but were told through the *minjung*, grandmother to mother and mother on to daughter. Therefore, subaltern consciousness helps the subaltern to recognize herself as the agency, per se, as Alison M. Jaggar, a postcolonial feminist, asserts. She comments, "Only by creating a collective identity with other women in similar situations, perhaps with other daughters and mothers can the subaltern even come to see herself as subaltern and in this way can she break through the barriers to her speech."[67]

In the patriarchal structure, women have been traditionally recognized as the "Other" of the male Self. Regrettably, Korean women in the *Joseon* Confucian society were excluded from the public activities and leadership which is undeniably oppressive for women as the subaltern in the society along with lower class males such as *koja* [eunuch]. Even within the limitations of this social structure, however, one can still discover constructive points for recognizing women's subjectivity and agency. In the apparently male-dominated Confucian society, home for Korean women is actually their domain in which they exercise their actual rights as subjects of *salim*.

According to Confucianism, the basic structure of human relationships is the family as the foundation of all other relational structures of society. First, Korean Confucian society teaches that filial piety [孝, *xiào*] is the most important responsibility of human beings and it should extend into the larger community. A Korean feminist theologian, Lee Eun-Sun, observes that "family for Korean women is not only the context of oppression but also the living organism of maintaining life and education."[68] The Korean women's role in the Korean household has been undeniably important not only traditionally but also nowadays. In the Korean language, there are two words that can be used to refer to a husband and wife, "*bakat* [outside: society] *juin* [master]" and "*an* [inside: home] *juin* [master]." In other words, the husband works outside of the household as the one who supports the family and the wife manages the home as the master of the household. Certainly it is problematic to split men's and women's roles along a binary of the public and the domestic. Locating Korean women's subjective roles in this oppressive system might depend on the binary system of the public versus the private -- one that would problematize any dualistic essentialist roles. Literally, she is the master, not the servant of her husband. The Korean words for a wife are "*an-juin*" (안주인) or "*an* [home] *hae* [sun] (아내, 안해). This means that Korean housewives have functioned as the subjects of the household like the sun in the sky while men functioned in the public domain. As the subjects of *salim*, Korean housewives have never given up the key of the *Goggan* [barn] which is the place for keeping the food. Thus, Korean women have played an important role in the economic production and the management of the household. Korean housewives are literally the realistic subjects of their household. Korean women are not only the subjects of the family but also the subjects of the history as the *minjung* of *minjung* since *minjung* theology sees *minjung* as the subject of the history.

    As the *minjung* of *minjung*, Korean women actually are not solely powerless. That is, they have played significant roles which can be viewed as quite powerful. When we identify men in the patriarchal society as the powerful and women as the powerless, this homogenous interpretation fails to bear witness to the fluidity and heterogeneity of power. Instead, one has to consider the heterogeneity of power as articulated in Foucault's work. Foucault's analysis of modern power discusses the relationships between repressive "legal-sovereign power," on the one hand, and the modern descendents of productive "normalizing-pastoral power," on the other. According to Foucault, sovereign powers are essentially repressive and pastoral powers are essentially productive. In *The History of Sexuality I*, Foucault views sovereign power as representing itself as negating, legislative, prohibitive, censoring, and homogenous while he recognizes bio-power as always productive, immanent, exercised, capillary, and resisted.[69]

In this regard, I apply Foucault's heterogeneity of power as sovereign power versus bio-power to my postcolonial understanding of *salim* which is not the institutionalized legal form of power but rather the bio-power that is necessary for survival and life. Power also comes from the bottom of the structure which has been considered as the powerless: "Power comes from below; there is no binary and all-encompassing opposition between rulers and ruled at the root of power relations, and serving as a general matrix – no such duality extending from the top down."[70] Applying Foucault's analysis, power cannot be the possession of the colonizer only because where there is sovereign power there is resistance which is survival power. When I connect the Foucauldian bio-power to *salim*, the bottom of the hierarchy can be understood as also the powerful in the manifold relationships, according to Foucault, "in families, limited groups, and institutions that run through the social body as a whole."[71] In this regard, the complex differential power relationships can be extended to every aspect of social, cultural and political lives, including all manner of subjective positions. Then, the Korean women as *minjung* of *minjung* in their family as *salim* makers could be seen as the powerful, exercising the bio-power. Thus, I interpret power in terms of multiplicity and fluidity. In manifold relationships, the fluidity of power, both sovereign power and bio-power, are simultaneously deployed. In this way, power can be understood as deriving its effectiveness through a double conditioning or reciprocal enhancement of both. It is not a defensive statement to avoid the negativity of Korean women's role in their families but actually is a recognition of their role as the subject through a new interpretation of power, adopting the Foucauldian notion of power.

It is interesting that Foucault discovered the power of life and recognized a political value of life. According to Foucault, life (bio-power) is a political value which can be more powerful than the law (legal power) as he argues that power comes from below:

> Life as a political object was in a sense taken at face value and turned back against the system that was bent on controlling it. It was life more than the law that became the issue of political struggles, even if the latter were formulated through affirmations concerning rights. The "right" to life, to one's body, to health, to happiness, to the satisfaction of needs, and beyond all the oppressions or "alienations," the "right" was the political response to all these new procedures of power which did not derive, either, from the traditional right of sovereignty.[72]

Foucault claims that life is more than struggle or survival but it has the power to pursue happiness and satisfaction not from the sovereignty but from living, which is, indeed, more powerful than sovereignty. Despite its very foreign location in the defining dynamisms of western modernity, Foucauldian bio-power is close to *salim*, since *salim* as living is an enhancing movement in terms of quality beyond survival. Thus, any hierarchical structure has double or multiple conditioning and reciprocal enhancement of both powers which I would like to refer to as hybrid power or the hybridity of power. Bhabha analyses the Foucauldian multiplicity of power to interpret Afro-American subalternity as follows:

> Foucault would say the relations of discourse are of the nature of warfare. Both gentleman and slave with different cultural means and to very different

Decolonizing Life

> historical ends, demonstrate that forces of social authority and subversion or subalternity may emerge in displaced, even decentered strategies of signification. Indeed the exercise of power may be both politically effective and psychically affective because the discursive liminality through which it is signified may provide greater scope for strategic maneuver and negotiation.[73]

Hybridity in terms of power needs to emphasize mutuality and negotiation as Wonhee Anne Joh asserts, "The relationship between the colonized and the colonizer is complex and nuanced because of contradictory patterns of psychic affect in colonial relations, such as desire and fear of the other. The colonial experience is not just an uninterrupted experience of oppression."[74] I would suggest here that the legitimate power and the survival power bring two or multiple narratives within the same period of hierarchy in which the powers and the narratives are being negotiated and intertwined. Then, in terms of the multiplicity and the hybridity of power, *minjung* women are, indeed, not powerless, even though they are generally excluded from the sovereign power.

Korean *minjung* women's efforts to survive in the oppressive Confucian system has been the source of their power which can be understood as bio-power, the power of resistance, the power of life, the power of *salim*. It is not a hegemonic power that is visible in the public but it represents a resistant power for survival, *salim*.

As I see the *minjung* women as the subjects of history, Spivak also refers to women as the gendered subaltern "historical agents."[75] For our analysis, it is important to clarify whether Spivak is self-contradictory *vis-à-vis* both the silence of the subaltern and the agency of the subaltern. How can a silenced subaltern who cannot really speak of anything be an agent of history? According to Spivak, if the subaltern can speak, "the subaltern is not a subaltern anymore."[76] Kwok Pui-lan points out that Spivak's pessimistic conclusion can be subjected to criticism for seeing the subaltern woman as a silent object, with no possibility of escaping from the totalizing discourse of western and patriarchal domination.[77] Spivak's response to feminist critiques on her notion of the speechless subaltern emphasizes whether the subaltern can be heard and under what conditions not whether the subaltern can speak. She asserts that it is important to acknowledge our complicity in the muting. She analyses her own essay, 'Can the Subaltern Speak?' (1988), in her book, *A Critique of Postcolonial Reason* (1999), as a compelling explication of the role of disappearing in the case of Indian women in the British legal history.[78] She is concerned with the condition that muted women's voice than women's capacity of speech: "The subaltern as female cannot be heard or read. She *has* spoken in some way."[79] The muting of the subaltern and not speaking are different. Spivak's point is that subaltern women are allowed no discursive position from which to speak. That is, as gendered subalterns, women have had no access to symbolic and political power, even though they have been written about and represented. Thus, "the subaltern cannot speak" means that when the subaltern makes an effort to the death to speak, she is not able to be heard. In other words, the silence of the subaltern might be used as a refusal to speak because they cannot find their own language code with which to express themselves. When Spivak uses the silent subaltern, she always uses a singular noun to depict the woman who has disappeared, been silenced, or distorted, and therefore, no longer exists because the so-called "woman" is a construction of the patriarchal perspective. She problematizes the term, woman, in the colonial context as a sexed term. The woman as widow is the sexed subject between the Hindus (patriarchy) and British (imperialism) is lost and over determined.[80] She claims that *sati* [widow self-immolation] is neither a social mission nor superstition but a crime.[81] In the name of good wife (the term, *sati*, simply means good wife),[82] the woman as a widow is not only silenced but is forced to sacrifice her life. Spivak asserts that there is no virtue in global laundry lists with 'woman' as a pious item.[83] Then, again I ask Spivak, "With what voice-consciousness can the subaltern speak?"

Spivak analyzes critically the position of the subaltern women in terms of sovereign (hegemonic) power in the patriarchal structure. "Between patriarchy and imperialism, subject-constitution and object-formation, the figure of the woman disappears, not into a pristine nothingness, but into a violent shuttling which is caught between tradition and modernization."[84] Thus, one can see that Spivak discovered the unfair structures of power and found the real voices of the subaltern in the heterogeneity of power. She insists that "the colonized subaltern subject is irretrievably heterogeneous."[85] Spivak evaluates the Foucauldian notion of heterogeneity of power as "an unquestioned valorization of the oppressed as subject": "Foucault adds that the masses know perfectly well, clearly. They know far better than [the intellectual] and they certainly say it very well."[86] Defining women as the new subaltern, Spivak discovered "women's history" from a postcolonial perspective with her "subaltern consciousness."

For Spivak, nonetheless, subaltern women are agents of history although women's history has been hidden and muted. Spivak discovers the fact that the subaltern actually speaks, instead of engaging silence. Beside male-oriented historiography, she finds rumors and narratives as women's history as she states, "I bear witness to the storying of the vanishing present, the piecing together of characters so that a detailed sequence may seen to exist. I might as well beg the question and call them *historical agents*."[87] She claims, "various rumors about illicit love affairs circulate even as self-styled subalterns and oral history investigators assure each other in print that the subaltern can, indeed, speak."[88] She responded to the criticism of her essay, "Can the Subaltern Speak? (1988)" in 2007 at the Drew Transdisciplinary Theological Colloquium that it should have been clear that she was speaking of the abominable example of *sati* (the self-immolation)[89] in Hinduism. The woman in the essay who hanged herself was her grandmother's sister who is an example of the muting of the subaltern which is very different from their "not speaking." Spivak commented that the issue as presented in "Can the Subaltern Speak?" was not a mistake. Rather, it provokes a response from people who claim to be subalterns, indicating "I am speaking, so therefore *the subaltern can speak.* ... This is subalternity. *She told me. She tried to speak.* ... Gayatri Spivak suggesting that the oppressed and dispossessed of *the world are mute!*"[90]

In this regard, I apply the same logic to Spivak's question, regarding the plight of Korean women. Thus, I raise the question, "Can Korean *minjung* women speak?" "Yes, they have spoken, cried out, shouted through the history as the subjects of history." However, the problem is that the male dominant society did not want to listen. Also Spivak's argument urges women to speak against the silenced figure of the "woman" who has been ahistoricized from the phallocentric tradition. Consequently, she insists on the so-called decolonization of the subaltern: "Subaltern historiography must confront the impossibility of such gestures for the figure of woman which is linked to silence."[91]

Thus, even though the voice of the subaltern has been eliminated from legitimate history from the hegemonic discourse, they do not simply represent the speechless in her analysis. As postcolonial subjects, the subaltern has power and voice, both of which are involved in the bio-power and the voices from the previously silenced. Spivak's notion of subaltern is not a word pertaining to class for the strict dual structure of the oppressed and the oppressor. Rather, Spivak finds the subaltern in a place of in-betweenness: "The subaltern is the buffer group between the people and the great macrostructural dominant group, is itself defined as a place of in-betweenness."[92] Wonhee Joh calls the abject (excluded from the subjective role) subaltern and recognizes the power of the abject: "Contrary to Spivak's initial declaration that the subaltern cannot speak for it, the abject as subaltern does and is able to speak through the ruptures of the maternal semiotic power within the symbolic."[93] In this regard, with this in-betweenness and heterogeneity, the subaltern cannot be absolutized as one class on the bottom of the dualistic hierarchy. Rather, the subaltern embraces the whole body through the subaltern consciousness (or perspective). The subaltern consciousness that Spivak encourages is actually the "subject consciousness" on which she elaborates in terms of the core Hindu teaching "*tat tva asi* [you are that in Sanskrit]" from *Dharmasastra*.[94] She recognizes the subaltern subject as this indefinable "that-ness" is not an ontological fixity.[95] Spivak did not interpret *tat tva asi* beyond that point that she connects it to the subaltern consciousness. The Hindu teaching, *tat tva asi*, suggests the realization of the True Self. I would apply it for claiming the subaltern consciousness through the self-conscientization as the agent of history, not as the object. At that point, we can refer to the subaltern as *tat tva asi*, that is, the agent of life as the decolonizing subject. The subaltern, as the decolonizing subject, according to Spivak's own surprising initiative can be expanded to nonhuman nature which has also been colonized as a result of the anthropocentric worldview.

    I would like to develop Spivak's claim of women as a new gendered subaltern to see 'nature as a new ecological subaltern' and apply decolonization to nature, insofar as nature has been colonized by the anthropocentric world. Just as women's subalternity for Spivak occurs in an androcentric worldview, nature's subalternity also occurs within an anthropocentric worldview. One cannot deny the subalternity of nature, at this time, nonhuman nature. Nonhuman nature has been manipulated and recognized only in terms of its instrumental value, not in terms of its intrinsic value. Elaborating the Spivakian notion of the silencing of the subaltern, I can say that, "*nature is mute*," and has been for centuries of human domination. In this regard, McFague also suggests in *The Body of God* that we have to recognize "nature as the new poor" which means "bodily poverty" in the dualistic hierarchy of humanity over nature.[96] I would use Sallie McFague's metaphor to describe the mutation of nature as the new subaltern, "*This is the Body of G*d that cannot speak*." Nonhuman nature is not only bodily poverty as the new poor but also the sacred body of divine immanence. "We, humans, speak too much." Now is time to listen to the cry of the earth, its divine immanence, revelation, and warning. Behold and listen carefully to our planet with our planetary love and responsibility.

Even though Spivak does not explicitly name nature as a new subaltern, by recognizing the "river and forest as foundations of life," her planetary love seeks a "non-Eurocentric ecological justice."[97] From her planetary love, Spivak suggests the term, "the planet," rather than "the globe." In this way she warns against an anthropocentric view of nature: "The globe is on our computers. It allows us to think that we can aim to control it. The planet is in the species of alterity, belonging to another system; and yet, we inhabit it, on loan."[98] Renaming the globe as a planet and the environment as nature changes the paradigm of the world from an anthropocentric environmentalism to a cosmocentric planetarity. Through this new perspective, human beings are much like those whom Spivak refers to as "planetary subjects"[99] rather than global agents.

> In this era of global capital triumphant, to keep "responsibility" alive in the reading and teaching of the textual is at first sight impractical. It is, however, the right of the textual to be so responsible, responsive, answerable. The "planet" is, here, as perhaps always, a catachresis for inscribing collective responsibility as right.[100]

Thus, postcolonialism is neither nationalism nor patriotism over against colonialism. Today it must be "planetarity" which is "paranational" as Spivak suggests: "The Earth is a paranational image that can substitute for international and can perhaps provide, today, a displaced site for the imagination of planetary."[101]

However, she recognizes the limitation of the word, planet, which still could be understood as part of the world's resources, unless human beings avoid the anthropocentric mastery mind. When Spivak use the term, planet, it is actually from her ecological love for ecological justice. "I am completely in favor of ecological justice, it was not about ecological justice. I am happy I used the word planet, but I am also unhappy, because the word planet immediately brings to mind, especially in those of us with this urge to save the world, the ideas of using the world's resources well."[102] Thus, her focus is on love for the planet as a part of planet. Actually, her understanding of love is very similar to our understanding of ethical practice.

Spivak calls our attention to the planet, by calling on our collective efforts through love: "I have no doubt that we must learn to learn from the original practical ecological philosophies of the world. This learning can only be attempted through the supplementation of the collective effort by love. Love is not the name of the phenomenal affect. It is a name for the effort to call forth a response. And for that you really have to acquaint yourself in humility with the pattern of desire of the other."[103] For Spivak, what deserves the use of the word, love, demands effort. "How does one win the attention of the subaltern without coercion or crisis?"[104] Nonetheless, her planetary love is not one of romantic imagination but one that reflects the ethical practice of human beings as planetary subjects. Spivak suggests the term, *dharma*, as the word for nature which usually is translated as religion. As she calls Christianity *khristodharma* and woman in her nature, *stridharma* [*stri* means woman in Sanskrit],[105] I would call our ethical responsibility on behalf of nature, *eco-dharma*, through her suggestion of planetary love as *dharma*.

Spivak's planetary love suggests a new worldview, a non-Eurocentric ecological justice. Soliciting Spivak's hint of ecology, Catherine Keller also suggests a counter-imperial ecology of love. She writes, "The globality of the Christian perspective would therefore have the capacity and the obligation to confront the imperial globalism from within, but from an inside not enclosed but porous in space and time, carved out and complicated by its own diasporas and margins, embedded in a nonhuman and now also colonized nature."[106]

Anthropocentrism toward the planet actually refers to our imprudent attitude toward something other than ourselves that dares to consider humans as the master of the universe, as if we are all-knowing [*omniscience*] by defining, measuring, conquering, even destroying life. Therefore, it is a form of *jugim* [violence] against *salim* [enlivening]. In order to see the whole universe as the gigantic organism of *salim* – one that can never be completely discovered or conquered yet, always is already beyond our crude intervention. Ecotheologians, therefore, often claim that the planet is a sacred space which embraces all as part of its domain. The planet is the holy open space of *salim*. In *Donghak* language, the earth is *hanul* [the sacred]. *Salim* [enlivening] the planet, is our *eco-dharma* with planetary love. Within a complex organic macrocosm, all things together endlessly symbiotically create life. The planet can never be polarized from humans as "the Other" but as a body on which we live together.

The Hybridity of *Salim*: Spatiality of Planetarity
Between the apartments
in that empty space
the flower wind blows

In every apartment
in everybody's heart
the flower bud sprouts

Even to the life in prison
Spring will come
through this *teum*

Humans are
teum

All new things
always come out of *teum*[107]

Teum, a Korean term, signifies an intriguing hybrid space of spatio-temporality (or spatiality of palnetarity): it means a "blank" or a "margin" in terms of space as well as a "chance" and an "opportunity" in terms of time. Therefore, *teum* has both spatiality and temporality. *Teum* is a relational term because it refers to an interstitial time and space between at least two things. The Korean

Decolonizing Life

term, *teum*, is normally translated in English in terms of space, crevice, crack, gap, and/or opening; in terms of time, as spare time, an interval, opportunity and chance; and in terms of relationship, as friction, estrangement, and alienation. As an expression of space, *teum* can be used to articulate, for example, a crack [*teum*] in the wall. In terms of time, *teum* can be used to express, for example, finding a time [*teum*] for us or I have no time [*teum*] because I am so busy. In relationship, *teum* can be used to describe a gap [*teum*] or friction between two persons. *Teum* is a hybrid moment, place, or relationship which contains a before and after, a here and there, a reflection of one and/or the other. Thus, the best way to describe or interpret the Korean notion of *teum* in English is to refer to it as a state of in-betweenness.

As one reads his poem, *Teum*, saying that all new things always come out of *teum*, one gets the impression that for Kim, *teum* is a principle of *salim*.[108] Kim also suggests *teum* as a spatial and temporal womb for *salim*. Therefore, for Kim, *teum* is the precondition of *salim*. "Life works through *teum* as the condition. There will be no life without *teum*. Without *teum*, life cannot expand or be diffused. *Teum* means freedom as a condition of adaptation."[109]

Moreover, Kim Ji-Ha asserts that *teum* is not only the condition of creation but also the subject of creation. Following Su-Un's understanding of *hanul* [the divine], Kim throws the subject of creation into this indefinable space. His *teum* is very similar to the Whiteheadian notion of *chaos*: "emptying, a blank, an open space, non-being [無, *moo*],[110] freedom.... are those conditions simultaneously the subject of creative evolution? That is really true. The condition of the order of creation is, therefore, *chaos* which is accidental and spontaneous."[111] It is interesting that Kim uses the Greek term, *chaos* (χάος), directly without translation in Korean to explain the Korean term, *teum*. In the Greek myths, *chaos* is the original dark void from which everything else appeared. This mysterious *chaos* as the source of creation is actually *tehom*, as articulated in Keller's theology of creation in her Whiteheadian understanding which is similar to Kim's interpretation of *teum*. She notes, "*Tehom*, the bottomless indeterminacy, remains beyond good and evil. It remains the source and mystery, in its spontaneities, of both. It demands an apophatic response, yet a message from the deep drifts into our awareness. The unknowable edges the known."[112]

Just as for Keller the *tehom* is beyond good and evil, so too, Kim Ji-Ha sees in *teum* an ambiguity which can yield both good and bad, positive or negative things. Kim considers *teum* a creative space and time and, at the same time, calls all dualistic separations *teum*. *Teum* could also be a chance for the colonizer to take the other's *bab* [rice], or life. Kim refers to "*teum* against *teum*" by deconstructing the dualistic separation [*teum*] between heaven and earth, men and women, master and slave, and opening a new time and space [*teum*].[113] According to Kim, "*teum* against *teum*" is a declaration against submission and colonization. He further states, "*teum* against *teum*" is a boycott of the colonial force.[114]

I understand, Kim's notion of *teum*, as an indefinable hybridity. It is not a dualistic structure of either/or but one space and time for new beginnings. Kim Ji-Ha in a move rare and startling in its explicit linkage to this book's theoretical intertextuality, identifies *teum* with the Whiteheadian notion of *chaos* together with the Deleuzian *chaosmos*: "*teum* is a chaotic ground of cosmic orders which is therefore a new cultural concept of *chaosmos* by Deleuze."[115] Kim asserts that "beyond the materialistic understanding of chaos theory we have to expand *chaosmos* theory toward a new culture of creationist evolution or evolutionist creation which can be established to heal the culture of *jugim*."[116]

At this point, Kim analyses Su-Un's *hanul* as *ji-ki* [至氣, the ultimate energy] which brings a new creation and connects it to Deleuzian *chaosmos*. Kim writes, "Su-Un called *ji-ki* [the ultimate energy] the cosmic order of *chaos* which opens a new world [*hu-cheon-gae-byeok*]. *Ji-ki* the cosmic order of *chaos* is the subject of creative evolution that amazingly fits into the Deleuzian *chaosmos*."[117] Similarly, Deleuze develops a speculative *chaosmology* in his *Difference and Repetition*. For Deleuze, *chaosmos* is generated "from within," by a wholly immanent process of self-organization:

"The eternal return is not an external order imposed upon the *chaos* of the world; the eternal return is the internal identity of the world and of *chaos*, the *Chaosmos*."[118] Nevertheless, Kim points out that unless the Deleuzian notion of "self generating" transforms into the creative evolution, Deleuzian *chaosmos* would be only a repetition of a *chaos* without G*d; this in his perspective would be the limitation of the Deleuzian *chaosmos*.[119] Such a critique is of course sympathetic with any Whiteheadian or theological reading of Deleuze.

On a similar point, Tim Clark argues that Deleuzian *chaosmos* has no one overarching center of value, meaning and order; rather, patterns of meaning and order emerge gradually and unevenly from a multiplicity of value centers. Clark, thus, refers to Deleuzian *chaosmology* as "a fancy neologism for a neo-Whiteheadian naturalism for a cosmological system which lacks a God."[120] Much like the remarks pointed out above regarding the thinking of Kim and Clark, if Deleuzian *chaosmos* is a neologism of Whiteheadian notion of *chaos*, then, what is the role of the Whiteheadian G*d in the Deleuzian *chaosmos*?

In Deleuzian *chaosmology*, Whitehead's G*d would have a positive, indeed, an essential role to play. Deleuze understands the Whiteheadian G*d as Process which reflects the bifurcating path, as *chaosmos*:

> For Whitehead, bifurcations, divergences, incompossibilities, and discord belong to the same motley world that can no longer be included in expressive units, but only made or undone according to prehensive units and variable configurations. In a same chaotic world divergent series are endlessly tracing bifurcating paths. It is a *chaosmos* in which even God desists from being a Being who compares worlds and chooses the richest possible. He *becomes Process*, a process that at once affirms incompossibilities and passes them through. The world is a world of captures instead of closures.[121]

The Deleuzian recognition of Whiteheadian G*d as the bifurcating path is based on his reading of Leibniz's monadology which holds two conditions of closure and selection. Deleuzian world as the *chaosmos* is made up of divergent series that "opens" on a spiral in expansion that moves further and further away from a center. His suggestion of the world as an open spiral may explain his understanding of the Whiteheadian Process which is not one way but rather is a bifurcating (two or multiple) path with heterogeneous differences that is kept open much like a pair of pliers: "The two begin to fuse on a sort of diagonal, where the monads penetrate each other, are modified and make up as many transitory captures. We are discovering new ways of folding, akin to new envelopments, but we all remain Leibnizian because what always matters is folding, unfolding, refolding."[122]

As such, the Deleuzian world is not a closed circle but an open spiral that is, for Deleuze, *chaosmos*, "*chaos + cosmos, chaosmos*."[123] However, the world is not *chaos* but rather a composition of *chaos* as Deleuze suggests, "Art is not *chaos* but a composition of *chaos*."[124] Therefore, *chaosmos* is a composed *chaos*. For Deleuze, *chaos* is more than a neutral term. It is a most positive term. He writes, "*Chaos* is the most positive which contains all the complicated series. *Chaos* contains all. It is the divergent series which leads out and then pulls back in, as well as the differentiator which relates them, one to another.[125] In *chaos*, each is implicated by the others, constituting the enveloping and the enveloped, the solving and the solved of the system."[126] I understand the Deleuzian notion of the heterogeneous *chaosmos* as a womb of becoming, a state of complication, in which before and after, self and the other, here and there, are all complicated, prehended, synthesized (or hybridized), and in a way, included through the process of "folding, unfolding and refolding" as Deleuze expresses. Everything comes out of this process of the heterogeneity in *chaosmos*.

The heterogeneous dimension of *chaosmos* comes from the depths for Deleuze. Deleuze writes, "extensity as a whole comes from the depth."¹²⁷ *Chaos* is what boils under the surface of the deep, as Deleuze suggests, "depth as the heterogeneous dimension is the matrix of all extensity."¹²⁸ The Deleuzian depth insinuates *chaos* from which difference unfolds a *cosmos*.¹²⁹ *Chaos* is inseparable from an identifiable system from a *cosmos*, *chaosmos*. *Chaosmos* is identifiable when its excessive fullness is filtered, sustained, and contained. Such a containment process does not arise *ex nihilo*; it always already has elements of containment.¹³⁰

In the Whiteheadian theology of creation, creation emerges from *chaos*, not from nothingness [*ex nihilo*].¹³¹ *Chaos* is neither nonbeing [*nihil*] nor Satan [evil], yet, the womb of all becoming. Moreover, the Whiteheadian notion of *chaos* is beyond the duality of nonbeing and being, yet, is the process of becoming. According to Catherine Keller, *chaos* is "the heteroglossic Deep [*tehom*] which signifies a fluid matrix of bottomless potentiality, a germinating abyss, a heterogeneous womb of self-organizing complexity, a resistance to every fixed order."¹³² Keller analyses the term, "beginning," from its etymological origin, *ginan* which means "to gape, to yawn" as a mouth or an abyss.¹³³

As noted earlier, I am attempting to connect Keller's understanding of *chaos* as a gap (an opening), the face of *tehom* in the beginning, "the deep, salt water, *chaos*, and depth"¹³⁴ to Kim's notion of *teum* as the principle of *salim* in which he actually uses the Greek term, *chaos*. *Teum* can be generally interpreted in English as a gap in between two things which can be time, space, and relationship. It is a very hybrid term that includes both understanding neither beyond nor within but "in-between" as Deleuze interprets *chaos* as "neither foreseen nor preconceived."¹³⁵

While *chaos* is a positive term for Deleuze, for Kim Ji-Ha, *teum* is neither negative nor positive. Rather, Kim explains *teum* in terms of the negativity of *hanul*. When Kim interprets Su-Un's *hanul* [the divine], he explains that *hanul* is actually drawn into the empty space of unknowing because Su-Un refused to interpret *hanul*, yet, remained a blank for the meaning of *hanul*. He notes, "*Hanul* is in *teum* [in-betweenness] which means the emptying, blank, freedom, and *chaos*, that is, indeed, the condition as well as the subject of the creative evolution or the evolution creation."[136] Thus, Su-Un's *hanul* is evolving since it is in the blank, between becoming (subject) and change (location) together with all other events. Su-Un's cosmology is similar to Whiteheadian organic cosmology. According to Roland Faber's poetic description, "Whitehead's organic universe appears neither as an exemplification of eternal ideas nor as the empty whirring of dead particles but as *a colorful community of creatures full of life and relationary.*"[137] Whitehead interprets evolution as a causal-final development of complex organisms within their environment. Every organism is based on events and every event constitutes an organism that becomes an environment for the other as Faber writes on Whitehead, "The cosmos itself consists in a complex, internally interconnected organism of organisms."[138]

Connecting the notion of *teum* to Keller's *chaos*, *genesis*, the beginning, that which comes out of *chaos*, a gap, *teum*, the abysmal depth is unknowable as Su-Un's blank for *hanul* [the divine]. Keller makes a transition from the process *chaos* to the postcolonial third space through the unknowable depths of our *genesis*/becoming which actually is the language of negative theology. Keller makes a connection of her *chaos* and Trinh Minh-ha's spiritually resourced critical *non-knowingness* to the third space of postcolonial theory. As Trinh Min-ha states that the process of infinite beginnings emerges from and dives into *the abyss of un-naming*,[139] the creation that emerges from the third space of the *chaosmos*; indeed, it would be the *chaosmos*. Creation comes to be an open infinity not just of relational signs but of signifying relations.[140]

In Keller's postcolonial understanding of *chaos*, the deep can be understood as hybridity. Keller writes, "hybridity has for at least a decade played a key role within conversations theorizing the cultural complexity within which progressive movements might learn to forge more effective alliances."[141] Homi Bhabha adopts the concept of hybridity for the subversion of authority in colonial discourse and resistance against the dominant imperialist power of the colonizer. To Bhabha, hybridity is defined as "a problematic of colonial representation" that reverses the effects of the colonialist disavowal, so that other denied knowledge enters upon the dominant discourse and estranges the basis of its authority.[142] Hybridity deconstructs the binary logic and melts away the difference between 'Self' and 'Other,' White and Black, West and East, but involves a newfound interdependency. As such, hybridity seeks a "third space"[143] beyond the polarizations and deadlocks of identity politics. Keller asserts Bhabha's example of "the hybrid moment of political change" in terms of the disputes between class and gender analysis.[144]

Keller finds a theological meaning of hybridity by studying *chaos* theory. She argues that the doctrine of *creatio ex nihilo* is a tool in the repression of *tehom* as mere *chaos*. In the doctrine of *creatio ex nihilo*, as Keller points out, whatever threatens the purity of the Origin gets marked as chaotic -- as out of control, beyond the bounds, mixed up and marauding; or as nothing at all, *nihil* and fair game for nihilation. Observing this *chaos* theory, Keller sees that hybridity can be construed as the cultural opening where "the ocean of heteroglossia"[145] has already leaked into the system:

> Thus, the water deeply threatens any theological mononarrative. The *hybridizations* where the sea leaks through convey the threat of the Deep itself. This tehomic depth washes out any notion of depth as mere interiority, contained within a self—it undermines any fixed boundary of inner and outer, us and them, the subject and its objects, the west and its others. It is not that it is threatening to wash out distinctions: on the contrary, *tehom* is sabotaging the rigid boundaries of all power drives.[146]

In Christian monotheism, G*d is the One who creates by speech alone, whose creation is mere order, and whose speech is the giving of orders. Keller insists that the "God-construct" requires a radical rearrangement theologically. Keller recognizes a place of hybrid as a nondualistic third space: "The hybrid is the complex, not the chaotic, but is often indistinguishable from *chaos*. Perhaps we may reinscribe the edge of *chaos* as the face of the deep. Perhaps the actual relation of oscillation between surface and depth, form and formlessness, wind and water, insinuates the theological depth of Bhabha's Third space."[147]

For Bhabha, the "Third Space" is a hybrid place of newness for both the colonizer and the colonized. The Bhabhan Third Space is that place which has no primordial unity or fixity, and therefore, a place where one creates a newness, hybridity: "The Third Space constitutes the discursive conditions of enunciation that ensure that the meaning and symbols of culture have no primordial unity or fixity; that even the same signs can be appropriated, translated, rehistoricized and read anew."[148] Like *teum*, the Third Space is actually excluded from the preexisting fixity (that could be time, space, people, structure, relationship, and ideology) yet, has the capability of being in terms of productive of endless newness.

I understand *teum* [gap] as an in-betweenness which is located at the edges of the two, touching two ends and creating the infinite new beginnings. The hybridity coming out of *teum* contains both ends but none of them are quite the same. Kim's *teum* and the Bhabhan Third Space, despite their different textual traditions, are very similar. "To that end we should remember that it is the 'inter'-the cutting edge of translation and negotiation, the in-between space- that carries the burden of the meaning of culture. And by exploring this Third Space, we may elude the politics of polarity and emerge as others of our selves."[149]

When Bhabha recognizes the hybridity of the Third Space, Bhabha challenges hegemonic historiography by denying the essentialism which comes from either the genealogical tracing of cultural origins or the representational act of cultural translation. Bhabha sees hybridity as an active moment that challenges dominant power relations and transmits the zone of transition from a source of conflict into a productive element, opening the Third Space. The Third Space for Bhabha is the "in-between space" that carries the burden and meaning of culture that makes the notion of hybridity so important.[150] Bhabha notes, "All forms of culture are continually in a process of hybridity. But for me the importance of hybridity is not to able to trace two original moments from which the third emerges, rather "hybridity to me is the third space" which enables other positions to emerge."[151] Furthermore, for Bhabha, hybridity is not only important for the Third Space but also hybridity *is* the Third Space.

> This third space displaces the histories that constitute it, and sets up new structures of authority, new political initiatives, which are inadequately understood through received wisdom. The process of cultural hybridity gives rise to something different, something new and unrecognizable, a new area of negotiation of meaning and representation.[152]

And within the intertextual filed of this chapter, the Bhabhan Third Space insistently echoes the Korean concept of *teum*. Kim Ji-Ha interprets *teum* as *chaos* and Keller connects *chaos* to postcolonial hybridity in the Third Space. Like the Korean term, *teum*, it emerges when two different things encounter each other. It can also be viewed as the gap between two different things, A and B. *Teum* creates new things which are neither A nor B but a newness which contains both A and B and, at the same time, deconstructs their oppositional duality. In this interstitial space, the One and the Other can encounter one another and possibly reconcile with each other. Therefore, *teum* could be a spatial and temporal gap that creates bridges between the past and future or the One and the Other. Likewise, Bhabha notes,

> Such assignations of social difference where difference is neither One nor the Other but something else besides, in-between- find their agency in a form of the future where the past is not originary, where the present is not simply transitory. It is, if I may stretch

a point, an interstitial future, that emerges in-between the claims of the past and the needs of the present.[153]

The Third Space for Bhabha is the "in-between space" that carries the burden and meaning of culture that makes the notion of hybridity so important.[154] Like Bhabha's Third Space, *teum* is the "in-between space" and the "interstitial space and time" which refuses to be included in any of two oppositions, yet, rejects the binary structure.

However, the binary structure is not the condition of becoming. Rather, it is a dipolarity of two (or many) events that, itself, is moving as a rhythm of oscillation between becoming and change. *Teum* can also be considered this space and time of *chaos*. Therefore, becoming *chaosmos* in which the *cosmos* evolves through hybridization. A process ecotheologian, Roland Faber connects *chaos* and *cosmos* as his organic cosmology: "A dipolarity of events constitutes the *cosmos*. Physical objects are always a result of this oscillation of dipolar events."[155] Faber sees the *cosmos* as a living organism. And it must be understood in terms of interconnectedness as a symbiotic becoming in the structure of microorganism and macroorganism. Faber continues,

> Every event nexus simultaneously constitutes an organism that becomes an environment for others. The *cosmos* itself consists in a complex, internally interconnected organism of organisms. In this sense, the entire world becomes an environment to itself insofar as every new generation of organisms relates directly within its own becoming.[156]

Life only appears in this interstitial space along with the orders of *chaos* where all the structures are "rhizomatically"[157] (or multifully) connected and broken where they become maps with cracks [*teum*].[158] One could therefore say that *teum* reflects a spatiotemporal environment of becoming. In this understanding of *teum*, all new things come into being, and therefore, are becoming: *genesis*. That is, *teum* is the place and moment of regenerating, thus becoming *salim*.

Chapter IV

A Process Ecotheological Reading of *Salim*

In this chapter, I propose an interstitial dialogue between the life-centered philosophy of *Donghak* and ecocentric process theology by comparing Su-Un's *si-cheon-ju* [侍天主, embracing *hanul*)] and John B. Cobb's *Life* as G*d. The Korean notion of life as understood in the philosophy of *Donghak* is comparable to the Whiteheadian understanding of G*d and life, the non-dualistic understanding of spirit and body, of the organic and inorganic. Hae-Weol's notion of reverence [敬, *Gyeong*] and Jay McDaniel's deep ecological understanding of process theology also resonate with each other. Hae-Weol's notion of *bab* as *hanul* is a good example of *gyeong-mool* [reverence toward nonhuman bodies] which Kim Ji-Ha relates to Jesus' body as bread for life. As McDaniel finds a postcolonial connection of *bab* hybridity in the Whiteheadian notion of concrescence, the *Donghak* process-like notion of *hanul* as part-whole can be considered a manifestation of hybridization, a becoming together through the *salim* process: *si-cheon-ju* [embracing *hanul*], *yang-cheon-ju* [caring for *hanul* with reverence], and *bab* as *hanul* [sharing *hanul*]. In the context of a process-*donghak* dialogue, *hanul* the endless becoming of life and *salim* as the process of becoming.

Su-Un's *Si-cheon-ju* [侍天主, embracing *hanul*] and John Cobb's Life as G*d

侍天主 造化定 永世不忘萬事知
[*shi-cheon-joo-jo-wha-jeong-young-sae-bul-mang-man-sa-ji*]:
If one embodies *Hanul*, one will be creatively transformed.
If one never forgets *Hanul*, one will know the mystery of everything. (translation mine)

This passage is known as the Incantation of *Donghak*. Founded by Su-Un, his teaching is condensed into these thirteen Chinese characters. Su-Un taught his followers to repeat and recite the thirteen words of incantation and subsequently interpreted each word. Yet, he never attempted to explain the word, *hanul* [*cheon*, 天, the divine]. Who or what is *hanul* for Su-Un? Why did Su-Un leave the term, *hanul*, without explanation?

For Su-Un, *hanul* is the word that represents ultimate reality. However, Su-Un chose not to define *hanul*. Rather, he opened a *teum* [interstitial space] for the word as a mystery. *Hanul* is the word for G*d in Korean. Nevertheless, based upon his elliptical comments it is evident that Su-Un's *hanul* is neither an ontological G*d in terms of traditional Christian theology nor does it reflect the western understanding of pantheism.[1]

One can look at Su-Un's *hanul* through his epiphany experience in *Donggyeong Daejeon*:

> A voice came from Heaven and it seemed as if the earth trembled. The voice said: "My heart is your heart [吾心卽汝心], yet how could humankind know

this? They may know Heaven and Earth, but they cannot understand the Spirit [鬼神]. I am the Spirit. Now you shall realize the Eternal Way, cultivate it, study it, record it and teach it to all humankind.[2]

Similar to the typical theophanies in the Old Testament,[3] Su-Un also experienced a mystical encountering of *hanul* which was auditory and visual, accompanied by some natural cataclysms. *Hanul* is described by Su-Un as the Spirit who is the external reality that descended on him and taught him the Way. In this way, Su-Un's *hanul* is a personal G*d who is other (or the Ultimate Other) than himself, and able to converse with him. It could be understood as evidence of *seohak* [Christianity, western learning] influence. However, Su-Un's *hanul* is a personal G*d and, at the same time, G*d of embodiment in everything who is "becoming together" with the world, including humans and more than humans. As the external reality, *hanul* becomes internalized within Su-Un by saying, "My heart is your heart [吾心卽汝心]." John B. Duncan, a scholar of Korean religions, interprets Su-Un's epiphany indicating that this identification of the human heart with the divine heart implies a fundamental equality of all human beings not to be found in either the Chinese or the indigenous heritage.[4] Moreover, in Duncan's perspective, the Eternal Way will be cultivated and taught by those encountered who now has the heart of the eternal. This shows that *hanul* also comprises the embodiments of *hanul* and becoming, working together with the embodiments.

Pyo Young-Sam points out that Su-Un was the first theologian who recognized G*d as both "becoming and embodiment" in the world.[5] Both Su-Un (1824-1864) and Whitehead (1861-1947) lived in the 19th century. It is interesting the notion of G*d as becoming in Su-Un and Whitehead emerged at the similar time in the East and the West without any academic exchange. Su-Un initiated *Donghak* in 1860 and wrote *Donggyeong Daejeon* [*The Great Text of Donghak*] in 1861, the year Whitehead was born, Whitehead later published *Process and Reality* in 1927.

According to Kim Kyung-Jae, a Korean process theologian, panentheism[6] would be a better description of the theism of Su-Un.[7] For Kim, Su-Un's concept of *hanul* can best be understood as panentheism as it overcomes the problems of theism and pantheism.[8] Kim comments on Su-Un's *hanul* stating: "Su-Un's *hanul* is not an ontological G*d who judges good and evil. If a human being lives right, s/he will gain a divine personality. However, a human being cannot overcome the condition of living. Therefore, living itself becomes *hanul*. Su-Un experienced *hanul* not as heaven for worship but as life, itself, for living as *hanul*."[9] Thus, Kim metaphorically analyses the traditional Christian theism as a stage of a play in which G*d is the director, the world is the stage, and human beings are the actors. He points out that, in theism, the world becomes just matter which is not only absolutely distinguished from G*d but also differentiated from human beings.[10] Kim Kyung-Jae claims that "Su-Un's notion of *hanul* is a highly developed panentheism which is life as living beyond an individual being but a whole which connects G*d-human-world as one organic body."[11]

Nevertheless, I am concerned that the distinction between pantheism and panentheism remain a western approach that cannot quite explain Su-Un's theology of *hanul* [the divine]. For Su-Un, *hanul* is not an object of worship but an internalization [*mosim, si,* 侍][12] of *hanul* in one's body, that is, of the embodied self. Su-Un's notion of *hanul* can be better understood through his notion of *si-cheon-ju* [embracing *hanul*, 侍天主] which is described in *Donggyeongdaejeon*: "Don't trust in me but trust in *hanul* who is embodied in you. If one realizes that you are an embodiment of *hanul*, you will be wise and good."[13] A *Donghak* scholar, An Sang-Jin, interprets *si-cheon-ju* as an "interiorization of G*d" through which all humans become deified regardless of status or class.[14] Su-Un's declaration of *si-cheon-ju*, indicating that humans are, in fact, *hanul*, was a decolonizing or liberating message to the *minjung* [the oppressed] of the *Joseon* dynasty (1392-1897)[15] which classified humans according to a range of hierarchal classes. Therefore, Su-

Un's notion of *si-cheon-ju* represented a salvific voice to people in the lower classes and women in the feudal patriarchal social structure.

In Su-Un's notion of *si-cheon-ju* [embodiment of *hanul*], women also are *hanul*-embodied. Therefore, they should be revered and respected as *hanul*. Su-Un, himself, freed his slaves and adopted one of the slaves as his own daughter and another became his daughter-in-law.[16] Su-Un's practice of *si-cheon-ju* is an illustration of his thinking which embraced all, regardless of gender and class. In this regard, a Korean *Donghak* scholar, Chung Ki-Yeol views Su-Un's concept of *hanul* through the lens of *si-cheon-ju* [embodiment of *hanul*] is "a *minjung*-centered, liberation-oriented and socially-transformative religious revolutionary concept"[17] that declared the equal dignity of all human beings: Humans are *hanul*. As we know through his practice of *si-cheon-ju* in his life, Su-Un invited those considered outcasts as *hanul* into the community of *hanul*. Thus, *si-cheon-ju* [embracing *hanul*] is not only internalizing *hanul* in oneself but also sending an endless invitation to others for becoming *hanul* as a community.

Thus, one must understand Su-Un's *hanul* [the divine] in his non-dualistic oneness of the universe which includes all subjects as one organic body. Yoon Seok-San, a *Donghak* scholar, explains Su-Un's non-dualistic worldview as follows: "Su-Un taught the oneness of self and the cosmos, *hanul* and self, the universe and self through harmony and unification toward the endless sea of a new heaven."[18] Kim Yong-Ok defines Su-Un's notion of *hanul*, claiming that "*hanul* is the eternal self (as individual) in the eternal body (as universe)."[19]

I understand Su-Un's notion of *hanul* as becoming, an extensive (temporal) as well as expansive (spatio) organism, which endlessly embraces all expression of life – human and non-human, including nonorganic bodies in which a part of the whole is *hanul* and the whole, as well, is *hanul*. One embraces the other as the whole and *vice versa* in this spiritual organism of the part-whole. This oneness of *hanul* is different from the traditional western monotheistic G*d who tends to be imagined as transcendent and beyond the world. Rather, the oneness of *hanul* including the whole cosmos is understood as one organic body in the cosmological hybridization (or becoming together) of *hanul* as the part-whole.

The Korean concept *hanul* [한울, the divine] in its etymology means one bound: *han* means oneness as well as greatness and *ul* means bound. *Han* of *hanul* does not mean suffering. *Han* in *hanul* used as an adjective while *han* [恨] as a noun means suffering, though they are pronounced in the same way. *Han* of *hanul* functions as an adjective that describes "*ul,*" and means 'one', 'infinite,' and/or 'gigantic.' The Korean letter, *han* (恨), has no end and means the infinite in process. That is, all different boundaries are becoming, together, and endlessly, as one, according to the letter, *han* (恨). *Hanul* (한울) for Korean means literally a magnificent unity which includes everything in terms of togetherness. Therefore, when we use the term, *hanul,* it indicates neither the physical sky nor the transcendental G*d who is beyond us, but the whole cosmos as one organic body, the whole process of the cosmic life.

Su-Un's *hanul* is not beyond the universe that is transcendent from space and time but is in the process of the world and actually the becoming in time, not beyond time. As humans are living in time and space, the cosmic life is living and becoming endlessly with humankind as *hanul*. *Hanul*, the cosmic life is thus living together with every tiny body as one unity. Finally, Pyo Young-Sam also notes, "Su-Un's *hanul* as becoming, therefore, the process of the cosmic life, existed even before the Whiteheadian G*d in process."[20]

Su-Un wrote in his *Podeokmoon*, the following, describing *hanul* as becoming, "I (*hanul*) had 'no work (no achievement, 勞而無功)' before I met you (Su-Un), therefore, I brought you out to people to teach the Way of *hanul*. My work is done through you."[21] As one can see in Su-Un's teaching, *hanul* is not a personal ontological G*d for worship. *Hanul*, as becoming together with its embodiments, has no work by itself. Only *in* and *through* a living embodiment in the process of life, with all engaging together as one body, is *hanul* living and working. Therefore, in this process, there is no completed accomplishment of creation as "the end," but only exists in the process of becoming. Thus, Su-Un pointed out that there is no task that is completed because all is essentially incomplete and unfinished. In a spirit of becoming, it is infinite.[22] Betraying my over-exposure to western culture, I see this whole process of life like an 'unfinished symphony' of *hanul* through which all movements play together. Actually, this unfinished symphony will never finish but will forever continue to evolve and change. Thus, through reading Su-Un's notion of *hanul*, I propose to define '*hanul* as the cosmic life in process,' which can be realized over and over through the body (meaning all bodies not only human beings) in the process of embodiment [*si-cheon-ju*, 侍天主] and becoming.

According to Kim Ji-Ha's reading of Su-Un's notion of *si-cheon-ju* [embracing *hanul*], embracing [*si*] is an expression of humanness as spiritual- organic.[23] Kim mentions that "embodying *hanul* is working. *Hanul* is living through working humans and working through their works. Thus, a person working for life is *hanul*."[24] As Kim recognizes, *hanul* is a human working on behalf of humankind while embracing the cosmic life. In this one character, *si* [侍], Su-Un taught what it means to be a human as an embodiment of *hanul*. In other words, the human is human when s/he embraces *hanul*. Through this interiorization of *hanul*, the human becomes *hanul* and *hanul* works through humans as an expression of life.

In the process of life, all movements of living, not only by and through human beings but also by all different entities, are considered as *salim* and the life as part-whole in the movements as *hanul*. I understand *hanul* according to the understanding of Su-Un who pointed out that it is both the cosmic life and its embodiment as part-whole. In the previous chapter I defined *salim* as the process of life. In this process of life, that which Su-Un left without any definition, *cheon* [天, *hanul*], is filling and emptying endlessly because *hanul* cannot be known without knowing the movements of life through *hanul*. Through the endless movements of embracing others (not only humans but also all other forms of body) so as to be enlivened together, *hanul* becomes *hanul* and is realized. Therefore, I would define this indefinite character of *hanul* [the divine] as becoming, G*d in process.

Su-Un's notion of *hanul* as part-whole can also be understood as such that the whole organic body, including individual bodies to the smallest individual units are becoming together. Therefore, in this interconnectedness and interdependency of symbiotic life in *hanul*, both the whole body as well as the individual units can be referred to as *hanul* in terms of 'symbiosis.' That is, the relationship between the macrocosm and microcosm of *hanul* [the divine] is similar to Whitehead's understanding of G*d as "the actual entity" and the world is in the process of becoming the "actual entities (also termed actual occasions, individual units)."[25] These actual entities "are the final real things of which the world is made up. There is no going behind actual entities to find anything more real."[26] An actual entity is not an inert and permanent substance, but a relational process of becoming: "*how* an actual entity *becomes* constitutes *what* that actual entity *is*. Its being is constituted by its becoming. This is the principle of process."[27]

This process of becoming is also a creative synthesis into one actual entity of its many relations to other actual entities. This process can also be described as continuing on and on. A womanist process theologian, Monica A. Coleman, summarizes continuity as follows: "Everything is constantly in the process of synthesizing a vast diverse past into a subjective, momentary unity. As soon as a new unity is achieved, the new entity contributes itself to the world and becomes one of the many that will be synthesized into a unity in the next moment of experience."[28] In the context of a process-*donghak* dialogue, I can describe "*hanul* as the endless becoming of life" and "*salim* as the process of becoming."

Nevertheless, the juxtaposition of Su-Un's notion of *hanul* as part-whole and the Whiteadian becoming in process does not mean that the process G*d and *hanul* are identical. For Whitehead, G*d exists in process and change. G*d is an active agent for Whitehead by the distinction between the Primordial and the Consequent Nature of G*d. Whitehead associates G*d's immanence with the Primordial Nature as "being with all creation," luring it toward beauty by providing potentials in the form of its initial aim.[29] Viewed as

Primordial, G*d is the unlimited conceptual realization of potentiality. However, G*d is not before all creation but *with* all creation. From the Consequent Nature of G*d, G*d is the principle of concretion. Whitehead's notion of G*d's immanence is sharing (feeling) creation: "God shares with every new creation its actual world; and the concrescent creature is objectified in God as a novel element in God's objectification of that actual world."[30] Thus, for Whitehead, G*d is the presupposed actuality of conceptual operation, in unison of becoming with every other creative act. In other words, G*d shares with every new creation its actual world; and the concrescent creature is objectified in G*d as a novelty in G*d's objectification of the actual world.[31] On the other hand, *hanul* for Su-Un is 'what changes in process' as he identifies working subjects as *hanul*. In this sense, one can say that Su-Un is more nondualistic than Whitehead.

For Su-Un, there is nothing beyond the world one experiences. *Hanul* is every working subject in the world. Hae-Weol referred to a working human being who was weaving cloth as *hanul*: "The one who is weaving cloth now is *hanul* [the divine], not your daughter-in-law. There is not one thing which is not *hanul* in the world."[32] Thus, *si-cheon-ju* [embracing *hanul*, 侍天主] means embracing or working *hanul* into one's life. *Hanul* is usually called *hanul-nim*. In the word, '*hanul-nim*,' the ending, *nim* referred to the honorific ending designating an honorable person warranting respect, such as *seonsaeng-nim* [teacher], *bumo-nim* [parents], *imkeum-nim* [king], etc. *Hanul-nim* is the word used in former times for *haneun-nim*, the term used nowadays in making reference to G*d. The '*Ul*' sound has been omitted in between *han* and *nim* which is common for other Korean words. Therefore, *hanul-nim* became *haneun-nim* with *eun* as a long extension of *han*. *Haneun* (하는) literally means "working" in Korean. Following this meaning, *haneun-nim*, therefore, means "a working G*d." Even though *hanul* is a word for G*d in Korean, Su-Un's notion of *hanul* is that of "G*d who is working" rather than G*d who simply exists in the physical heaven or sky. A Korean process theologian, Kim Sang-Il, identifies the active concept of "*haneu-nim*, 하느님, as that of "a working G*d" very similar to Whitehead's concept of "Creativity."³³

I agree with Kim Sang-Il's comparison between "*haneu-nim* or *hanul*" of Su-Un and the "creativity" of Whitehead as embracing the same notion of the Ultimate. With 'one' and 'many,' Whitehead includes 'creativity' as the principle of novelty in the category of the Ultimate.³⁴ G*d is not in the category of the Ultimate but creativity is. Whiteheadian cosmology recognizes the Ultimate in unity, multiplicity, and creativity. The term, 'one,' and the term, 'many,' presuppose each other and are linked with creativity together in complex unity. "Together presupposes the notions creativity, many, one, identity and diversity."³⁵

This triad structure of the Whiteheadian Ultimate is comparable to Su-Un's *hanul* as a working G*d. Su-Un explains the Spirit [*jiki*, 至氣] in *Nonhakmoon* (1860), "*Jiki* is the empty Spirit that becomes endlessly, works in everything, and hard to describe the forms, may be heard but cannot be seen, that is the energy of life in everything everywhere."³⁶ For Su-Un, the Spirit can 'only' be working when it is embodied. Without embodiment, the Spirit is just empty, therefore, can be localized but not limited in the endless process of becoming through emptying and filling. It is called *heoryeong* [the empty Spirit, 虛靈] *changchang* [creating and creating, 蒼蒼], an endless becoming and creating through the endless openness of opennesses. *Hanul* is endlessly becoming together through the process of embodiments. This endless creating process of emptying and filling [虛靈蒼蒼, *heoryeong changchang*] reflects the movements of Life, *salim*.

In this sense, *hanul* as the Ultimate and *haneu-nim* (하느님 or 하는님), as the "working G*d," one can understand *hanul* is actually very similar to the Whiteheadian "moving whole." Roland Faber describes it well in his book, *God as Poet of the World* (2004), stating: "The universe as a 'moving whole' becomes within this unity. A unity emerges as creative novelty out of multiplicity; this unity is relativized into one unity among many in a universe that is precisely and creatively renewed. Whitehead's universe is an ecological process of integration and relativization, a process of processes."[37] The triad structure of one and many through creativity endlessly creates through the process of becoming and perishing, diffusion and conversance.

In the notion of the Whiteheadian Ultimate, the G*d which Whitehead points out is the actual entity, therefore, "a creature transcended by the creativity."[38] For Whitehead, "there is no meaning to 'creativity' apart from its creatures, and no meaning to 'G*d' apart from the 'creativity' and the temporal creatures, and no meaning to the temporal creatures apart form 'creativity' and 'G*d.'"[39] Nonetheless, it does not appear that creativity is another name of G*d for Whitehead. But one can say that G*d can be G*d when s/he creates. David Ray Griffin points out that Whitehead's term, creativity, provides a new understanding of the previous philosophers' notion of "being" or "being itself. Griffin affirms that the "Whiteheadian God is not simply being itself, but the ultimate embodiment of this power, creativity."[40] Consequently, the Whiteheadian G*d is G*d in action, under construction or in process, therefore, a working G*d [*haneu-nim*, 하느님] in process. For Su-Un, *hanul* is under construction as well as the construction workers (that could be humans and nonhumans) are *hanul* as well.

The Korean process theologian, Kim Kyung-Jae, also notes that "Su-Un's *hanul* is not a transcendental being but One who is becoming (*sangseong*, 生成, which can also be translated as generating or creating). That is, G*d is revealed in the process of creating which is G*d's breath of life."[41] As mentioned above is the understanding of Su-Un that *hanul* is the endless becoming of life.

In this study, I metaphorically compare the relationship between G*d and creativity for Whitehead to that of a lamp and light. That is, there is no meaning for a lamp to be a lamp without light, even though we can still call a lamp a lamp, even if there is no light. However, if a lamp does not give any light, the lamp has lost its function. Thus, if we call a lamp that does not give light a lamp, that does not fulfill the meaning of a lamp. Just as providing light is the essence of the lamp, creativity is the essence of divine actuality since

Whitehead introduced G*d as the Ultimate actuality. Then, is G*d more ultimate than creativity? Jay McDaniel clarifies that the ultimate reality of the universe is not G*d but rather, Creativity. For him, the process understanding of G*d is actually G*d's relation to Creativity. For him, Creativity is the ultimate reality; G*d is the ultimate actuality.[42] "Creativity is not reducible to the choices of a single divine creator."[43] In this understanding, creativity does not belong to only G*d. Rather, as the ultimate reality beyond good and evil, creativity is manifested in all individual beings, including those who have capacities for creative responses, in which case, creativity can be understood as their own self-creativity.

According to John B. Cobb, "Whitehead understands creativity, God, and the world as all equally essential to the creative process. He will not subordinate the world to either creativity or God any more than he will subordinate God to creativity. Whitehead's definition of creativity as 'the many become one and are increased by one' is much the same."[44] John Cobb understands Whitehead's G*d as 'creative love' and identifies it with 'the Primordial Nature of G*d' that can be called '*Logos*' [Christ].[45] Cobb distinguishes Christ as the incarnate *Logos* from Jesus in traditional Christology as the sole incarnation of Christ 'once and for all.' He writes,

> The incarnate *Logos* is Christ. Christ is present in all things. It is in living things that the proper work of the *Logos* is significantly manifest. *Logos* is to be discerned, the decision of the creature becomes increasingly important. This means that the extent of the effectiveness of the *Logos* in these creatures is largely decided by the creature. Christ is present to a greater or lesser extent as the creature decides for or against the *Logos*. Christ is most fully present in human beings when they are most fully open to that presence.[46]

Cobb's understanding of Christ is quite similar to Su-Un's notion of *si-cheon-ju* [侍天主, embracing *hanul*]. According to Cobb, Christ is not only present in all things but also is dependent upon the openness of all things. In sum, all things, including human beings, are fully subjects of incarnation. Cobb's Whiteheadian notion of G*d's immanence, as Christ in all things, can be compared to Su-Un's understanding of *hanul*. In his view, *hanul* is 'internalized in everything' [*si-cheon-ju*] as the embodiment of *hanul*. Then, not only is *hanul* in everything but also everything can be considered as the embodiment of *hanul* [the divine]. When Su-Un called, "You are *hanul*!," he implied the whole organic unity.

In this sense, *hanul* is 'the becoming' of the part-whole instead of the sum of everything. Therefore, I would say that *hanul* includes everything and *more than* the sum of everything. That can be a clue that Su-Un's theology can neither pantheistic nor panentheistic. *Hanul* is identical to the world (pantheism), and yet, embraces more than the world because *hanul* is evolving and becoming. *Hanul* is in the world (panentheism), and yet, not limited because of the endless openness of opennesses [*heoryeong changchang*].[47] Thus, for Su-Un, pantheism and panentheism are not contradictory but both make sense in different ways. Comparing Cobb's notion of Christ's incarnation, *salim* is more like creative transformation and *hanul* is more like the transformative creativity in terms of *si-cheon-ju* [when one embraces *hanul*, one becomes *hanul*]. Creative transformation requires creative and responsive love according to Cobb as Christ means love incarnated.[48] Life as *salim* rejects *jugim* and creates love and peace. For my analysis on Cobb's Christ as transformative creativity and creative transformation, creative transformation reflects actual movements (*salim*) while transformative creativity implies potential capacity which can be realized or incarnated as becoming (*hanul*).

Park Jong-Cheon, a Korean Christian theologian, interprets Su-Un's notion of *si-cheon-ju* [侍天主]: "In *si-cheon-ju* [侍天主], the concept of *cheon* [*hanul*, 天] is not a personal monotheistic G*d but 'the Grand Cosmic Life' itself who is present in the creative evolution of the cosmos."⁴⁹ Kim Ji-Ha also recognizes *hanul* as "the Cosmic Life"⁵⁰ which is working in *minjung* through his meditation on the thirteen words of Incantation of *Donghak*,⁵¹ as noted earlier in this discussion.

Hanul as 'the Cosmic Life' is similar to John Cobb's Christ as 'creative transformation' "which can be found in all things and especially wherever there is life."⁵² Moreover, Cobb recognizes 'Life' as G*d. Cobb distinguishes 'Life' from life as an abstract noun or collective reference to all living things. Instead, he indicates that 'Life' is the central religious symbol. Hence, he uses a capital 'L': "The Spirit of God is God. God is the Spirit. If it is the Spirit that enlivens us, we may equally say that it is God who makes us alive. If the Spirit is the true Life within us, then God is that Life." ⁵³

As Kim Ji-Ha refers to *hanul* as the Cosmic Life, Cobb refers to Life as cosmic power which creates by bringing order out of *chaos*. Therefore, Life is creator, according to Cobb. Cobb understands that Life as the central religious symbol is G*d. Cobb himself acknowledges that his understanding of Life as G*d is indebted to Whitehead. "The Whiteheadian idea of God is appropriately called Life not only because the immanence of God in the world is the life-giving principle but also because the life-giving principle is, itself, alive."⁵⁴

In Cobb, the relationship between G*d and the world, in terms of Life, is symbiotic and panentheistic. Unlike the pantheistic aspect of *Donghak*, which declares one is *hanul*, Cobb does not identify the world as G*d. Rather, he clarifies that G*d is not the world and vice versa. However, he also notes that G*d includes the world and the world includes G*d. The world and G*d are creating and perfecting each other. When he says that there is no world apart from G*d and *vice versa*, one can say that his G*d exists within relationship to the world. In other words, the existence of G*d depends upon the existence of the world as the world depends upon G*d. However, paradoxically,⁵⁵ Cobb also states that "whereas no world can exist without God, God can exist without this world."⁵⁶ It does not mean that G*d exists all alone without this world but rather that there must be something (some sort of world) which is Life with and in G*d, then Life/G*d will continue.

Cobb's notion of Life as G*d is not just a life which can be good or bad. It is Life as purposeful and loving. It is very close to "life as *hanul*," *salim*, which is in everything:

> Life is the cosmic aim for value. Life has achieved
> rich value in dolphins as well as in human beings.
> Life is not only purposeful in itself, but it is the source
> of all the derivative purpose in living things. Life
> favors all living things including both the fox and the
> hare. Life's aims for us envisage the good of human
> societies, the species, and even the whole community
> of living things, but they include immediacy of
> enjoyment and personal greatness in the individual
> person now as well as in the future.[57]

Apparently, Cobb's Life as G*d is different from ordinary life, in general, and is understood as 'the Consequent Nature of G*d.'[58] Basically, Cobb's Life as G*d is Life that redeems, loves, creates, aims for us and everything toward the fullness of all existence, which can be defined as *salim*, meaning quality of life. *Salim* is not just a life that can be viewed as bad, neglect, abandoned, useless, or violent, etc. *Salim* is more like a hopeful survival for a better life. Therefore, it is more than survival. Whitehead proposed that all living things live with three hopes: "(i) to live, (ii) to live well, (iii) to live better. In fact, the art of life is first to be alive, secondly to be alive in a satisfactory way, and thirdly to acquire an increase in satisfaction."[59] Thus, to live better does not mean to have more in terms of quantity but rather, to live in qualitatively rich ways in community with others, in ways that include openness to new possibilities.[60] *Salim* includes Whitehead's three hopes of life yet endlessly pursues 'a quality of living in *satisfaction*.'

In Whiteheadian thinking, G*d is immanent within all living beings as a lure to live with *satisfaction* that Jay McDaniel calls the process of hybridity, "The very impulse to live with satisfaction relative to the situation at hand, which lies at the very heart of life, is an ongoing process of hybridizing."[61] McDaniel asserts that process theology offers a cosmological background for considering the more specific type of hybridity with which postcolonial thinkers deal: "All of us are already hybrids many times over in the actual living of our lives. We are never simply one thing but always already many things. We are always already a process of the many become one."[62] As such, *salim* is living in satisfaction with all others in the symbiotic part-whole [*hanul*] through the process of hybridizing, becoming together.

I would assert that the Whiteheadian "Life as G*d" is *salim* in the sense that *salim* reflects true life [or the very meaning of life] against *jugim* [violence] which enlivens humankind and not only pursues survival, but also hopes for the abundance and fullness of life with beauty, goodness, and truth in harmony and balance in an organic web of life. This is what Roland Faber calls the Whiteheadian "ecological doctrine of G*d" which understands G*d as a concrete event within the process of processes.

> God now emerges as the 'happening' that encompasses the universe in its ecological relationality and creative motion, as *the empowering and saving event per se* and in which the universe, as the process of processes, creatively constitutes itself, ecologically enters into its network of relationships, and acquires enduring character even amid its perishing.... Whitehead's ecological doctrine of God became the initiator, driving force, and catalyst for the subsequent development of process theology.[63]

Salim, the dynamics of life, is the very process of empowering and saving as Faber interprets Whitehead's ecological G*d (which I prefer to refer to as "eco-G*d," yet, Faber refers to G*d, "the poet of the world," following Whitehead)[64] as the happening, the empowering and saving events. Thus, the Whiteheadian Life as G*d is the whole process [*salim*] of the universe as a moving part-whole [*hanul*]. In process-*donghak* language, if Christ is creative transformation and love incarnated, I would replace *Logos* [Word] with *salim* and G*d and the world together as the unity of *Life* with *hanul* to rewrite a variation of John 1:1-4.

> In the beginning was *Salim*, and *Salim* was with *Hanul*, and *Hanul* was *Salim*. All things came into being through *Salim*, without *Salim* not one thing came into being. What has come into being through *Salim* was *Hanul*, and *Salim* was the light of *Hanul*.

Hae-Weol's *Gyeong-Mool* [敬物] and Jay B. McDaniel's Reverence for Life

Beyond a poplar tree
is the sky.
At the end of the sky
is a popular tree.

Stand up on high,
then realize that mountains are high

Oh, my heart,
beat fast,
when I see a woman
in front of children.
Oh, Heart,
The cosmic seeds
live in all places.

Love is reverence.
Love flows,
when it reveres.

Stand up on high,
then realize mountains are high.

Realize mountains are high.
An end of a poplar tree is sky.
Love flows,
when it lowers.
  —*Gong Gyeong* [恭敬, *Reverence*], Kim Ji-Ha[65]

Su-Un's *si-cheon-ju* [侍天主, embracing *hanul*][66] theology was highly developed and practiced by Hae-Weol's notion of *yang-cheon-ju* [養天主, living *hanul*] which can be described by three practical approaches: reverence toward heaven [敬天, *Gyeong-Cheon*], reverence toward human beings [敬人, *Gyeong-In*], and reverence toward everything [敬物, *Gyeong-Mool*]. As a species that has invited *hanul* [the divine], in order to keep *hanul*, humankind needs to be faithful and moral in living which is *yang-cheon-ju* [養天主, living *hanul*] according to Hae-Weol. *Yang* [養] literally means to raise and to nourish. Only the person who lives *hanul* is the person who has embodied *hanul*. The *Donghak* scholar, Pyo Young-Sam, connects Su-Un's embracing of *hanul* and Hae-Weol's living *hanul* with a seed analogy. He writes, "*Hanul* is like a seed of the cosmic life. We plant a seed of the cosmic life and raise it mindfully. We keep and live *hanul* through the practice of *Do* [道, the Way of *hanul*]."[67] Thus, I interpret the *yang-cheon-ju* [養天主, living *hanul*] as a more process-focused life, living *hanul*, which means living the divine which is similar to the term, "godding," in English. The term, "godding," is used for living the divine, though it could be used in reference to all diverse religious acts. Then, how could we live through the divine according to Hae-Weol? What could be the guideline for "godding" in Hae-Weol? The answer is reverence.

  Hae-Weol's notion of reverence is first directed toward heaven and human beings, and reaches everything on the earth, including organic bodies and non-organic things. The anthropocentrism of western theology can be challenged by Hae-

Weol's *Gyeong-Mool* theory which is life-centered and bio-centric, and is comparable to Jay McDaniel's notion of openness toward G*d and reverence toward life.

Jay McDaniel expresses his deep ecological concerns in his theology of life. For him, reverence is not just an act of thinking but an act of feeling the presence of the surrounding world with respect and appreciation. His suggestion of reverence toward gods, people, animals, and the earth, including both organic and non-organic beings from his ecological sensitivity, gives a clue to interpreting the notion of life in *Donghak*, theologically. Both McDaniel and Hae-Weol understand the earth as an organic unity in which all things are interconnected and interdependent. Therefore, we are a life community, which I would like to refer to as a *salim* community.

Then, what is *hanul* [the divine] for Hae-Weol? For Hae-Weol, *hanul* is the subject of living. For Hae-Weol, living means working. His famous sermon is "the weaving *hanul*" [*cheon-ju-jik-po-seol*, 天主織布說]. When Hae-Weol called the woman who was weaving the cloth, *hanul*, Hae-Weol's *hanul* is not that of an ontological G*d, an object of worship, but the movements of life itself. This meaning of *salim* resembles living and enlivening rather than the word, life as a noun. It seems that, Hae-Weol recognized *hanul* as the movements of life, living and working not as an object of worship. Hae-Weol viewed it as a working subject, *hanul*. Using such logic, one can say that everything is involved in some kind of movement. There is nothing immobile in the world in a certain sense. However, this movement should not be *jugim* yet, it must be involved in creating and recreating *salim*. In this sense, it is possible to say that everything is *hanul*, if it is related *in* and *for* life, following Hae-Weol's definition of *hanul*. Therefore, the subject of *salim* is *hanul*.

Consequently, Su-Un's notion of embracing *hanul* can be accomplished by Hae-Weol's notion of living *hanul* through the practice of three types of reverence: reverence toward heaven, reverence toward human beings, and reverence for all things. Then the first step of living *hanul* should be that of embracing in this process. Kim Ji-Ha calls *si* [侍, embracing] the principle of *salim*.

He emphasizes that every movement of life should be that of embracing, *si*, 侍. Kim Ji-Ha's interpretation of Su-Un's embracing, *si*, 侍, is not just one quick step but is the continual process of serving and living *hanul* [the divine] throughout life.[68] Kim's notion of embracing *hanul* is, therefore, living *hanul*. We can recognize that Kim combines Su-Un's *si-cheon-ju* [侍天主, embracing *hanul*] and Hae-Weol's *yang-cheon-ju* [養天主, living *hanul*] as he interprets embracing *hanul* as living *hanul* by practicing the three forms of reverence which Hae-Weol taught. As Kim mentions embracing and living *hanul* as the principle of *salim*, *salim* suggests living *hanul* with reverence toward life.

Among the three forms of reverence, Kim Ji-Ha evaluates *Gyeong-Mool* [reverence toward everything, 敬物] as the highest human virtue and calls it "eco-ethica."[69] I understand Kim's notion of *mool* [物, things] as that of following Hae-Weol's notion of *Gyeong-Mool* [reverence toward everything, 敬物] in which *mool* is neither a static dead matter nor the Kantian "things in themselves."[70] I can say that *mool* in the understanding of Kim Ji-Ha and Hae-Weol does not reflect the Kantian notion of "things in themselves" [物自體, *Ding an sich*] which refers to those that are independent from us, yet exist by themselves as *noumenon* distinguished from our worldly phenomena.[71] The Kantian notion of *Ding an sich* exists by itself, separately, beyond or before our experiences, *a priori*. However, Kim's notion of things, *mool* [物], is interconnected and interdependent as the whole massive and organic spiritual body. From a western perspective, one could say that it is very close to the monistic understanding of body and spirit rather than that which is dualistic.

Kim Ji-Ha's notion of things, *mool* [物], is nondualistic because he sees life in terms of nonorganic matters as well. This is possible because he understands the movements of life as oscillation, expansion, circulation, and generation in which everything (of course, nonorganic things as well) is involved.

> Things are life and the character of life is spirituality. Living is knowing and knowing is *salim*. The whole process of generation of the cosmos of matter to spirit can be summed up in one word, "the cosmic life."[72] I believe that not only organic things but also non-organic things are living. Though there is no reproductive function, all of the motions of oscillation, expansion, circulation, and generation are spiritual activities, the movements of life, *salim*.[73]

As Kim Ji-Ha discovered "the cosmic life" in things (so-called matter), the whole process of all the activities of life in the whole cosmos is actually a non-dualistic macrocosmic living organism. In the first section of this chapter, I referred to the notion of *hanul*, the cosmic life as part-whole, and *salim* as the process of life. In the web of life, there is no separation of matter and spirit but only spiritual organism and organic spirit. It is difficult to say that things are dead or nonorganic, when we just consider that there is no life in our anthropocentric sense. As Whitehead observed, "At the lower end of the scale, it is hazardous to draw any sharp distinction between living things and inorganic matter."[74] In a way, one can say that everything is living in this living organism. In this sense, there is nothing in the world that is not involved in *salim*, the process of life.

Kim Ji-Ha interprets Hae-Weol's *hanul* as "the cosmic life" which is in all things, including non-organic things. In this sense, everything can be called *hanul*. Hae-Weol's eco-centric cosmology is similar to the thinking of Jay McDaniel. For him, *hanul*, the cosmic life, can be comparable to "G*d's indwelling lure" which is in cats, birds as well as "pelicans."[75]

> For Whitehead, God is not the supreme exception to inter-being but rather the supreme exemplification of it. God is in all things, and all things are in God, such that neither can be sharply separated from the other. Of course, this indwelling lure-God- is not within

humans alone. It is also within plants and animals, hills and rivers, plants and stars. In Whitehead's philosophy, God is not merely anthropocentric; God is eco-centric and each living being has its own unique relationship to "the cosmic lure." Dogs respond to the lure of God by barking, cats by purring, fish by swimming, and birds by flying.[76]

For Hae-Weol, G*d is indwelling (embracing according to Su-Un) in the sense of the woman who was weaving the cloth. *Hanul* [the divine] can be recognized not only in human subjects but also in birds and even in non-organic things, so-called materials. Everything is embracing G*d while G*d is indwelling in everything. The difference between these two sentences is the working subject. When referring to the latter, G*d as the subject is working through the embodied. For Hae-Weol, the working subject (it could be nonhuman nature and nonorganic things) is "godding," living the divine as *hanul*. Hae-Weol's understanding of Su-Un's notion of embodying is reflected well in his poem about living *hanul*, through reverence toward all things from human beings to the dust in the world:

> Hear!
> That is also a sound of *si-cheon-ju* [侍天主, embracing *hanul*].
> Marvelous,
> How wonderful the Way of *hanul*
> Penetrating everything.
>
> Everything is the glory of the way of *hanul*,
> From the sun and the moon in the sky
> To the dust in the earth
> When human beings pray to mountains and rivers,
> They answer our prayers because
> There is no place where the Way of *hanul* is not indwelling.
> — Hae-Weol (translation mine)

This is one of the famous lessons by Hae-Weol along with *cheon-ju-jik-po-seol* [天主織布說, the weaving *hanul*].⁷⁷ According to Hae-Weol in his preaching, everything in the world has the marvelous divine quality. It is not exceptional to a human being, to a bird, or even to a tiny dust particle. In this sense, everything contains a divine quality throughout Hae-Weol's two sermons. Hae-Weol even called rice and salt *hanul* as well as human beings. "How come only human beings can embrace *hanul*? Everything in the earth is *hanul*. Human beings eat foods which are *hanul*. Therefore, *hanul* eats *hanul*."⁷⁸

> Don't hit children. That is against *hanul* because it is hitting *hanul*. When a guest comes to your house, don't say that a guest is coming but just say that *hanul* is coming.⁷⁹ (translation mine)

In the category of everything that Hae-Weol indicated as *hanul*, it is possible to say that Hae-Weol is pantheistic as well as panentheistic in his notion of *hanul* because Hae-Weol not only suggests that *hanul* is indwelling in everything but also directly named everything *hanul*. Nevertheless, I would assert that *Donghak* is neither completely pantheistic nor completely panentheistic but contains both aspects on two points. First, in the sense that Hae-Weol not only called all things *hanul,* but also treated them exactly as *hanul*, it is possible to call *Donghak* pantheistic. Secondly, it is possible to say that Hae-Weol was amazed by *hanul*'s indwelling in all things which have embodied *hanul* [*si-cheon-ju*, 侍天主] and lived through the Way of *hanul* in them [*yang-cheon-ju*, 養天主]. Then, his notion of *hanul* is panentheistic as well. Even though Hae-Weol pointed to everything as *hanul, hanul* as the cosmic life cannot be reduced to one particular thing because *hanul* is not limited to one embodiment but the endless life in everything in its fullness. Likewise, Jay McDaniel uses G*d to name the bird, but he claims that

G*d is not reducible to the hopes of the human beings and other animals:

> A bird may be an indwelling lure within the universe as a whole, inwardly animating each creature to seek its unique form of beauty and well-being and yet beckoning the whole of creation toward new forms of order that build upon inherited forms-living cells from molecules, and then people and penguins. The song of the bird may be the song of the universe. In using the word God to name the bird I do not mean that God is reducible to the hopes of human beings and other animals.[80]

When we call a singing bird and a working woman *hanul*, the signifier and the signified are transformed through the process of divine hybridity. There will be a shift from the object to the subject and both are in continuous process of becoming together as one. McDaniel considers G*d an act of hybridity, influenced by all that happens in the world, forever composed of those happenings in the creation of an ongoing as the Deep Listening. For McDaniel, "Deep listening is not an act of *knowing about*. Rather, it is an act of *knowing with*."[81] In the process of listening is the process of hybridization as McDaniel notes, "In genuine listening, the dichotomy between subject and object is eliminated, because at a certain level of the listener's psyche, we become the other, the person listened to."[82]

Indeed, listening is a very hybrid process of becoming the other. Through the process of listening, one transcends him/herself to become the molecule's level to empty (allow) a space for embracing the other immanently within her. In this sense, Deleuze says that "all becomings are molecular," becoming animals, flowers, stones and women. Becoming-woman is not imitating this entity or even transforming oneself into it.[83] Then, what does a genuine becoming mean?

For Deleuze, becoming woman must first be understood as a function of something else not imitating or assuming the female form but emitting particles of a microfemininity that produce in us a molecular woman. In a molar entity, Deleuze asserts, the man also becomes or can become a woman. By the same token, we may say that the becoming-woman of the man is like becoming-animal of the human. "For everybody is the molar aggregate, but becoming everybody is another affair, one that brings into play the cosmos with its molecular components. Becoming everybody/everything [*tout le monde*] is to world [*faire monde*], to make a world [*Faire un monde*]."[84] Thus, becoming is always double as Deleuze says that "One who becomes becomes no less than the one that becomes."[85]

This kind of becoming for Deleuze is, therefore, a becoming minor, becoming the one that cannot become, for its being is already major. The Deleuzian becoming can be seen as "experiences of the impossible: experiences of radical alterity"[86] suggested by Spivak who names "a deconstructive embrace" for embracing the other (one who is radically different such as becoming woman of man) within oneself.[87] Becoming understood in this way leads to the deconstruction of the concepts of the self-conscious male: a becoming-woman, a becoming-animal, a becoming-stone, and "a becoming-the earth" that I would suggest. Adapting Spivak's notion of embrace, humans embrace the earth (the embraced) and both humans and the earth transcend themselves (the old self) in becoming immanently the other (a new self).

In its very molecular level of radical immanent becoming the other, humans should be able to feel (share) all that happenings in the earth as a part of the body that feels the whole body. McDaniel argues that an ecological spirituality is a spirituality that listens.[88] To listen to the earth is to feel the earth as G*d feels her, from the inside rather than the outside. It is to hear the earth through the heart of G*d. There was an episode that Hae-Weol felt broken-hearted when he heard a harsh stepping sound on the ground and worried and cried for the earth because, in his view, the earth is *hanul*'s face as he taught, "Do not spit on the ground for that is *hanul*'s face."[89] Hae-Weol's care for the earth can be recognized as divine care. If I use Hae-Weol's triad reverence [*gyeong*] of *hanul*, I can reiterate Hae-Weol's episode that a human-*hanul* cares for the earth-*hanul* with *hanul*-love. Similarly, McDaniel writes that "We become participants in the divine life, experiencing love without jealousy which characterizes God's care for the world. In so doing, the image of God within us becomes a likeness of God."[90]

Nonetheless, according to McDaniel's witness, "Today humanity is indeed spitting on the ground, and with substances much more dangerous than saliva."[91] It is basically from the anthropocentric worldview that focuses on the territoriality of the earth as just matter. In this perspective, the earth is something human beings can possess and conquer. The materialistic and imperialistic view toward the earth of the human beings has caused many ecological crises. People contaminate the earth by the irresponsible disposal of chemicals and trash. Both Hae-Weol and McDaniel agree with the fact that the earth is G*d's body which needs to be revered. For McDaniel, the earth as G*d's body includes our own bodies as well as the rocks, wind, water, fire, and all things of nature. As he declares, "God is the psyche, the heart, of the universe, and the universe is God's body."[92] Then, whatever humankind has done to the earth is something we do to G*d as well as to ourselves because we, as human beings are a part of this cosmic body. Actually, the earth is our body and also our home.

When I use this analogy of the earth as home, I exclude the image of a patriarchal household in which the head of a household is actually male. Rather, I would use the Korean concept of *hanul* as one cosmic body in which everyone is biologically related. The Korean term, *hanul*, means not only the divine but also "one community" which could be a family (or home), a country, the earth as one massive body. The *Donghak* scholar, Kim Hyeong-Ki interprets Su-Un's *hanul* as the expanding cosmos, nature itself, in which human beings endlessly expand the eternal self.[93] *Hanul* can be understood as this oneness of all other bodies like the community of communities. Thus, the boundary of *hanul* is immeasurable because the name, *hanul*, is a more encompassing concept, embracing the whole cosmic body in which the earth can be referred to as *hanul* as well as human beings and rocks along with other entities of the entire cosmos.

The earth as *hanul* is a shared community. We live in one another's lives and die one another's deaths. We feed and raise one another. Everyone's life depends on the lives of all others. This symbiotic family lives together and dies together as the *salim* community. Therefore, I view '*hanul* as a *salim* community.' The traditional usage of *salim* means all the productive activities in a household such as the interior of the home, raising plants, cleaning the house, managing the home, its economics, as well as cooking and feeding the family. If we see this planet as our home, all the productive activities in our planet could be understood as *salim* and actually that is the broad meaning of *salim*. Trees and squirrels are also our household members. Renaming the planet "home" (a vast planetary house) *hanul*, the boundaries of the household are expanded as well as activities and meaning of *salim* as they relate to the whole planet. *Salim* is not just caring for our children in one patriarchal household but the all-encompassing caring for everything in this planet as an organic unity. *Salim* in this sense reflects 'planetary love,' 'an eco-caring energy.'

When Jay McDaniel applies the term, *oikos*, to the earth, it is not a reference to the patriarchal household. Rather, McDaniel hopes for "a postpatriarchal community" in which he suggests deconstructing two ideas, "(1) that men must be stereotypically masculine, given the image of masculinity just described, and (2) that God is a sovereign, all-controlling expression of an exclusively masculine spirit."[94] McDaniel's hope for a postpatriarchal community echoes Kim Ji-Ha's hope for a *yin*-world which has less masculinity and more femininity. When McDaniel and Kim indicate masculinity, they refer to a social value in the patriarchal society which has been idealized as a human value, opposing femininity. Both scholars try to avoid overpowering one gender character as the standard by which to define G*d and human beings. Even though it could be criticized as an essentialistic and also dualistic approach to use the old stereotypical values of femininity and masculinity, it is important to regard the problems of the patriarchal world which emphasize a single value which is masculinity. Similarly, Catherine Keller suggests talking about a wide range of wombs such as *creatio ex utero* [creation out of womb] or *tehom* [the deep as a feminine symbol]. She writes, "As long as the transcendent phallogocentrism runs deeper than law, it continues to requisition every origin. So it must be countered just there, where the origin betrays its dark secret: its deep down there."[95] Likewise, both Kim and McDaniel suggest the plurality of values and give more power to the one that once was powerless to make a more balanced world, a postpatriarchal world, the *yin*-world. G*d's *oikos* which McDaniel describes following the era of patriarchy has six characteristics: "(1) value-pluralistic thinking and care, (2) a logic of relational power, (3) a nondualistic approach to reason and feeling, (4) the self as creative, relational, and dynamic, (5) nature as evolutionary and ecological but not mechanistic, and (6) God is Heart."[96]

I would like to focus on McDaniel's G*d as Heart. By suggesting a postpatriarchal household, McDaniel wipes out my ongoing worry related to *oikos* for the earth in a way that legitimates masculine power over a patriarchal household. It is a new household which is no longer occupied by a male G*d but is cared for through the Heart of G*d. McDaniel's G*d is one of feeling. As such, the heart, is recognized as emotion which is used as word contrary to reason and is placed on a lower level than the mind in the dualistic hierarchy as the so-called "feminine." McDaniel refers to the earth as our home of homes, as "an all-encompassing, womb-like matrix" that includes the earth and is *more than the earth*.[97] McDaniel uses a female pronoun to indicate G*d when he explains the fluidity of G*d who becomes the world.

> The fluidity of God has important implications for how we conceive her. God assumes the character that is most needed by the creature at issue, given its

circumstances. For pelicans, God becomes in her own heart, a pelican; for cockroaches, a cockroach; for cats, a cat; for earthworms, an earthworm; for humans, a human. The fluidity of God allows us to say that God becomes the kind of person that is most needed by the person at issue in order for that person to find wholeness and help others to become whole. It is to trust in the flow of her grace, to trust that whatever situation we are in, she will be there as a companion working to guide us toward the fullness of life.[98]

McDaniel's woman identification with the earth shows his deep ecofeminist view to hope for a new earth as a womb that might be a symbol of "becoming together" with the other whom she symbiotically embraces in her. What McDaniel suggests is 'a bio-centric community.' However, this bio-centric, eco-centered, nature-oriented community is apparently different from the patriarchal community and, for a long time, the term, nature (or bio, etc.) has been used as an attribute of femininity. Since everyone is nature and everything is life, the traditional definition of femininity does not have to be used only for women nor for only humans. Therefore, this is, indeed, a bio-community not a matriarchy. It is one organic body as a part-whole, *hanul*. In this massive organic body, humans are a part of living with other living things and all other things which are considered as non-organic. Nonetheless, if one sees the earth as organic, then, nothing is dead or mere matter in the world because the earth as the macrocosm is alive, and therefore, organic. For McDaniel, the earth is G*d's own body including human beings, rocks, wind, water, and fire. "The earth is the immediate content of God's experience, therefore, God's own life."[99] For him, "God is the Sacred Whole of the universe, a Life in which all lives are gathered together in wisdom and compassion."[100] In my view, McDaniel's G*d as feeling or Heart can be compared to *hanul* as the cosmic life and the symbiotic body as the part-whole organic community (household) since McDaniel's G*d is heart and the earth is G*d's body.

McDaniel recommends panentheism as an ecological way of thinking about G*d in relation to the universe.[101] In the pan*en*theistic worldview, everything is *in* G*d and G*d is *in* everything and yet, the universe is not identical with G*d but with the body of G*d. Therefore, we must insert "*en*: in" between everything [*pan*] and G*d [*Theo*] in order not to make G*d immediately everything (pantheism). Therefore, for McDaniel, it is possible to say that G*d becomes a pelican yet the pelican is not G*d" while Hae-Weol directly called the weaving woman *hanul* yet did not say *hanul* is becoming the weaving woman. Actually, she is both the embracing subject and embodied object and, as both, is recognized as *hanul*. Nevertheless, the process notion of panentheism is clearly distinguished from both the ontological theism and pantheism because G*d in panentheism is neither an external super person nor the universe, itself, but exists *within* the universe as the Spirit (or the psyche according to McDaniel) of the universe.

McDaniel distinguishes panentheism from dualism and pantheism by presenting three visual images: a horizontal spiral indicates the ongoing history of creation and a larger circle represents G*d. As we see these figures: in dualism, G*d and the history of creation go separately; in panentheism, the history of creation is actually in G*d. His process panentheistism image shows how creatures are immanent "within" G*d's interiority just as the earth is like a fish swimming "in" an ocean called G*d.[102]

| Dualism | Panentheism | Pantheism |

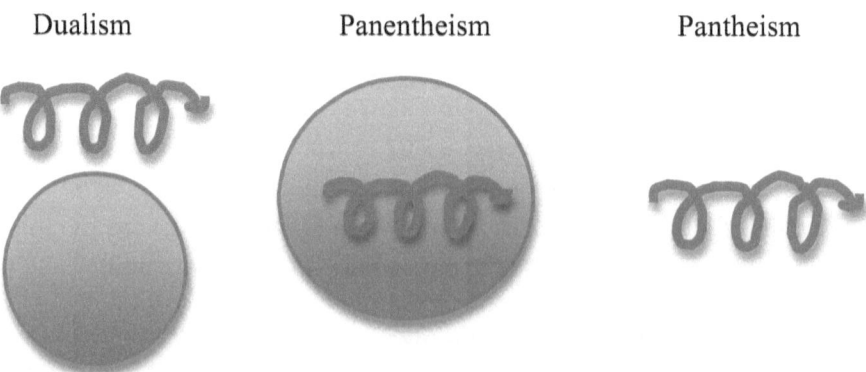

Can we apply these three visual images to explain the notion of *hanul* in *Donghak*? McDaniel's diagrams seem so understandable and accurate to explain the western categorization of dualism, pantheism, and panentheism as a process understanding of G*d and creation. Does this panentheistic circle fully describe the complexity and multiplicity of *hanul* as a symbiotic body, that is part-whole? The first figure is not even close to *hanul* as the cosmic life since that is apparently dualistic. The third figure as the equation of G*d and the creation does not tell anything about *hanul* as the sacred. There is no distinction between the sacred the secular but is only a single line which does not set the sacred apart from the secular. Although the second picture is the closest to *hanul* in terms of the notion of *si-cheon-ju* [embracing the divine] of Su-Un, as the process in G*d, it does not quite satisfy my sense of *yang-cheon-ju* [living as *hanul* not living in *hanul*] by Hae-Weol. Thus, I would like to elaborate on McDaniel's second picture to describe *hanul* as non-dualistic part-whole, as a picture combining the thinking of Su-Un and Hae-Weol's *hanul* through my Asian process rendition of McDaniel's interpretation.

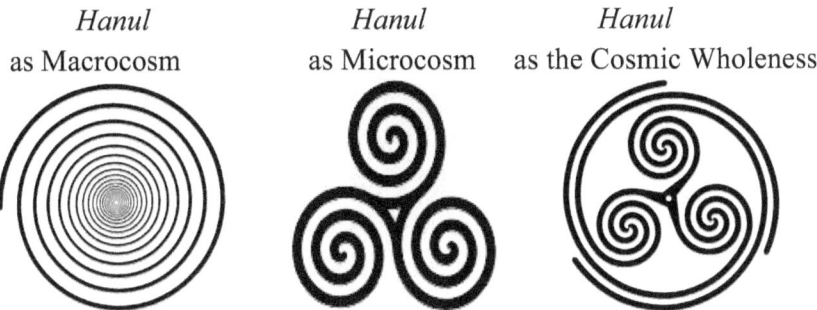

Hanul as Macrocosm   *Hanul* as Microcosm   *Hanul* as the Cosmic Wholeness

I understand the *hanul* of Su-Un and Hae-Weol through a process reading such that *hanul* reflects the cosmic life as one organic body which is the whole encompassing macrocosm and microcosm in the process of life, *salim*. In the first design, I draw *hanul* as a macrocosm with a huge circle without an end, a spiral that is open-ended. Thus, *hanul* as a macrocosm is evolving and expanding in process. One can see it as being more dynamic than in the spiral which reflects the movements of life, *salim*. Then, how would we draw *hanul* as a symbiotic body of part-whole? The ending of the spiral is not the end but continues to create, is becoming as an open-ended alternative within which there are endless, unlimited circles (spirals of spirals) we cannot even count. Our life is an ongoing process that can be described as *hanul*, a microcosm which could be depicted by the second picture, the multi-folded spiral.

As Hae-Weol describes *hanul* in three forms of reverence, I use the three-spoked spiral to symbolize the process of life in multiple directions (three symbolizes all directions which can potentially representing millions, multiplicity of multiplicities) in multiple forms not a single spiral moving in one direction within a circle. Thus, we can draw multiple spirals endlessly in the second picture signifying numerous branches of each spiral. I combine the two pictures in the third picture to depict *hanul* as the cosmic organism. In this process, *hanul* cannot be described by a definition. That is, a process that is incomplete: it is ongoing becoming. This aspect I would call convolution, evolving together as the whole cosmic organism in which the part is the whole and the whole is the part, henceforth, referred to as the part-whole. All is a part of *hanul* as Life.

Hae-Weol directly referred to everything in the universe as *hanul*. Nevertheless, Hae-Weol's notion of *hanul* is similar to McDaniel's panentheistic view of G*d as "the heart of the universe" and the universe "the body of G*d" in terms of the cosmic life of part-whole. Therefore, Hae-Weol is pantheistic, yet, at the same time, he can be described as panentheistic, if one intentionally classifies him in the western categorization of the relationship between the world and G*d in three aspects. Actually, his notion of *hanul* embraces both aspects and beyond them. Hae-Weol called everything in the universe *hanul*, including a women who is weaving cloth as *hanul*, children as *hanul*, and rice as *hanul*, because each embraces and lives *hanul* as the living part-whole.

I understand *hanul* not as one static being, regardless of whether that being is a human, bird, flower, rock, water, etc. Rather, *hanul* is an actual working (living) subject as singular as well as becoming subjects as plural in the whole set of living organisms of *hanul*. There is no boundary between a part and the whole as one macro-cosmic organism in which everything is involved in every other thing in the process of *salim* by touching and penetrating each other's boundaries. This complexity of life is actually the part-whole relation of the ecosystem in which one part cannot be divided or reduced from the whole and *vice versa*.

All the particularities of singularities shine by their own uniqueness and differences by their nature as Su-Un praises that "a red flower blooms red, therefore, so beautiful" in his poem, "*Chusaga*: A Song of A Retired Gentleman."[103] Similarly, Deleuze also notes the "rhizomatic" becoming of the cosmic whole with the multiplicity of multiplicities, "The Pink Panther paints the world its color, pink on pink; this is its becoming-world, carried out in such a way that it becomes imperceptible itself, its own line of flight, follows its aparallel evolution."[104] The Deleuzian notion of "becoming multiplicity" can may be illustrated in the figure three above – *hanul* as the cosmic whole, an open spiral embraces multiple spirals and *vice versa*. In the Deleuzian notion of becoming (more accurately, "becoming together"), each individual is an infinite multiplicity and "the whole of Nature is a multiplicity of multiplicities:" The part of the whole, the whole with its parts together, an infinity of particles is entering into an infinity of more or less interconnected relations.[105] If the whole is *hanul,* then, a part of whole in relation to the whole is also *hanul*, not one of *hanul* or one in *hanul* but *hanul*, itself. By the same token, Pyo Young Sam states, "from a tiny cell to the whole cosmos is one organic body, *hanul*. This means one becomes many and many become one. My body is life as a part and *hanul* is life as the whole between which there is no separation, even for a second."[106] When Hae-Weol referred to a working woman as *hanul* as well as a singing bird *hanul*, it is not to the static substance but to the actual changes, movements, living, life in dynamics, thus, to *salim*. Therefore, *hanul* is Life, becoming together. When we recognize life as the divine, we can recognize the face of G*d in nature, human and more than human, organic and nonorganic matters, which are *imago Dei*, the body of G*d, divine, indeed. Not only feeling the divine immanence 'in' everything but also recognizing nature 'life as the divine,' Hae-Weol transcended the western classification of pantheism and panentheism, saying that even "*bab* [rice, food] is G*d."

Bab [rice] is *Hanul* [the divine]

Bab is *hanul*
Bab is for sharing
like *hanul* can't be taken by one person

Bab is *hanul*
Bab is for everybody
Like everybody sees the stars in the sky

Bab is *hanul*.
When *bab* is eaten through one's mouth
We embrace *hanul* in our body

Bab is *hanul*.
Ah! Ah!
Bab divides up its body for feeding everybody. [107]

Hae-Weol points out that life is *hanul*. In his notion of *gyeong-mool* [reverence toward things] theology, food is not mere material but life which is *hanul*. For Hae-Weol, there is nothing that does not reflect *hanul* [the divine] in the world. Not only human beings but also animals and plants embrace *hanul*. This is not only for living things but also for non-organic things, including the dust in the world.

> Listen, everything embraces *hanul* and embodies
> *hanul*. Amazing! The mystery of *hanul* penetrates
> every single moment of the world. The Way of *hanul*

glorifies from the sun and moon in the sky to the dust of the earth.[108] (translation mine)

This fragment of Hae-Weol's preaching was written after he listened to the song of a bird. It is to say that everything in the world has *hanul* [the divine], including birds, as well as nonorganic things such as dust. Since everything has *hanul*, for Hae-Weol, everything including foods is, therefore, *hanul*. He writes as follows:

I always say that each thing is *hanul*. If you recognize this fact as right, *foods are hanul*. When you eat things then *hanul eats hanul* which could sound nonsense. That is because you see only from one side. If you view the whole universe as one body, you will recognize the fact that *hanul* feeds and raises *hanul* by sharing and helping to reconcile each other. By this whole process, we live together as one body with harmony and interconnectedness.[109] (translation mine)

Hae-Weol called the human being *hanul* as well as *bab* [rice, food in general]. Similarly, Kim Ji-Ha calls himself *bab* which is *hanul*. If we eat *bab*, that means we eat *hanul*. Therefore, a human being as *hanul* eats *hanul*. Consequently, it is possible to say that, "*hanul eats hanul*" [*eicheon sicken*, 以天食天] in Hae-Weol's symbiotic cosmology. Hae-Weol's notion of *gyeong-mool* [reverence toward things] is summed up in his *bab* theology: "*In a bowl of rice, the truth of heaven and earth exist. Serving bab, sharing bab, eating bab are the most sacramental ritual of all for life.*"[110]

In the same way that Kim Ji-Ha refers to '*bab* as *hanul*,' Kim declares, "*Bab* is G*d."[111] The traditional understanding of *bab* is very anthropocentric: *Bab* is only produced for human need. Kim Ji-Ha elevates *bab* to the sacred which had been only recognized for human need having only a material value. Kim's notion of *bab* [food] as the sacred [the divine] breaks down the binary structure of G*d and creation, humans and nonhumans, self and "the other," so that it can be viewed as a mediating function to connect everything to every other thing, symbiotically, as one cosmic body [*hanul*], in which everything is being fed and feeds one another. For Koreans, *bab* is the most important matter for life. Kim Ji-Ha suggests *bab* as a catalyzer of symbiosis which fills *teum* [gap] between One and the Other and connects them to open a new relationship.

Eating is a way of communication and relation to one another. Through this process, you become me and I become you. Therefore, I would say that eating is a process of hybridity. "Life feeds on life." This can be called *bab* hybridity which is a place where multiple forms of hybridity come together in the very act of cooking, eating, and sharing. Hae-Weol preaches, "In a bowl of rice, the truth of heaven and earth exist." Through eating, a person experiences a micro and macrocosmic union with all these universal elements. When we eat we become one with the materials, which have themselves become one from other materials. "The universe is present in a bowl of rice." In this activity, perhaps the several forms of hybridity can come together in some way such as the farmer, grains, the woman who cooks and serves, one who eats rice, etc.

锄禾

锄禾日当午,
汗滴禾下土。
谁知盘中餐,
粒粒皆辛苦。

Toiling Farmers
At noon farmers hoe up the crops in the sweltering sun,
Sweat dripping onto the soil beneath the crops.
Who knows that each grain of the meal is filled with hard work?

—an ancient Chinese poem

Jay McDaniel lists many forms of "*bab* hybridity:" "The multiple foods on the table are a kind of hybridity; our act of eating is a kind of hybridity; the identities we bring to the table are hybridities; the lure toward beauty within each of us, in whose listening all of this occurs; is a hybridity."[112] At the eating table, different stories are told, transmitted, retold, and created.[113] It brings people together simply to share food, drink, and friendship with joy and laughter. Every dining table is actually "a sacrament of the present moment."

However, eating does not only mean a peaceful sharing as *salim*. *Jugim* [killing] for survival also exists in the circle of life. Whitehead described this eating process as 'robbery.' He comments, "A living society is such an agency. The societies which it destroys are its food. All societies require interplay with their environment; and in the case of living societies this interplay takes the form of robbery. Whether or no it be for the general good, life is robbery. However, the robber requires justification."[114] The word, "robbery" for life, might be a harsh word or warning for every form of life since everything is eating and being eaten which is the circle of life because the conventional use of robbery nuances violence and exploitation of "the Other." The more complex the entity is, the greater the robbery from other entities as human beings eat more diverse foods than any other animal. Here we enter into the ethical dilemma of foods. However, life for Whitehead does not appear within the hierarchies of the organization of organisms, but their *edges* as Whitehead describes, "Life is a bid for freedom not captured by permanent characteristics but set free by originality."[115] Whitehead states that an entirely living nexus requires its immediate environment. Thus, every one becomes part of the environment of others. A hybrid prehension is the prehension by one subject of a conceptual prehension, or of an impure prehension, belonging to another subject.

In this hybrid process, "originality is both canalized and intensified."[116] This hybridizing process is happening in "empty space amid the interstices"[117] in the Whiteheadian language which resonates with Kim Ji-Ha's connection of *bab* and *teum* [gap]: "We eat each other's *edges* not the center or the whole body. Every new thing comes out of *teum*."¹¹⁸ Kim explains this connection of *bab* and *teum* as "a paradoxical circulation of symbiosis" for interpreting Hae-Weol's "life eats life":

> When we watch the process that an eagle eats a lamb, we can realize that the eagle targets a sick one among the flock. Similar to a tiger, when a tiger catches a rabbit, the tiger always growls as a signal before he eats, giving some other healthier ones can have a time to run away. It is the same as a fishnet that has holes that catches only big fishes. Therefore, the tiny fish can sneak out through the holes and live longer. Nature has always *teum* in which life finds its way of living. *Life eats life* but only *edges* of each other through *teum*. If one invades the other's center, then the paradox of the circulation of life will just be destroyed [*jugim*].¹¹⁹

Kim calls this paradox of the "sanctification of the food-chain"¹²⁰ which we human beings should learn from non-human nature, even though there are inevitable sufferings.

Unpacking the metaphor of robbery, we need to give consideration to the concept of life. Life contains beauty and suffering at the same time. If one just romanticizes life as only beautiful, how can we explain the bitterness of life? If *salim* hides the robbery of the horror of animals being preyed upon by other animals, how is it honest? Jay McDaniel agrees with the robbery concept of life by Whitehead and suggests another way to discuss it, though the term, robbery, already sounds brutal and violent which is a term resembling, *jugim* [killing, violence] rather than *salim* [enlivening]. McDaniel comments, "Because life is a type of robbery, ecological Christians must inevitably make decisions about whom to rob, when to rob, how to rob, and most importantly, how to minimize robbery."¹²¹ For McDaniel, it is necessary to distinguish degrees of intrinsic value among different kinds of organisms. Nevertheless, there is a danger of anthropocentrism in terms of the decision of degrees of intrinsic value among all things: Who is going to decide and for whom? Also important to this discussion is the undeniable hierarchy of the ecosystem: Can one say that an amoeba is more valuable than or has the same value as a human baby? What about plants and grains like rice?

In order to transform or reinterpret life of the ecosystem from this sad notion of robbery into the hopeful notion of *salim*, one has to recognize the intrinsic values of all living organisms rather than the instrumental values and respect their subjectivities as agents of *salim*, even when they are being eaten. Everything possesses some degree of subjectivity as Whitehead suggests. In his view, "Apart from the experience of subjects, there is nothing, nothing, nothing, bare nothingness."[122] It seems that Whitehead had already found a solution for his bold concept of robbery for life, when he referred to the food as "a catalytic agent"[123] which makes one and the other hybrid through the process of disturbance. For Whitehead, *teum*, in the process of eating, is an "empty space" which is not a space occupied by any corpuscular society but the statistical balance that has been disturbed. Whitehead states that life does not occur in the spaces already occupied by living societies but lurks in the interstices between societies; it approaches from an "empty space."[124] In other words, it is only through this empty space and by this occasion of robbery that all living societies are first related to one another, or that a living society is put in touch with its environment through the act of robbing it and destroying the organic societies that comprise its food.

Whitehead believed that the living cannot come from the dead; the living only come from that which is alive.[125] In the Whiteheadian sense, food is alive as is a mountain. Food is not just an object of the eater but also is a subject of *salim* as the feeder for life. In this sense, *bab* [rice, food] does not exist only for human beings but, as an agent of life, itself, it feeds other life. When life eats other forms of life, the ecosystem becomes a hybrid organic body based on symbiosis. When one understands *salim* as enlivening, then the whole process of eating and being eaten is a process of *salim*, feeding, sharing, caring, raising, etc. Kim Ji-Ha sees this symbiotic process of eating as the principle of *salim*:

> Therefore, "*hanul eats hanul*" [*eicheon sikcheon*, 以天食天] means "life eats life." It doesn't mean that a life destroys another life but a life penetrates into the *teum* [gap] of other life and eats the boundary of the other to produce new things and open a *teum* to others. In between the two actions, there is a *teum* which is a chain that connects one to another. That is actually the creative circulation of *salim*.[126]

Therefore, according to Kim Ji-Ha, *bab* is *hanul* [the divine] and eating *bab* [*siksa*, 食事] is a sacred process.

Nevertheless, traditionally, unlike Kim's notion of *bab* as the sacred, women and the handling and preparation of food had been degraded as being domestic rather than the public in the dualistic patriarchal hierarchy. Kim also mentions the sexist view on the traditional kitchen against women: "When I heard the names of elderly women who were separated from their families during the Korean War on T.V., I cried for the women who had no names in the old days as they were referred to only with kitchen-related names, *bab-punnae* [food server], *guk-punnae* [soup server], *boouk-daegi* [kitchen lady], etc."[127]

There has also been a gap [*teum*] between *siksa* [食事, eating *bab*] and *jaesa* [祭祀], rituals that usually suggest ancestor worship. *Jaesa* [祭祀] is Korean ancestor worship that was originated in the *Cheonsin* [heaven G*d] worship of Korean ancient religion and developed into its present form through the process of interaction and synchronization of the Korean shamanistic beliefs and the Confucianism and Neo-Confucianism of China. The Korean shamanistic worldview has provided an important foundation for Korean ancestor worship. Confucianism played an important role in adding, concretely, the ethical dimension to Korean ancestor worship, while Neo-Confucianism provided the metaphysical dimension.

Thus, ancestor worship, with its moral, ritual, and cosmological aspects, became a richly religious form of worship in Korea. Ancestor worship was no longer a ritual, exclusively belonging to the Confucian tradition. Rather, it became the most important and popular family ritual for all Koreans regardless of their religious affiliations, until Christianity was introduced. Nevertheless, Ancestor worship became the most well-accepted religious ritual among all Koreans.[128]

Only *jaesa* [ancestor worship] has been recognized as a sacred ritual, yet *siksa* [eating] has been classified as secular and unimportant. Therefore, *jaesa* and *siksa* are two fundamentally different processes in Korean traditional thinking. Interestingly, both *jaesa* [ritual] and *siksa* [eating] use *bab* [food] as an important catalyst to connect with one another. In *jaesa*, *bab* connects two realms, the dead and the living, while *bab* connects living people themselves in the process of *siksa*. Another step from which understanding can emerge is related to the conventional function of *bab*. One can view *bab* as a catalyst to connect *jaesa* as the sacred and *siksa* as the secular. Sharing *bab* can be seen as a hybrid process through which *jaesa* and *siksa* are not really separable but are interrelated becoming a sacrament.

Some Korean Confucian scholars such as Ro Young-Chan and Andrew Song-Min Paek evaluate *jaesa* as a beautiful tradition in Korea which holds the non-dualistic view between the spiritual and physical worlds and between this life and the afterlife.[129] Such thinking has validity since *jaesa* has the function to bring all the family members together for reunion and to remember their dead ancestors. Actually, the ancestors are treated just as their family members as they serve food [*bab*] for the ancestor and bow to the ancestor, showing reverence, as if they were still alive. Therefore, *jaesa* is a very hybrid moment and a place that connects life and death. However, Ro and Paek fail to see the misogynic aspect in the process of the *jaesa*.

Traditionally, for ancestor worship, women cook and prepare foods in the kitchen but are not allowed to participate in the worship, as only men are permitted to conduct the worship and are allowed to bow to the spirits of their ancestors. Therefore, men are the conductors of the *jaesa* and women are the servers of food. *Siksa* [eating] and women who cook *bab* have been always positioned in a lower realm, according to the traditional *jaesa* [ritual] custom in Korea. In this androcentric view, only male descendents have the privilege of conducting the ritual of *jaesa* and of communicating with the spirits of their ancestors. Therefore, people prefer to have male children to prepare for their future after death. Though women prepare the foods for *jaesa*, they are isolated from the ritual and even from the foods they have prepared. Instead of participating in the ritual, they are excluded to wait in the kitchen until the ceremony is finished. This *teum* [gap] between *jaesa* and *siksa* is a product of the dualistic separation of the sacred and the secular, the dead and the living, men and women. The question is then, how can this huge *teum* [gap] that exists between *jaesa* and *siksa* enjoy reconciliation? Kim Ji-Ha suggests that *bab* [food] can be the mediator to connect, fill, and transform the *teum* between these two different dualistic processes. Kim calls it "*teum* against *teum*."[130] Yet, how can this *teum* against *teum* happen?

    Traditionally, the dinner table for ancestor worship should be set facing the wall, not in front of the family members. The ancestral tablet is placed on the altar. All the dishes should be set on the table in a specific order and place: Rice should be on the west, soup on the east, meat should be on the west, and head of the fish on the east and tail on the west. The fruit should be in the first row, the meat and fish in the second row, and the vegetables in the third row, and cooked rice and soup in the last row.[131] Even the spoon and the chopsticks should be placed toward the wall because people believe that the ghosts take the food from the side of the wall. Therefore, in the traditional *jaesa* custom, *bab* should be placed toward the wall for the spirits which is known as *hyang-byeok-seol-wi* [to place *bab* toward the shrine, 向壁設位]. Thus, in the ritual of *hyang-byeok-seol-wi*, *bab* is prepared to feed the spirits in a respectable manner.

Consequently, there is a huge *teum* between the sacred altar and people's eating place, *babsang* [the dinner table].

Thus, *jaesa* becomes a dualistic separation which creates a hierarchy of the dead at the top and the living on the bottom, men at the head and women on the bottom, whereas it should be a time and place for a reconciliation of the whole family that is the beauty of *jaesa*. It is important to note that the meaning of *jaesa* is beautiful, yet, the process of *jaesa* creates a dualistic hierarchy in its practice because of the position of *bab* which is not prepared for the living but for the spirits.

As an alternative to this dualistic separation from *jaesa*, Hae-Weol created a transformative shift from the spirits of the dead to the living by switching the position of *bab* which is called, *hyang-ah-seol-wi* [to place *bab* toward the people, 向我設位] employing the following command:

> "What remains of the deceased parents' blood and spirit, I am heir to it." [父母之死後血氣, 存遺於我也]
> The disciples asked,
> "Then, how could we know that the spirit came and took the food?"
> Hae-Weol said,
> "It is evident that the spirit is living in you, when you feel hungry and want to eat food. That is your energy of life which is the spirit." [人之欲食之念, 即天主感應之心也][132] (translation mine)

Making reference to the former statement of Hae-Weol, "What remains of the deceased parents' blood and spirit, I am heir to it," can be stated in another way: "You who offer *jaesa* are the spirit and the place you stand is the place of the spirit because the spirit is embodied in you. So, you eat it!" It is from Hae-Weol's *gyeong* [reverence toward heaven, human, and things] theology of *hanul* which considers people as *hanul* and also the foods as *hanul*. In other words, if we do not feed the living for worshipping the spirits, we starve the living *hanul* [the divine].

As the Psalmist expresses the importance of living for worship (Psalm 6:5): "For the dead do not remember you: in the grave who shall give you thanks," Hae-Weol's notion of *hyang-ah-seol-wi* [placing *bab* toward people] seems to emphasize "living" more than worshipping [ritual] because there will be no worship without the worshippers. Actually, *bab* becomes a catalyzer that connects the dead and the living.

Through the ritual of *hyang-ah-seol-wi*, one can see a hermeneutical oneness of "the spirit-the people-the food" as one organic body of *hanul*. Thus, Hae-Weol's *bab* theology is nondualistic as it stands in the interstitial space between the spirit and the living body, human beings and the foods as non-human nature and the so-called material as one *hanul*. In this sense, I find a deconstructive aspect in Hae-Weol's *hyang-ah-seol-wi* [to place *bab* toward the people] in so far as it transforms the *teum* [gap] of *jaesa* [ritual] into a time and place of reconciliation connecting the spirit of ancestors and the living people, men and women, the shrine and the kitchen, the sacred and the secular. The altar becomes the people's dinner table and the offering becomes *bab* [food] for feeding people in life. Sharing food becomes the holy sacrament. Therefore, *jaesa* becomes *siksa* and, as a hybrid process, there is actually no distinction of the two absolute opposite processes.

Hong Gi-Seong, a *Donghak* scholar, refers to *hyag-ah-seol-wi* [to place *bab* toward the people, 向我設位] "a Copernican Revolution" in Korean history.[133] Kim Ji-Ha also recognizes the revolutionary declaration of *hyang-ah-seol-wi* as "*teum* against *teum*." In Kim's observation of *hyang-byeok-seol-wi* [to place *bab* toward the shrine, 向壁設位], there is a *teum* which does not cross the border between *hanul* [heaven, *cheon*, 天] who is working on the opposite wall and the people who are offering *bab* on the floor. He sees *hyang-byeok-seol-wi* [placing *bab* toward the spirits, the wall] as a disguise because it expands the *teum* [gap] between *hanul* [the divine] and the people, the subjects of *salim* [enlivening] who produce the *bab* [food]. Thus, the distance between *hanul* and the people becomes wider.[134] Kim mentions that "*hyang-ah-seol-wi* [placing *bab* toward the people] enables a repositioning of *bab* which is an outcome of the people's effort toward themselves who are actually *hanul*. Thus, *hanul* [the sacred] is not on the wall or on the table but in the people who are the subjects of *salim, hanul* themselves."[135]

Even though Kim points out a *teum* [gap] between the dead and the living when he interprets Hae-Weol's *hyang-ah-seol-wi* [placing *bab* toward the people], he misses pointing out a *teum* [gap] between men and women. The structure of the altar room does not create a spirit of *salim* for women. Therefore, there are two *teums* [*gap*], one between the spirit and its male descendants, and the other between males and females. *Bab* [food] is offered on the altar toward the wall and people are not allowed to eat the *bab* on the altar and need to wait until the spirits are fully served.

I would assert that *hyang-ah-seol-wi* [placing *bab* toward people] is a beginning of a new relationship, a new *teum* [interstitial space] which deconstructs the dualistic hierarchy of heaven and people and men and women by offering *bab* to people who are the subject of *salim*.[136] Recalling Hae-Weol's well-known proverb, "in a bowl of *bab* [rice], there are millions of meanings of life," so many people work to make the grain causing many people to be exploited for *bab*. Women work for *bab* and cook and feed *bab* to their family. For *salim*, people work for *bab*, cook *bab*, eat and feed *bab* that is the process of living which connects everything to every other things symbiotically. This whole process, one could say, can be related to the Eucharistic, the holy communion, as Kim mentions the sacred nature of *bab*, "*bab* is truth, the movement of life, and life itself, therefore, G*d."[137]

Though Kim Ji-Ha focuses and emphasizes the act of "eating," he does not mention the act of "feeding." If there is an act of eating, then, there must be an act of feeding. Feeding the family is the women's task in a traditional Korean household. "*Bab ul hada* (밥을 하다)" means "cooking meal" in a broad translation. "*Hada* (하다)" a verb means "to do" not "to cook." Therefore, in a direct and more accurate translation, "*bab ul hada*" means "doing *bab*" which is often accepted as "*salim hada* (살림하다)," "doing *salim*."

Thus, women are the subject of doing *bab* and doing *salim* in the Korean household. They are in charge of feeding the family. Not only women who cook *bab* but also the *bab*, itself, is being offered its body to be eaten by others, thus, be life itself, in *hanul*. According to Hae-Weol, *hanul* is embodied in *bab*. Therefore, *bab* is *hanul* for Kim Ji-Ha who follows Hae-Weol's notion. Thus, when we eat *bab*, we can say that "life eats life, *hanul* eats *hanul*."[138] It also means that life feeds life, *hanul* feeds *hanul*." Therefore, by eating *bab* and feeding it, life is involved in life through this full macrocosmic body in the web of life, a symbiotic bio-community.

Kim Ji-Ha and Hong Gi-Seong's discovery of a Copernican Revolution in Hae-Weol's *hyag-ah-seol-wi* [placing *bab* toward people] focuses on the shift of the location of *hanul* from the wall to the worshippers themselves. In addition to their discovery, I found three shifts in *hyag-ah-seol-wi*: The first is a shift from being worshipped to the worshipper. *Hanul* [the divine] becomes the worshipper her/himself. *Hanul* is no longer the object of the worship but the subject of the worship by "embracing *hanul* in her/his body" [*mosim, si-cheon-ju*, 侍天主]. Second, there is a shift from the participants (male descendants) of the ritual to that of the outsiders (females in the kitchen). Women do not need to wait in the kitchen but they can share *bab*, in the same place and time, as members of the community of *salim*. Also, women become the subjects of *salim*, that is, they are those who cook *bab* to enliven others. The last one is a shift from the object of the eaters to the subjects of *salim, hanul*. *Bab* is not a mere material but is *hanul* which was offered for our life. Therefore, *bab* becomes a subject of *salim* as well. Thus, the objects traditionally at the bottom of the hierarchy now become the subjects of *salim* as *hanul*. Not only the females who prepare *bab* in the kitchen but also *bab*, itself, is *hanul* in this process. Therefore, through these counter-hierarchal movements, *hyang-ah-seol-wi* [placing *bab* toward people] is a process of *salim* which feeds and is fed to maintain life abundantly in the oneness of "heaven-human-food" as one organic body, *hanul*. Consequently, *hanul* [heaven, 天], *saram* [human being, 人間], and *bab* [food] are all subjects of *salim* in the symbiotic process of life. Therefore, in this organic community of *salim*, all are being sanctified as *hanul*. In Kim Ji-Ha and Hae-Weol, *bab* is *hanul*. *Bab* is the source of life. Without *bab*, there is no life.

There is a poem which calls "G*d grain" similar to Kim Ji-Ha's poem, "*Bab* is G*d," by an anonymous Indian woman:

> Every noon at twelve
> In the blazing heat
> G*d comes to me in the form of
> Two hundred grams of gruel.
>
> I know G*d in every grain
> I taste G*d in every lick
> I communicate with G*d as I gulp
> For G*d keeps me alive, with
> Two hundred grams of gruel.
>
> I wait till next noon
> and now know G*d had come:
> I can hope to live one day more
> For you made G*d to come to me as
> Two hundred grams of gruel.
>
> I know now that G*d loves me-
> Not until you made it possible.
> Now I know what you're speaking about
> For G*d so loves this world
> That He gives His beloved Son
> Every noon through You.[139]

This poem illustrates the fact that when starving people eat *bab*, they experience G*d. This poet confesses that Jesus was being offered for us, like two hundred grams of gruel through which she experiences G*d's love. When she chews the grains, she feels and tastes G*d's love in each grain. The food in this poem symbolizes Jesus Eucharistic body which was being offered for people. Jesus not only offered his body as *bab* but also called himself *bab*: "I am the *bread of life*." (John 6:48)

Bab is such an important matter in Jesus' ministry. A Korean *minjung* theologian, Park Jae-Sun, writes in his book, *Jesus' Movement and the Community of Bab* (1988), that the kingdom of G*d about which Jesus preached was actually a peaceful community where all G*d's children could eat together abundantly.[140] The Israelites confessed *YHWH* as their G*d, when they were fed abundantly: "I have heard the grumbling of the Israelites. Tell them, at twilight you will eat meat, and in the morning you will be filled with bread. Then you will know that I am the LORD your God." (Exodus 16:3, *NIV*)

The kingdom of G*d is actually, a place where all G*d's children can eat enough *bab* peacefully, without struggle, according to Park Jae-Sun. He has same notion of *bab* as Kim Ji-Ha. For Park, *bab* is the source of life which feeds people (life), therefore, *bab* is life. According to him, the kingdom of G*d is actually "*babsang gongdongche*" [the community of *bab*].[141] Park quotes Isaiah: "On this mountain the LORD Almighty will prepare a feast of rich food for all peoples, a banquet of aged wine—the best of meats and the finest of wines." (Isaiah 25:6, *NIV*)

Park Jae-Sun understands Jesus' movement as a movement of "*babsang gongdongche*" [the food table community] on three points: First, Jesus ate with sinners and considered himself as their friend (Mark 2:16, Matthew 11:19, Luke 7:34). Jesus shared *bab* and his life with the outcasts in the society and established a new sharing community of *bab*. Secondly, Jesus offered the miracle of sharing (Luke 6:30-44, Mark 8:2,3). The miracle of the loaves and the fish was Jesus' feast to feed the hungry, the *minjung*. They became a *babsang gongdongche* [the food table community]. Third, Jesus offered his body as *bab* for people at the last supper which was the actual practice of the Jesus movement and realization of *babsang gongdongche*.¹⁴² "Then he took the bread, said the blessing, broke it, and gave it to them, saying, "This is my body, which will be given for you; do this in memory of me." (Luke 22:19, *NIV*)

Kim Ji-Ha's Christological point is in this declaration just as Park Jae-Sun points out in Jesus' ministry. According to Kim Ji-Ha, when Jesus refers to himself as *bab*, there are two points: "The first point is that I am the *bab* [food] of heaven which should be shared by *minjung* as a result of their labor, therefore, they become empowered to work again. The second point is that I am your food. Therefore, if you want me, do whatever you want to me."¹⁴³ On this point, Kim sees that Jesus is both spiritual and physical food for people. Actually, Kim's notion of *bab* is not merely physical but also spiritual. He understands life as a unification of the spirit and matter which are not really separable: "*Bab* is life. In life, there is no distinction between spirit and matter because it is a holistic body. Life has intrinsic unity and, therefore, life is *bab*."¹⁴⁴

Nevertheless, by making the assertion that "Jesus is *bab*" and referring to "*bab* as *hanul*" are different. It is not a process that can be switched automatically. There is actually a difference between the two different processes of incarnation (embodiment) and sanctification. From my perspective, when Jesus refers to himself as *bab*, Jesus is being materialized (incarnated) in *bab* (panentheistic incarnation); however, when Hae-Weol said that *bab* is *hanul*, *bab* is sanctified as the sacred, heaven. It does not mean only that *hanul* is in *bab* but also *bab* can be viewed as *hanul*. Before Jesus humbled himself as *bab*, for Hae-Weol, *bab* as nature was already the sacred, holy, heaven as *hanul*. It is precisely from Hae-Weol's deep ecological cosmology, that *Gyeong-mool* cosmology [敬物, reverence toward everything including non-organic things] emerges.

The whole process of cooking, eating, and sharing *bab* is *salim* process, having multiple forms of hybridity in a bowl of *bab*: "I offer you a bowl of rice; you take some; I take some; I hope you like it; I made it just today; and you chopped the onions; thank you; here, shall we say a blessing beforehand; it's OK, if we don't; but if we do that would be good, too. Take, eat and remember today."[145] When we offer a prayer at the beginning, we will thank the earth and the plants and the animals, the people who prepared the food and who served it, the farmers and people who brought the food to market. We will remember that we are nourished physically and spiritually by the lives of so many others, without whom we would not exist. And in our moment of gratitude some of us may sense a greater harmony in which all lives are enfolded. Through eating *bab*, one transcends herself and encounters the Other, which is a process of hydridization.

Consequently, through such a hybridizing process of *bab*, the sacred becomes matter and the matter becomes the sacred. That is the process of *salim* [enlivening] -- when life eats life, all become hybrid, you become me and I become you, and we are becoming together as part-whole. In this process, incarnation is sanctification as well as sanctification is incarnation. The dualistic opposition of heaven and earth, the sacred and the secular, is deconstructed here through sharing: By this transmission of hybridization the originality is being canalized and intensified.[146] The *teum* [interstitial space] between the sacred and the secular becomes the hybrid openness of endless new beginnings within the context of *salim*. These two processes happen simultaneously yet, they are not opposite but two sides of the same coin. As Whitehead states, "The many become one, and are increased by one,"[147] the macrocosm is scattered into numerous pieces (diffusion) to be shared and the microcosm becomes unified with macrocosm (convergence) and again and again repeated and generated endlessly, together as an organic body of *salim*. This whole process brings the miracle of life, the circulation of creation [*changjo*, 創造, creation] and the re-creation [*gaebyeok*, 開闢], realizing a new heaven and earth.

The life as part-whole does not mean a temporal lifespan or a life form of one living individual but the wholeness of all lives, including non-organic things. Before I was born and even after I die, life that was will continue. The whole continual process of life is *salim*. We all share this life symbiotically as one organic body beyond birth and death. As one organic body, the microcosm of the macrocosm, is evolving, decolonizing, creating, recreating, recycling, expanding, which is the process of life, *salim*. In this process, everything is holy and sacred as a part of life. Therefore, everything is *hanul* because the part is whole, actually, a part-whole. However, one cannot explain the whole but it contains the whole and *vice versa* in the mystery of life. Hae-Weol discovered the mystery and the holiness of life working creatively as Kim Ji-Ha finds the holy power of sharing (communion) when we eat *bab* as a way of living and enlivening, *salim*. If *hanul* is life, everything can be called *hanul* because there is nothing that is nonliving in a certain sense. Most accurately, when life is viewed as the "whole," everything is then connected to every other thing. In this symbiotic web of life, one shares everyone's life through the process of *salim*. Therefore, it is possible to say that I will live more than a million years, when I share life with others as part of the whole.

> How old am I?
> When I count,
>
> Since life has started on the earth, I am 350 million years old,
> Since the universe has formed, I am 1500 million years old,
> If I count from before and after it happened, I am eternal.
>
> Ah~ eternal...
>
> I am endlessly dying;
> but ceaselessly living
>
> There will be no fear

Today
I will love a plant.
I will love myself.

—Kim Ji-Ha, *Saebom*, "A New Spring"

Chapter V

Salim for All:
Toward a Postcolonial Ecofeminist Theology

Su-Un's notion of embracing *hanul* [*si-cheon-ju*] was integrated in Hae-Weol's notion of reverence in a practical way of living toward heaven, human beings, and all things which Hae-Weol referred to as *yang-cheon-ju* [living *hanul*]. Through the process of embracing *hanul* and living *hanul* with three forms of reverence, the whole universe can exist creatively in the process of transformation, which Su-Un called *jo-hwa-jeong* [造化定, creative transformation with peace and harmony]. Such thinking points to the very content of *salim* [enlivening] as *shalom* a quality of life, whether or not there is any ancient etymological linkage, the resonance is startling: *shalom* suggests a quality of life like that toward which Su-Un points as a way of living in a new heaven and a new earth known as *hu-cheon-gae-byeok* [a beginning of a new world]. Su-Un's eschatology is comparable to Catherine Keller's "eco-eschatology" which requires that humans take responsibility (*eco-dharma* in Spivak) to make a new eco-world of becoming (*eco-topia* in McDaniel and *eco-cracy* in Kim Ji-Ha). The last chapter of this book points out the necessity for repentance and responsibility for taking care of this planet, and suggests a new world, an eco-community characterized by the continuing creation of the cosmo-organic body of *hanul* [the divine] which endlessly evolves toward a better life.

Salim as *Shalom*[1]:
Jo-hwa-jeong [造化定: Creative Transformation]

The next step of the process of life in Su-Un after *si-cheon-ju* [embracing *hanul*] is to engage the process of *jo-hwa-jeong* [造化定, creative transformation with peace and harmony]. Actually, *jo-hwa* [造化, wondrous becoming] is the most important process to bring about a new world in the sense of Su-Un. The word, *jo-hwa*, refers to a peaceful state of living in which everything is well-harmonized. When one understands *Donghak*'s deep eco-centered philosophy, one can recognize the importance of *jo-hwa-jeong* [造化定, creative transformation] for our symbiotic life as *hanul* [the one organic body]. Thus, *Jo-hwa-jeong* can, in fact, represent the actualization of *si-cheon-ju* [embracing *hanul*] in the practice of *salim* [enlivening].

The state of *jo-hwa* [wondrous becoming] is similar to the relational and cooperative peace which Jay McDaniel discusses in his book, *Gandhi's Hope*. In this text, McDaniel analyzes the deepest level of peace with an improvisational jazz concert.

> The music at such a concert consists of a creative and evolving harmony of sound produced by different musicians who have the material wherewithal to purchase their instruments and who are cooperatively responding to one another in an ongoing live performance, often in surprising and joyful ways. Peace is like this. It can be unpredictable, filled with creative tensions, and it can have its sad and mournful moments. But it is cooperative and creative, surprising and sometimes joyful, and its competitive dimensions do not degenerate into violence.[2]

In my reading of McDaniel's jazz concert as an analogy of peace, to make beautiful sound, peace, with a creative harmony, much collaboration is needed with values such as responsibility, joy, surprise, endurance, good will, forgiveness, unpredictability, creative tension, sadness, cooperation, creativity, compatibility, and nonviolent competition. According to McDaniel, these activities are found in one word, "listening." Thus, McDaniel beautifully introduces his own *genesis*, "In the beginning is the listening, and this listening is with God and is God."[3] Jay McDaniel considers God an act of hybridity, influenced by all that happens in the world, forever composed of those happenings in the creation of an ongoing as the Deep Listening. For McDaniel, "Deep listening is not an act of *knowing about*. Rather, it is an act of *knowing with*."[4] Indeed, "listening" is a very hybrid process of becoming the Other. Through the process of listening, one transcends him/herself to become the molecule's level to empty (allow) a space for embracing the other immanently within her. Listening is a practice to let others engage their own nature which is opposite to governing others. As McDaniel recognizes listening as a divine quality, 'listening is a prerequisite of peace.'

In order to have peace, we have to follow nature's way, the way as everything is, which Kim Ji-Ha calls "biocracy."[5] Thus, Kim interprets *jo-hwa* as *wuwei* [無爲, nondoing]. The whole meaning of *jo-hwa-jeong* [creative transformation with peace and harmony] is through Kim's suggestion of 'biocracy,' that is, that life participates in harmony for making peace, when we all follow the way of nature rather than having one govern the other. Therefore, Kim's suggestion of nondoing for peace is that of engaging in "doing-nondoing" [爲無爲, *wei wuwei*] as a constructive practice rather than as a form of lazy on looking with folded arms or abandonment. Kim asserts, "We have to practice *wuwei* intentionally, intentionally not interrupting the way of cosmos, intentionally not governing the nature, therefore, we can participate in the way of the cosmic life."[6] I understand Kim's notion of *jo-hwa* [wondrous becoming] as *wuwei* [nondoing] that can be viewed as synonymous with McDaniel's notion of listening. Significantly important, listening requires patience and thoughtful consideration of others which is a constructive practice for becoming together as part-whole.

Just as all instruments have their own unique sounds and qualities, everything has its own uniqueness and value which are irreducible. It is difficult to say that a rock is more valuable than a human being. However, it is also difficult to say that human beings can measure the value of all other things in terms of hierarchy from an anthropocentric point of view. Going back to the concert analogy, I am reminded of a friend who plays cymbals in an orchestra. I was wondering why he plays a less popular instrument, which seemed very minor in my ignorant understanding. I asked him, "Why don't you play a more noticeable instrument like violin or cello? "He responded by asking me, "Why should I play the violin? I am a cymbalist." I said, "You play them only a few times in the concert." He said, "I play the music for the whole time by listening. Even if I make a sound for just one moment, I still play the whole song." As a cymbalist does not play the violin, a bird cannot be a cow. For a bird, flying is its fulfillment, therefore, the value is fulfilled. When we hear the song of a bird, we realize the aesthetic quality of life as *hanul* as both Whitehead and Hae-Weol poetically shared their thrilling impressions from the sound of a bird. As McDaniel observes Whitehead's reading of Emily Dickinson,

> The bird is not simply biological or terrestrial but also cosmological. The bird may be an indwelling lure within the universe as a whole, inwardly animating each creature to seek its unique form of beauty and well-being and yet beckoning the whole of creation toward new forms of order that build upon inherited forms. *The song of the bird may be the song of the universe.*[7]

The deepest level of peace that McDaniel proposes can therefore be likened to the state of *salim*, the hope of hopes in Whitehead to live a better quality of life.

As the quality of life, McDaniel suggests "peace" which is not the absence of violence but the presence of the fullness of life.[8] When we learn about *jo-hwa-jeong* [creative transformation with peace and harmony], we can notice that harmony is the condition of peace and *vice versa* through the listening to others. As Kim's nondoing is actually "doing nondoing" as a constructive practice for *salim*, McDaniel's peace is not simply inner serenity. We have to understand peace in terms of relationship to others in this whole cosmic body as one organic community. According to McDaniel, as a practice, peace does not come automatically but by mutually enhancing relationship of the "give and take." McDaniel describes peace as harmony of life with the earth and other living beings, by making space for the whole of life to flourish, therefore, for the realization of an *ecological well-being*.[9] He also states that peace can be referred to as *shalom* (שָׁלוֹם), utilizing the Hebrew word. The state of *shalom* means living in harmony and security toward the joy and well-being of every creature, not only for human beings but for those other than human beings. One can see McDaniel's symbiotic vision of life in his understanding of *shalom* (שָׁלוֹם): He writes, "*Shalom* is that harmony which would inform a community that has realized this vision. This harmony would be a feature of the communal order itself, and of the subjective lives of the individuals constituting that order. *Shalom* is harmony externally observed and internally felt."[10]

> "Seek the *shalom* of the city where I have sent you,
> for in its *shalom*, you will find your *shalom*." -
> Jeremiah 29:7

Shalom is the Hebrew word meaning peace and well-being, and can be used for greeting persons in situation of both hello and goodbye much like the Korean term, *an-nyeong* (안녕).[11] *Shalom* reflects a perfect state of life, the best life we could hope for on the earth in our history, not in the life of an after-life, somewhere other than this cosmos. Thus, the term, *shalom*, represents the wholeness of life. As for Catherine Keller, "*Shalom* is not for life without death but for a long, full life, lived under the shade of one's own vine and in the fullness of a community healed from the alienation from nature and culture."[12] I understand *shalom* is our urgent need and nonapocalyptic eschatological hope for life which *salim*, as the process of life, always pursues.

Though there is perhaps no way to make a case that *salim* and *shalom* are etymologically connected, it is surely meaningful that the Hebrew term, *shalom* and the Korean term, *salim* are pronounced so similarly, and that both signify peace and the well-being of life. *Salim* has the same root with the Korean term, *saram* [사람, human], in the Korean verb, *salda* [살다, to live]. *Salim* [살림, enlivening] is the gerund of the verb, *salida* [살리다, to save, to enliven]. Then, connecting *salim* to *shalom* is not about etymology but about the similarity of its meaning. More accurately, "*salim* is life as *shalom*," living with peace; *shalom* is peace and represents the well-being of life. In this regard, one can speak of *salim* [enlivening] for *shalom* [the fulfillment of life] or *salim* as *shalom*. Then how do we attain *salim* as *shalom*?

Jay McDaniel identifies peace with Whiteheadian "beauty" which contains the two qualities of harmony and intensity. For him, "Harmony is what we feel when we are at one with other things; intensity is what we feel when we are filled with creativity and zest. From a Whiteheadian perspective, a more adventurous peace will be both harmonious and intense, neither to the exclusion of the other."[13] For the Whiteheadian beauty of creation, the harmony and intensity can be recognized as a cosmological hybridity. In this sense, hybridity can refer to the process of experiencing itself, as expressed in all living beings, humans and those other than humans: amoeba, penguins, and people. This can be the Whiteheadian term, "concrescence." It is the activity by which all the living beings prehend many influences and gather them into the unity of a single moment in their ongoing life. Their activities are themselves in terms of *salim*, life as living and enlivening. In this symbiotic living together, we may say that they are hybridizing, all the while seeking whatever harmony and intensity are possible for them in the situation at hand, penetrating each other's interstitial spaces. The very impulse to live with satisfaction relative to the situation at hand, which lies at the very heart of life, is an ongoing process of hybridizing for a better living in future.

In his essay, "How Newness Enters the World" in *The Location of Culture*, Homi K. Bhabha states, "Hybridity is neither One nor the Other but something else, *in-between*, finding its agency in a form of the *future* where the past is not originary, where the present is not simply transitory."[14] Bhabha points out the temporality of the present and marks the openness of the future which can be reiterated in the process term, *becoming*: "The present of the world appears through the breakdown of temporality, signifies a historical intermediacy; the future becomes once again an open question, instead of being specifies by the fixity of the past. The interactive time of *the future is a becoming once again open*."[15]

For Bhabha, thus, hybridity is a form of future which is becoming. *Salim* as an ongoing process of hybridizing deals with situations at hand (to live) and hopes to understand *salim* as *shalom* (to live better in quality) for becoming (the future which is radically open). As Whitehead characterized life as having three qualities, to live, to live well, and to live better, *salim* in its broad aspect contains all these three. Nonetheless, what *salim* aims and hopes for is to live better, to have a quality life, and an abundant life, which is a fully connected set of beauty, harmony, and goodness that actually signify peace, therefore, *shalom*.

For Whitehead, peace reflects the "harmony of harmonies" which shall bind together the other four qualities of truth, beauty, adventure, and art.[16] In this aspect, peace is a relative value with all other qualities and shall basically contain them. Thus, I understand Whiteheadian notion of peace as a better quality of life, *salim* as *shalom*.

> No element in fact is ineffectual: thus the struggle
> with evil is a process of building up a mode of
> utilization by the provision of intermediate elements
> introducing *a complex structure of harmony*.[17]

However, this peace is not achieved automatically but is achieved by yearning and endeavoring to accomplish it in a non-peaceful situation. Where there is a lack of peace where disturbances such as *jugim* [distortion, disguise, murder, violence, fight, war, etc.] exists, we yearn for peace. In this sense, Whitehead said that, "Peace is not anesthesia. Peace is most clearly understood by considering it in its relation to the tragic issues which are essential to the nature of things. Peace is the understanding of tragedy and, at the same time, its preservation."[18] Thus, Whiteheadian peace is paradoxical as a reaction or an outcome of violence: "The meaning of peace is most clearly understood by considering it in its relation to the tragic issues which are essential in the nature of things. Therefore, Peace is the understanding of tragedy, and at the same time its preservation."[19] By the same token, the power of *salim* springs out from situations of *jugim* [violence] because life pursues living, living well, and living better. The *salim* [enlivening] tendency of life against *jugim*, a value I would like to call, bio-power, following Foucault, and which Whitehead referred to as peace: "This survival power in motive force, by reason of appeal to reserves of Beauty, marks the difference between the tragic evil and the gross evil. The inner feeling belonging to this grasp of the service of tragedy is Peace -- the purification of the emotions."[20]

Just as hope occurs in hopeless situations according to the Pauline notion of hope,[21] for Whitehead, suffering becomes already a sign of peace as he mentions: "Suffering attains its end in a harmony of harmonies."[22] I would like to relate the Whiteheadian notion of peace as the harmony of harmonies in suffering to Su-Un's notion of *jo-hwa-jeong* [造化定, creative transformation with peace and harmony]. Creating peace in the midst of suffering is the process of life, a process which is here interpreted as the meaning of *salim*.

Whitehead's discovery of peace out of suffering can be understood as *salim* for *shalom* through *jo-hwa-jeong*. If something is too high, it is lowered and *vice versa*. If there is violence and *jugim*, we yearn for peace and *salim*. As creative transformation, *salim* is generated in the process of creating peace. Therefore, as much as life is so difficult, hope for peace becomes greater. As Whitehead affirms that peace is not "anesthesia,"[23] peace does not mean a static immobility with no change which is stagnation or dullness, rather than peace.

Likewise, our ecological crisis nowadays is a vivid and serious problem of *jugim* [killing, disturbance of peace]. Confronting the ecological crisis, all the spontaneous movements and intentional endeavors to restore life are directed toward peace with the harmony of harmonies. Therefore, the whole process of creating peace is *salim*. In so doing, *salim* is directed toward the healing of suffering and a declaration of peace against the disturbance of peace, *jugim*. Mending the wounds of the earth is engaging in *salim*, wishing *shalom* to all, that is, peace to all.

Dialectically, *salim* as a survival for the process of life springs from the situation of *jugim* [evil, distortion of life] as antithesis. As *shalom salim* suggests a better quality of life with beauty and harmony. It is a synthetic aspect of living which we hope will be realized not only for human beings but also for all creation. In this sense, *jo-hwa-jeong* [creative transformation with peace] is *salim,* a process which aims for better living, the beauty of life with peace.

As one of the qualities for peace, beauty for McDaniel who is following Whitehead reflects *wuwei* [無爲, non-doing] as we learned from Kim's notion of non-doing[24] in Ch II: "Birds walk in beauty when they fly; fish walk in beauty when they swim; cats walk in beauty when they purr."[25] McDaniel suggests that human beings walk in beauty when we love which is our vocation and responsibility for the communities.[26] Therefore, peace in beauty as McDaniel understands it is viewed as our responsibility in which practice "doing non-doing" [爲無爲, *wei wuwei*] rather than staying in a static immobility.

Doing non-doing [爲無爲, *wei wuwei*] is the principle of *salim* for *ecotopia* (an ecologically livable world). According to the doing non-doing principle, not only do we not harm our bio-community but we also actively keep the beauty of nature from being destroyed by the *jugim* culture. Nowadays Korean ecological activists [*salim-kun*] resist the Grand Canal Project mandated by the Lee Myung-Bak government that will involve disrupting four rivers that flow throughout South Korea. Regarding this project, there is a discrepancy between two sides. From the perspective of the government, this project is publicized by the government as a *salim* project for four rivers; on the other hand, from the Korean ecological activists, it is known as a *jugim* [killing] project that will destroy the eco-system of four rivers.[27] This project got underway in 2008 by the Lee Myung-Bak government, as so-called "The Korean Green New Deal Project." Han Seung-Su, the prime minister in Korea at the time (2008), stated, "This project will enliven our economy, culture, and environment."[28] Nonetheless, the beautiful curves of the rivers have been straightened and the bottoms of the rivers have been dug by forklifts and cranes, which have brought a tremendous amount of ecological damage. In the name of economic progress, this project destroys the beauty of nature and threatens the circle of life. In order to carve out the waterway, already numerous trees have been cut.[29] I would call the Grand Canal Project of four rivers 'a *jugim* project' that destroys the beauty of life. "In process theology beauty is understood to be the very aim of the universe and the aim of God. To wantonly destroy beauty in the name of progress is itself a for of SIN,"[30] Jay B. McDaniel writes. It is a denial of human responsibility, in Spivak's term, a refusal to be "planetary subjects." It is, by no means, *jugim*, therefore, SIN.

The Grand Canal Project in Korea focuses on the economic development rather than on the ecological aims that Lee Myung-Bak promised in his presidential manifesto, "This will revive our economy."[31] It is a negative catachresis of the term *salim* for *jugim* because what the government does for the rivers actually *jugim* in the name of *salim*. People live by *Nak-Dong* River can no longer drink the water and eat the apples, which were the natural resources of their living. It reminds Gayatri Spivak's warning about ecological loss for economic growth.

> What we have to notice here is that the developing national states are not only linked by the common thread of profound ecological loss, the loss of forests and rivers as foundations of life, but also plagued by the complicity, however apparently remote, of the power lines of local developers with the forces of global capital.[32]

The Grand Canal Project (so-called the *salim* project of four rivers) can be an example of "old-style imperialism" according to Spivak, which does not regard the possible ecological loss but only focuses on economic development. Against such structure, Spivak encourages "non-Eurocentric ecological justice." She explains that the old-style imperialism takes the European Economic Community as a model.[33] Even though the Grand Canal Project undertaken by the Korean government with little regard for nonhuman nature, it still can be viewed as a postcolonial issue. In this case, the state exercises its power to domain the nonhuman nature which has been greatly devastated. Eventually, humans have been affected as well. Under the state power (governmental power), nature (including humans) has been *groaning together in the pains of childbirth until now* (Romans 8:22). This ecological domination is being exercised in the interest of full participation in a global economy defined by western neoimperial agendas. This can be an example of human's colonization over nonhuman nature.

In the scope of postcolonial studies, decolonization is not limited to the condition of colonialism. The postcolonial theologian Stephen Moore argues, "Imperialism denotes the multifarious, mutually constitutive ideologies that impel a metropolitan center to annex more-or-less distant territories, and the determine its subsequent dealing with them."[34] In the one organic web of life, the complex unity of economy and ecology has created a mode of *jugim* toward ecology when the state misuses its power in the name of *salim* for the economy, though it will eventually be evaluated as destructive for all. Ecological crisis cannot be separated from economic development as Edward W. Said states, "We live in one global environment with a huge number of ecological, economic, social, and political pressures tearing at its only dimly perceived, basically uninterpreted and incomprehended fabric."[35] Decolonization of nonhuman nature can also be considered the redemption [*salim*] for humans as part of the incomprehensible fabric reflecting the complexity of life as (part-) whole. Our planetary life is an organic body of which human beings are a part. The earth is one organic body of life as part-whole that cannot survive without the other. The planet is then understood as one vast ecosystem, or bio-system, affiliated through this amazing *Gaia* connection. In this symbiotic web-like system (body), everyone's life is involved with that of others, each affects another. Everything is interfused into every other thing. We are being hybridized by the presence of one another. This natural world is basically "Life," the full movements of "becoming together."

When we see all things in harmony in terms of *shalom*, life with peace in harmony is not a lonely life but a symbiotic life, living together as one organic body in terms of independence and interconnectedness, as the literal meaning of *hanul*: one magnificent [*han*] body [*ul*, we as one body who are bound together]. Thus, the meaning of *hanul* literally indicates one macrocosmic organic body that embraces all the bodies together as a bio-community (or eco-community). *Hanul* is the place where the sacred is found in life. Jay McDaniel's *ecotopia* can be said in other word *hanul*. According to McDaniel, this homelike community is called *ecotopia*, "global village" which is not arranged for human life alone but is a community of biotic communities.[36] In fact, in this symbiotic life of the web in the ecosystem, everything we do to others, including to animals and plants on the earth or earth, itself, is what we do to ourselves. Therefore, to establish the *ecotopia* in this global village as McDaniel suggests, we have to apply the golden rule, "Do to others as you would have them do to you" (Luke 6:31, *NIV*), that is, to everything on the earth not only to other human beings. Traditionally, the Christian golden rule has been accepted as a rule for the way in which we engage human relationships. Beyond the anthropocentric golden rule, we need to set up an ecocentric golden rule which can be understood as a negative golden rule, based upon the principle of (*wei*) *wuwei* [爲無爲, doing non-doing]: "Do not hurt others as you do not want to be harmed."

Nonetheless, I understand *ecotopia* not as an ideal static world but as this world which is becoming better in process. Thus *ecotopia* is an unfinished divine symphony unceasingly played by 'the infinite creativity of life' [*salim*], "*Salim Symphony.*" Similarly, *ecotopia* is likened to jazz according to McDaniel in his writings in *Jesus, Jazz, and Buddhism*:

> It is the image of people coming together, listening to one another, respecting one another's talents, and trying to creating something beautiful together. They are free to express themselves as individuals, having been given the opportunity to develop their unique creative potentials. And yet they also have the humility to let others solo without having to be the center of attention. They are accountable for themselves and to one another, yet they are also forgiving, making the best of their own and other's mistakes. Most importantly they have faith. As they play together they trust in the availability of fresh possibilities.[37]

McDaniel's notion of jazz is the idea of sustainability. It would be a good idea if people lived this jazz-like way. Jazz is a beautiful metaphor to describe harmony among people and planet. And certainly it would help if they tried to make music with other animals and the earth honoring the unique voices of the more-than-human world.

Ecotopia literally reflects an ecological *eutopia*. *Eutopia* is derived from the Greek εὖ, "good" or "well," and τόπος, "place," meaning a place of perfection rather than nonexistence. When *eutopia* meets *eco*, it overcomes anthropocentric idealism and become a cosmocentric process. If we shift our anthropocentric paradigm to an ecocentric one, an *ecotopia* can be practiced and constructed one step further. We should view our planet as an *ecotopia*, and thus practice our vocation and responsibility as McDaniel suggests above, toward nonhuman forms of nature through doing non-doing (not a static immobility but an active mobility). It is for this reason that I have identified *ecotopia* as our *eco-dharma* which should be actively engaged through our living in a new heaven and a new earth everyday, again and again, ...

How then can we best construct our *ecotopia*, our new heaven and new earth, through living? I would like to suggest the way of *salim*. Kim Ji-Ha understands the principle of creation as becoming by practicing doing non-doing. "Everything lives a way of life, transforming, managing, deciding, and creating spontaneously which means that non-governing is the best practice of politics."[38] It is important to distinguish between "doing non-doing" from having a passive attitude of doing nothing. I think that both Kim's notion of "doing non-doing" and McDaniel's notion of peace [*shalom*] as our vocation for *ecotopia* call for our active and positive practice to protect the symbiotic life of our home planet not only as a way of preserving or conserving but also as a way of becoming "better" in a process sense.

I discovered a process worldview in Su-Un's notion of *jo-hwa-jeong* [造化定, creative transformation with peace], which is not just peace in harmony but the principle of creation. The Chinese character '造' (*jo*) means 'creating' and '化' (*hwa*) means becoming. The comparative theologian and *Donghak* scholar Lee Hyo-Dong translates *jo-hwa* as "wondrous becoming." I would say that *jo-hwa* means "becoming creation" or "creation in process." Through creating [造, *jo*] and becoming [化, *hwa*], things find peace with a right balance and harmony [定, *jeong*]. The intentional effort to keep everything natural and livable from the power of *jugim* [killing] could be described as "*jo*" [造, *creating or making*]. The spontaneous changes of nature through nature could be "*hwa*" [化, becoming]. These two Chinese characters, *jo* [造] *and hwa* [化], actually explain two important principles of *salim*, intentionality and spontaneity. All the spontaneous as well as intentional movements undertaken through the spirit of *jo-hwa-jeong* [creative becoming of peace and harmony] toward the evolution of our quality of life are, therefore, *salim*.

    Jo-hwa-jeong [造化定, creative transformation] through *mu-wi-i-hwa* [無爲而化, becoming through non-doing] is, therefore, the process of Life, which I would like to call *salim*. *Jo-hwa-jeong* is the sanctification of everything as an individual and the whole to satisfy the cosmic way of life, both spontaneously and intentionally. I would like to connect McDaniel's *ecotopia* with Kim's *ecocracy*, living principle for all which can also be described as *salim*. "*Salim* as *shalom*" (for all) is the living principle of *ecotopia* that is *ecocracy*. *Salim* is more fundamental than any *ism* we can imagine: religionism or atheism or modernism or postmodernism or humanism. Life can never be contained in our ideologies, and yet it is always concrete, as enfleshed in the lives of living beings, cats, dogs, butterflies, flowers, and trees like us. Together, we can creatively realize the optimum point as the part-whole which is the cosmic-self-realization. The meaning of *salim* is not just life, but it suggests a quality of living, the enhanced life, becoming better, restoring, healing and mending, decolonizing, and bringing about reconciliation, sanctification, and therefore, salvation for a new creation, a continuing genesis, that is, an *ecotopia*, Su-Un's *hucheongaebyeok* [後天開闢, opening a New Heaven and a New Earth]. Su-Un's thinking of '(new/re) *beginning of heaven and earth*' on the advent of a new world was a religious alternative to overcome the colonial difficulties, particularly associated with the infiltration of the western powers, which the *Joseon* (*Yi* Dynasty) society faced in the 19th century. *Hucheon* [後天] means new heaven and *gaebyeok* [開闢] an opening of a new beginning which implies the deconstruction of the old one and the proclamation of 'a new genesis.'

Salim Eschatology: *Hu-cheon-gae-byeok* [後天開闢, a New Creation]

"Then I saw a new heaven and a new earth. The former heaven and the former earth had passed away, and the sea was no more." (*Revelation* 21:1)

We must be still and still moving
Into another intensity
For a further union, a deeper communion,
Through the dark cold and the empty desolation,
The wave cry, the wind cry, the vast waters,
Of the petrel and the porpoise.
In my end is my beginning.
—T.S. Eliot, *East Coker*, 1959[39]

Su-Un's *hu-cheon-gae-byeok* [後天開闢, opening a new heaven and a new earth] and McDaniel's *ecotopia* are resonant to point out a new world here on earth in which our ecoethical responsibility reflects our process of life. The world Su-Un pursued through *si-cheon-ju* [embracing *hanul*] and *jo-hwa-jeong* [creative transformation with peace and harmony] is the process of *hu-cheon-gae-byeok* [opening a new heaven and a new earth]. Su-Un distinguished a new heaven and a new earth from the first heaven and the first earth. He referred to the first heaven and the first earth, *seon-cheon* [先天], such that the new heaven and new earth will become *hu-cheon* [後天]. *Gae-byeok* [開闢], referring to transformation, literally indicates a huge opening of the earth. Thus, *hu-cheon-gae-byeok* [後天開闢] implies transformation from the first heaven and earth to a new heaven and a new earth.

However, Su-Un's new world was not a strange world which is separated from the current world. Rather, he emphasized a huge metamorphosis of the old world into a new world. Therefore, he was not talking about the end of the world. In his time, Su-Un's new world was neither apocalyptic (the end of the world, a life after life) nor nostalgic (returning to the old age) but a practical transformation of the world, a desirable change for living better. He considered his new world as a proper result and a right change through practice doing non-doing. He saw an end of a historical period at that time. The Confucian culture, as the leading philosophy and moral system in the *Joseon* (*Yi* Dynasty, 1394-1910) had become corrupted and institutionalized, manipulating the *minjung* under the strict aristocracy. The system of *Oryun* [五倫] that classifies the five basic relationships of Confucianism between king and servant, husband and wife, teacher and student, parents and children, and friend and friend for harmony of the community. However, the Confucian virtues had become an oppressive tool for the higher class to control the lower class and served as a justification of the system of hierarchy. Furthermore, Buddhism had barely influenced people since the *Joseon* Dynasty harshly persecuted Buddhism as result of the severe corruption of Buddhism, the most powerful religious institution in the *Goryeo* Kingdom (918-1392). In Su-Un's time (1824-1864), the life style of the *minjung* had impoverished by both the oppressive aristocracy and the colonial Japan and the imperial west. Su-Un did not distinguish Christianity from the west. Su-Un recognized Christianity as the philosophical foundation of the western imperial power.[40] Thus, Buddhism and Confucianism, together with Christianity could not really give hope for *minjung*, including Su-Un who deplored the corrupt conditions of the religions of the past, stating, "the fate of Confucianism and Buddhism for the thousands of years is up now."[41] For Su-Un, social transformation was an urgent need for the Korean *minjung* in order to survive the oppression of the corrupted Confucian aristocracy and the imperial threats from the west and Japan. The Korean *minjung* were internally and externally suffering. Therefore, Su-Un proclaimed the need for *gae-byeok* [開闢, transformation] at the time as a solution or a hope for the Korean *minjung* to point out a practical new heaven and a new earth.

In Chapter III, I defined the *Donghak* movement as a decolonizing movement. *Donghak* is a postcolonial hybrid of Asian philosophies and religions through the perspective of the colonized against the Japanese colonization and western imperialism. *Donghak* as a hybrid of the process of mimicry, problemitized both the internal corruption and the external colonization in Korea, resisted against both authorities.   Since the western imperial powers had enforced Korea to open its doors for westernization or modernization, there were voices for social reformation [改革, *gae-hyeok*]. One of the famous reformations by the *Joseon* government was *Gab-o-gae-hyeok* [甲午改革] that occurred in 1894 and which is characterized as a modern reformation of Korea.[42] Through this reformation, the *Joseon* aristocracy was deconstructed and the government cabinet was reformed according to the western style, distinct from the Confucian system of social order.[43] However, it was not a reformation by the Korean people themselves but rather by the *Joseon* government which was controlled by the Japanese imperial power that chose to taste western modernization. The *Gab-o-gae-hyeok* finally became a seed to bring about the Japanese invasion (1910-1945).

Su-Un's notion of *gae-byeok* [transformation or beginning] can be interpreted as a postcolonial strategic *catachresis* that reiterates the term *gae-hyeok* [改革, reformation] in the colonial situation. Literally, *Gae-hyeok* means reformation. Yet, the goal or the aftermath of *gae-hyeok* was *gae-hwa* [開化, modernization] at that time which was enforced by the trifold 'colonial power lines,' the *Joseon* government, Japanese colonialism, and western imperialism. In the midst of this flow of modernization, Korean people had to accept the so-called reformation, whether they wanted to or not.

The term, catachresis, has been adapted by Gayatri Spivak as a postcolonial strategy. Catachresis [κατάχρησις] is originally a Greek rhetorical figure denoting misuse or misapplication of words. In *Post-Colonial Studies*, Bill Ashcroft states that catachresis is the process by which the colonized take and reinscribe something that exists traditionally as a feature of imperial culture.[44] As employed by Spivak, the term catachresis, denotes the process by which the colonized strategically appropriate and redeploy specific elements of colonial ideology.[45] Spivak asserts that the colonized have the ability to catachretize the colonial words much like that which occurs in a parliamentary democracy. That is, in her thinking, catachresis is the insertion and the reinscription of something which does not refer literally to the correct narrative of the emergence of parliamentary democracy.[46] In this sense, catachresis can be understood as a practice of resistance against the colonizer through an act of usurpation. A postcolonial theologian, Stephen Moore, defines catachresis as "a practice of resistance through an act of creative appropriation, a retooling of the rhetorical or institutional instruments of imperial oppression that turns those instruments back against their official owners."[47] As Moore employed the term catachresis to mean "an act of counter-appropriation,"[48] Su-Un declared *gae-byeok* [transformation, beginning] against the colonial *gae-hyeok* [reformation, modernization] and appropriated the term, *gae-byeok*, to proclaim a new beginning of Korea over the original *gae-byeok* [the beginning of the world] and can referred to as a practice of strategic misrepresentation. Using the same term, *gae-byeok*, Su-Un made a clear distinction between the first creation and a new creation by speaking of transformation and *dasi-gae-byeok* [transformation again, a new beginning] in his *Ansimga*, referring his mystic experience of meeting *hanul*.

> *Hanul* said, "Since the first heaven has opened for fifty thousand years, I had no work until I met you. You are the first one enlightened, so we both made this success. Thus, the bad fortune of twelve empires will see a new beginning [*dasi-gae-byeok*]."[49] (translation mine)

Literally, *gae-byeok* means the beginning of the world like *genesis* (γένεσις) in Greek. For Su-Un, *gae-byeok* happened fifty thousand years ago at the beginning of the world. Nevertheless, Su-Un added the word, "*dasi*" [again and again, ...], to *gae-byeok*, as *dasi-gae-byeok* [transformation again], reflecting his understanding of a new genesis. The Korean word, *dasi* (다시), is an adverb, and means "again" not one more time but endless tries, "again and again,

....." The Korean term, *dasi-gae-byeok*, does not reflect a complete creation once and for all. Rather, it suggests on-going creation and the transformation of this world.

Transformation [*gae- byeok*] for Su-Un was a practical revolution of the current society in his time. As discussed in previous chapters, *hanul* [the divine] is an organic body which includes everything in the cosmos as being integral to the cosmic body. Transformation is the endless becoming of *hanul*. Therefore, the evolution of *hanul* in which the subject of transformation refers to actually each individual who invites *hanul* as *hanul*, as we read from his *Ansimga*, *hanul* cannot make any change nor can it control the world without being embodied in a subject individual who can bring forth movements of life: for example, "until I met you, I had no work." Consequently, *hanul* can be *hanul* when it is embraced by *hanul*, and works as *hanul* through *hanul*. Thus, *hanul* as a subject of transformation does not have to refer only to humankind but includes all forms of life as parts of the cosmo-organic body not statically but with some fluidly, since life does not reside only in one particular form.

I understand Su-Un's notion of *gae-byeok* as the cosmic evolution of life. As the whole cosmo-organic body, *hanul* is continually evolving. Thus, transformation reflects the evolution of *hanul* which includes the organic evolution and quality of the evolution of life, *salim*. In this sense, *hanul* is not the creator who alone created the heaven and the earth but is both a creator and the created, together with all the expressions of *hanul*. That is, *hanul* is the self-transforming creativity and everything in the world is the expression of that creativity. Su-Un's new creation implies the continuing creation of the cosmo-organic body which endlessly evolves toward a better life.

> Everyday "little by little [*cha-cha-cha-cha*],"[50]
> practice what we study.
> Spread the virtues before the endless harmony.
> First, set a new law and write the way of life.
> People who enter in the new way will become sages.

> Here you are, *hanul* in this world through doing non-doing.
> – *Gyohoonga*, 教訓歌, "A Song for Teaching"[51]
>
> (translation mine)

As we see in his *Song for Teaching*, Su-Un wanted a practical transformation of life in his time. Thus, a new creation will and should come by people's effort and change. As McDaniel mentioned, *ecotopia* is our vocation and responsibility.[52] Human beings, as a part of the cosmic body are *hanul*, and, therefore, are interconnected. In this sense, if this change happens to one individual, then it will bring a change to the whole cosmic body. Su-Un, through this *Song for Encouraging Study*, made it clear that a new creation is in this world through the transformation of life. Thus, he suggested a new paradigm of life.

The new creation that Su-Un suggested is not the end of the world in an apocalyptic sense but refers to a gradual change "little by little [*cha-cha-cha-cha*]," therefore, becoming a new creation. That change is a very real and tangible one which should be a *kōan* [公案, a question in history] and an encounter with the question. Su-Un confronted his own historical *kōan* in his time and struggled for it. A new heaven and a new earth for Su-Un represented the endless process of becoming which meant faith, hope, and zeal for life, living in a spirit of *salim* in the place in which he was living. In his poem, *Yongdamga* [龍潭歌, *A Song for Dragon Pond*], Su-Un described a new world, praising the beauty of nature in Korea:

> *Joseon* [朝鮮][53] is the name of our country.
> Oh! Beautiful rivers,
> Wonderful mountains!
> Behold!
> People of the whole world,
> come and see such a sacred place.
> This place longs through the ages.
> Discover the everlasting way of life
> through this beautiful place.

> This place longs for fifty thousand years.
> Even if I become a heavenly man,
> I would live here at the beautiful *Yongdam*.[54]
> (translation mine)

Through reading his poem, one can see his love for nature in the place he lived, his country, *Joseon* (Korea) and his hometown, *Yongdam*. Shin Il-Cheol, a *Donghak* scholar, sees that "Su-Un's eschatology is eco-oriented and this world focused is nothing about a new world in a strange place but a good change of his own place in his time."[55] Thus, Su-Un looked for a new world in the midst of his old world by transforming the way of living of his people. This commitment was based upon his process worldview as creative evolution that does not replace this world with the other world but mends and cultivates the new world for becoming a better world in its quality of life, *cha-cha-cha-cha* [little by little]. Consequently, Su-Un's new world can be understood as represented by the process of transformation (becoming). In his notion of a new heaven and a new earth, creation becomes a new creation (or re-creation) and the old world becomes a new world *with* and *for* all, together, as one cosmic organic body, evolving together (convolution) and working together (synergy).[56] This very process of evolving and working together can be referred to, therefore, as *gae-byeok* [開闢, transformation of the world] in the process of life, *salim*.

Su-Un's ecocentric process eschatology can be fruitfully compared to Catherine Keller's *eco-eschatology*. Both Su-Un and Keller focus on the issues faced in their temporal and spatial situatedness, their *sitz-im-leben*. Keller recognizes earth as our home. Therefore, she states that suggesting other places as our home and talking about the end of the world is actually "the ultimate case of homelessness."[57]

> With the apocalyptic emphasis upon the new heaven and earth, this new creation comes about by the supernatural intervention of the omnipotent God. Is

> not the new earth, with its new Jerusalem, so incomparably more perfect than the first creation as to make this one out to be a crummy little earth ball?[58]

Keller suggests a new heaven and a new earth here on earth in our time making a link between ecology and eschatology, in her newly developed eco-eschatology. In her writing, Keller is not talking about apocalyptic eschatology but eco-eschatology. As Su-Un had concern on the issues of everyday living in his time, Keller's concern is on life, itself, not on a life after life. "As theological practitioners, our mission is not to a life after life but to life itself."[59]

Su-Un yearned to reconstruct a new society amidst the corrupted living conditions which could not give any hope to people's lives, neither from Confucianism nor from Buddhism. Su-Un did not run away from the problems which the society actually faced yet, he confronted them by educating and challenging people, helping them to recognize themselves and others as *hanul*. I discovered that the urgency of Jesus' mission and that of Su-Un's mission bore some resemblance to that of Keller's theology.

As Su-Un pointed out, *hu-cheon-gae-byeok* [後天開闢, a new heaven and a new earth], Jesus' mission was that of the *basileia tou theou* [kingdom of G*d] that had been a long-term expectation of a new Jerusalem for the Israelites. However, according to Keller, Jesus was incapable of accomplishing his mission to bring the kingdom of G*d to satisfy the people's ancient yearning of the new Jerusalem. It is very important to see the fact that Jesus obviously failed his mission to build a new Jerusalem as the notion of kingdom of G*d from a process theological perspective. In my process view, the mission cannot be completed in any way because there should not be the apocalyptic end of the world. Actually, on this point, not only Jesus but also even the Christian creator G*d is unable to really complete the mission because, as long as life continues, everything is continually creating and recreating as *creation continua*[60] through which the process G*d is still creating the world *with* and *through* her creation that never has been completed.

In this sense, it is necessary to reinterpret a new heaven and a new earth from a process eschatological view of the end of the world. That is what Keller calls 'the recycling of eschatology.' According to her practice of recycling theology, she declares that the "New Jerusalem can be placed in the context of prophetic hope for a radical renewal of *THIS* creation."[61]

In her view, "The task of theologians at the end of millennium is to take responsibility for defusing the self-fulfilling prophecy of worldly doom. Thus the recycling of eschatology becomes precisely a means of the *metanoia* [μετάνοια, repentance] of theology itself: of its return to the earth."[62]

> And saying, the time is fulfilled, and the kingdom of God is at hand: *repent ye*, and believe the gospel: καὶ λέγων ὅτι πεπλήρωται ὁ καιρὸς καὶ ἤγγικεν ἡ βασιλεία τοῦ θεοῦ· μετανοεῖτε καὶ πιστεύετε ἐν τῷ εὐαγγελίῳ. (Mark 1:15)

It is interesting that Keller interprets the Markan *metanoia* as the recycling of eschatology and replaces a supernaturalist conception of the new Jerusalem with that of a radical transformation of this world. Keller's recycling of the term eschatology confronting the apocalypse could be an example of strategic catachresis as well. The announcement of the *basileia* comprises the core of Jesus' message and mission. The Markan description of 'kingdom [βασιλεία]' requires people's transformation at the time through *metanoia*. Stephen Moore points out that Mark's deployment of the term, *basileia*, may also be deemed a stunning example of what the postcolonial theorist, Gayatri Spivak, has dubbed as catachresis. Moore interprets *basileia* (βασιλεία) in *Mark* as "empire" rather than "kingdom," especially referring to the Roman Empire.[63] Proclaiming the kingdom of G*d by using the same word as that of empire, Mark urged people to repent to bring about a new world while, at the same time to resist against the Roman Empire. Stephen Moore interprets Mark's practice of catachresis, as it pertains to *basileia*, can therefore be said to border on the periodic. Mark writes, "The time is fulfilled, and the Empire of God has come near (Mark 1:15)." Moore comments as follows: "Mark's ragtag peasant protagonist proclaims, marching through the remote rural reaches of southern Galilee, and drawing assorted other peasant nonentities in his wake, fellow builders-to-be of this latest and greatest of empires."[64] The Markan catachresis of the term, *basileia* (βασιλεία), was used similarly in *the Book of Revelation*: "The empire of the world [*he basileia tou kosmou*] has become the kingdom of our Christ (11:15)." On this behalf, Stephen Moore asserts that *the Book of Revelation* would appear to be "an anti-imperial text" which announces the transformation of the world *imperium* from the Roman Emperor to Christ.[65] As Spivak's notion of postcolonial catachresis, reclaiming of the term *basileia* (βασιλεία) for G*d in *the Book of Revelation* could be a challenge to Rome's claims to kingship.

Keller makes one step further toward an ecotheological hermeneutics on *the Book of Revelation* 11. "Now is the time… for destroying the destroyers of the earth (11:18)." She points out that this warning is sounded explicitly as "the nations rage (11:18)" for while they war the planet could be seen already to be dying.[66] The planet's destruction is not the will of G*d. From her ecological perspective, she suggests one to read this passage as G*d's love toward the first creation which G*d will take care of our ecological crisis for which human beings are responsible. This warning is, therefore, G*d's promise that "the earth (the first creation) will be saved."[67] Likewise, for Su-Un, *seon-cheon* [先天, the first heaven] and *hu-cheon* [後天, a new heaven] are not opposite concepts. Yet, the former results in the latter as a right consequence in the process of life just as the postmodern follows the modern.

The Greek word, *meta*, means after and beyond. Therefore, *metanoia* requires something beyond regret that means change, and therefore, transformation. What Su-Un hoped for was not a totally different world that is not of this earth but a continual transformation of the first heaven into a new heaven and a new earth in *THIS* world in his very time. I would assert that the principle of *metanoia* as it relates to "deconstruction" is the same notion as that of decolonization. Without transformation, that is not real *metanoia*. Deconstruction is not a creation out of nothingness but a transformation of things that already exist by deconstructing the old structure and constructing and altering a new paradigm, therefore, transformation. Therefore, *metanoia* is a radical process of becoming. Roland Faber declares that *metanoia* is in fact revolutionary: "Everything that can be said besides becoming can be said only with becoming or in the process of becoming."[68]

Su-Un's notion of *hu-cheon-gae-byeok* [後天開闢, a new heaven and a new earth] could count as a 'historical eschatology' which responded to the divine call in his era. As Rosemary Radford Ruether mentions in her book, *Sexism and Godtalk*, "historical eschatology takes seriously the realities of our present temporal existence and holds up a just and livable society as normative in this age, rather than subjecting ourselves to the tyranny of impossible expectations of final perfection."[69] For Su-Un, the term *gae-byeok* [the beginning of the world] was used as the time of creation of a new nation. Its overtones suggest the dawn of a new era of history. Su-Un appears to be writing the history of Korea from a new perspective to save it from its present state of corruption, decline, and vulnerability in the face of the foreign imperial powers.

What could be a historical eschatology in our time? As Keller suggests, it is *eco-eschatology* which also fits into Su-Un's hope to transform the old heaven into a new, better, and livable world of becoming, according to his life-centered philosophy. It is not about the final perfection. Actually, there cannot be perfection in the sense of completion, stasis, or flawlessness. By nature, everything comes to an end, generating a continuous beginning which we call change. Su-Un pursued a meaningful transformation for life which comes and should be realized everyday, not only on one particular day (or someday) in a strange place, "little by little [*cha-cha-cha-cha*]."

Thus, I believe I am justified in referring to Su-Un's historical eschatology as a process eschatology. Following my study of the process ecotheological rendition of *salim*, I found a sweet correspondence between three words: Jay McDaniel's *eco-topia*, Kim Ji-Ha's *eco-cracy*, and Catherine Keller's *eco-eschatology*, since they all point to an ecocentric new world here on the earth in a process sense of becoming together. The process eschatological perspective teaches that the new does not displace the past, nor does it take place in mere discontinuity with it. Rather, it creatively transforms. It is not one of total annihilation of the world but rather a continual transformation of this world in the process of life, *salim*. Therefore, in the process eschatological perspective which both Su-Un and Keller pursue, a new heaven and a new earth mean a continual transformation of *THIS* creation. Thus, mending the creation is our urgent task rather than moving on to another "mansion" by "abandoning our home."[70] In such a process we are rebuilding (reconstruction through deconstruction) our home [*oikos*]. And that is our "homework," according to Keller. "The question is whether Christian hope in collaboration with other, earth-friendly traditions can also energize the needed homework."[71] The homework is humans' responsibility to the earth community. Keller's homework could be understood as my Spivakian notion of *eco-dharma* in a postcolonial sense in which we should decolonize humans and nonhumans or more than humans from the colonization of nature, from all the *jugim* [killing] activities. In this sense, *salim* is the principle of decolonization. *Salim* is indeed our *eco-dharma*.

The power to renew our home is within us in life as *hanul* [the sacred]. That is the power of *salim* as well as *salim* is the process of life. *Hanul* is the macrocosmic organic body of the universe and the process of life is its endless creative evolution, which Su-Un called *hu-cheon-gae-byeok* [後天開闢, a beginning of a new heaven and a new earth]. That state is actually the state of *shalom* which cannot stay in one place at one time, yet, coming and becoming always occurs in terms of "newness." Life generates hope and brings with it a *good-newness* through decolonizing, hybridizing, surviving, enlivening, sharing, healing, reconciling together as becoming or becoming together, endlessly. A body encounters another body and the two multiply and generate newness. This is the mystery of life and the secret of opening a new heaven and a new earth. Everything delivers some other thing, feeding, nurturing, embracing, and raising one another, all of which comprise *salim* in Korean. If it is a part of our "feminine nature" According to a traditional essentialism, then, even without the stereotype, everything can be considered metaphorically a mother in the whole cosmic womb-like body, the maternal universe. *Salim* is the process of life which not only expands its boundary in quantity but also deepens its relationship in quality as a quality evolution of life.   If the quality of life is *shalom*, then, *salim* reflects the movements and the process to bring forth *shalom* for all in a symbiotic sense. The earth, our home, including us as the cosmic organic body which is *hanul*, the sacred, divinely hopes to maintain life, and furthermore, pursues a better living by renewing and regenerating, together in the process of life, *salim*. Our future will never be the same as Heraclitus put it first in the west. "We cannot step into the same stream twice." "There is the possibility. The future can be different from the past. Therefore, there is hope. *Where there is life, there is hope*."[72] We need to call on a new heaven and a new earth everyday, again and again, for the well-being (be*com*ing) of life, *shalom* for all.   *Salim* is the very PROCESS of LIFE.

> *The spring sunshine has not yet been coming,*
> *though I have been waiting desperately for spring.*
> *There is the spring sunshine always*
> *yet the time has not yet arrived.*
> *When the time comes,*
> *Spring will come eventually.*[72]
> *Last night through the spring wind,*
> *all the trees bud simultaneously.*
> *One day, one flower blooms,*
> *two days, two flowers,*
> *three hundred sixty days, three hundred sixty flowers…*
> *Every body is flowering and every house is becoming spring.*
> — *The Spring Sunshine* [春光好], Su-Un[73] (translation mine)

Glossary of Korean Terms

bab   Bab [밥, rice] is the daily meal of Korean people which literally means rice, indicating the daily meal. The word, *bab*, is often used to indicate food in general. In Korea, *bab* has traditionally been served by women for their families. Cooking *bab* is also called *salim* but in a narrow sense, that is, of feeding and enlivening life. Kim Ji-Ha understands "*bab* as *hanul* [the divine]."

donghak   Donghak [동학, 東學] is a Korean modern religious experience. *Dong* [東] means "the East" and *Hak* [學] means "learning." Therefore, *Donghak* can be translated, literally, "Eastern Learning," which is indigenous to Korean people. In the middle of the nineteenth century, in the midst of colonization and westernization by Japanese and Christian imperialism, Su-Un initiated a national religion of Korea, called *Donghak* which was influenced by other Asian philosophies, i.e. Confucianism, Buddhism, and Daoism as well as Christianity which Su-Un called *seo-hak* [西學, western learning]. Three Asian religions were Koreanized and syncretized in *Donghak* for Korean people. One can say that at its inception *Donghak* was inter-religious, inter-cultural, inter-ideological, and inter-traditional. Therefore, *Donghak* was already holistically inclusive tradition as a philosophical and religious hybrid.

hanul   Hanul [한울, the divine] is the word for G*d in Korean. The Korean concept *hanul* in its etymology means one bound: *han* means oneness as well as greatness and *ul* means bound. *Han* of *hanul* does not mean suffering. *Han* in *hanul* used as an adjective while *han* [恨] as a noun means suffering, though they are pronounced in the same way. *Han* of *hanul* functions as an adjective that describes "*ul*," and means 'one', 'infinite,' and/or 'gigantic.' The Korean letter, *han* (恨), has no end and means the infinite in process. That is, all different boundaries are becoming, together, and endlessly, as one, according to the letter, *han* (恨). *Hanul* (한울) for Korean means literally a magnificent unity which includes everything in terms of togetherness.

hu-cheon-gae-byeok I translate *hu-cheon-gae-byeok* [후천개벽, 後天開闢] as "opening a new heaven and a new earth" that points out a new world (I call it "ecotopia") here on earth in which our ecoethical responsibility reflects our process of life. Su-Un's thinking of 'Re-Beginning of Heaven and Earth' on the advent of a new world was a religious alternative to overcome the difficulties, particularly associated with the infiltration of the western powers, which the *Joseon* (*Yi* Dynasty) society faced in the 19th century. The world Su-Un pursued through *si-cheon-ju* [embracing *hanul*] and *jo-wha-jeong* [creative transformation with peace and harmony] is the process of *hu-cheon-gae-byeok* [opening a new heaven and a new earth].

hyang-ah-seol-wi Hae-Weol created a transformative shift from the spirits of the dead to the living by switching the position of *bab* which is called, *hyang-ah-seol-wi* [to place *bab* toward the people, 향아설위, 向我設位].

hyang-byeok-seol-wi In the traditional *jaesa* [ritual] custom, *bab* [rice] should be placed toward the wall for the spirits which is known as *hyang-byeok-seol-wi* [to place *bab* toward the shrine, 벽설위, 向壁設位]. Thus, in the ritual of *hyang-byeok-seol-wi*, *bab* is prepared to feed the spirits in a respectable manner.

jaesa *Jaesa* [제사, 祭祀], Korean ancestor worship, originated in the *Cheonsin* [천신, heaven god] worship of Korean ancient religion and developed into its present form through the process of interaction and synchronization of the Korean shamanistic beliefs and the Confucianism and Neo-Confucianism of China. The Korean shamanistic worldview has provided an important foundation for Korean ancestor worship. Confucianism played an important role in adding, concretely, the ethical dimension to Korean ancestor worship, while Neo-Confucianism provided the metaphysical dimension. Thus, ancestor worship, with its moral, ritual, and cosmological aspects, became a richly religious form of worship in Korea.

jo-hwa-jeong   The usual translation for *jo-hwa-jeong* [조화정, 造化定] is "Creative Transformation. The word, *jo-hwa* [造化], refers to a peaceful state of living in which everything is well-harmonized. *Jo-hwa* [造化] can be understood to mean "wondrous becoming" which *jeong* implies harmony which ultimately brings "peace." I understand *jo-hwa-jeong* [造化定] in relation to *salim* as *shalom*, creative transformation with peace.

jugim   *Jugim* (죽임) is the contrary to *salim*, not only as an expression of killing but also as a term reflecting different forms of violence, in general, which disturbs all the intentional and spontaneous movement of *salim*. *Jugim* includes all the destructive activities such as oppression, exploitation, coercion, contamination, destruction, marginalization, killing, etc.

koja   *Koja* [고자, eunuch] was an official position for serving kings during the *Goryeo* (918~1392) and *Joseon* (1392~1910) dynasties. Their principal function was mainly to be responsible for the miscellaneous chores in the royal palace. They were the men who served the royalty. All women in the royal palace were considered the King's women. In order to prevent love affairs between the *koja* and the women in waiting in the palace, the *koja*'s genitals were castrated. They were the outcaste low class *minjung* [민중, the oppressed] in the society.

salim   *Salim* (살림) is a Korean term, literally meaning making things alive, restoring, and enlivening. *Salim*, in a narrow sense, and traditional, refers to women's tasks such as cooking, gathering wood, cleaning and washing, raising children, cultivating gardens, and managing household affairs. *Salim* can also include all diverse activities that make things alive and keep things living. However, *salim* has been gendered and degraded as exclusively women's tasks in Korea.

salim-kun   In Korean, someone who does *salim* is called *salim-kun* (살림꾼) which usually refers to housewives traditionally. Kim Ji-Ha called ecological activist *salim-kun* regardless of his/her gender. Chung Hyun-Kyung was inspired by Kim's notion of *salim* and *salim-kun*. Later she created the term, *salimist,* for referring to *salim-kun*. Through her declaration of "*Salimist* Manifesto," she indicated that her *salimist* ideas were greatly indebted by Kim Ji-Ha in her book, *Goddess-spell According to Hyun Kyung* (2002).

si-cheon-ju [시천주, 侍天主]   *Si-cheon-ju* can be interpreted as "*hanul*'s indwelling in life" or "embracing *hanul*." Hae-Weol referred to every working subject as *hanul*. Thus, *si-cheon-ju* [embracing *hanul*, 侍天主] means embracing or working *hanul* into one's life.

teum   The Korean term, *teum* (틈), is normally translated in English in terms of space, crevice, crack, gap, and/or opening; in terms of time, as spare time, an interval, opportunity and chance; and in terms of relationship, as friction, estrangement, and alienation. As an expression of space, *teum* can be used to articulate, for example, a crack [*teum*] in the wall. In terms of time, *teum* can be used to express, for example, finding a time [*teum*] for us or I have no time [*teum*] because I am so busy. In relationship, *teum* can be used to describe a gap [*teum*] or friction between two persons.

Bibliography

Process Ecotheology

Armstrong-Buck, Susan. "Nonhuman Experience: A Whiteheadian Analysis." *Process Studies* 18, no.1 (1989): 1-18.

_____. "What Process Philosophy Can Contribute to the Land Ethic and Deep Ecology." *Trumpeter* 8, no.1 (1991): 29-34.

_____. "Whitehead's Metaphysical System as a Foundation for Environmental Ethics." *Environmental Ethics* 8 (Fall 1986): 241-59.

Birch, Charles, William Eakin, and Jay McDaniel, eds. *Liberating Life: Contemporary Approaches to Ecological Theology*. New York: Orbis, 1990.

Cobb, John B. *A Christian Natural Theology: Based on the Thought of Alfred North Whitehead*, 2nd edition. Louisville: Westminster John Knox Press, 2007.

_____. *Christ in a Pluralistic Age*. NY: Wipf and Stock Publishers, 1998.

_____. *Is It Too Late? A Theology of Ecology*. Denton: Environmental Ethics Books, 1995.

_____ and David Ray Griffin. *Process Theology: An Introductory Exposition*. Philadelphia: The Westminster Press, 1976.

_____ and Charles Birch. *The Liberation of Life*. Denton: Environmental Ethics Books, 1990.

_____ and David Ray Griffin. *Process Theology: An Introductory Exposition.* Philadelphia: The Westminster Press, 1976.

_____. "Protestant Theology and Deep Ecology." In *Deep Ecology and World Religions: New Essays on Sacred Ground.* edited by David Landis Barnhill and Roger S. Gottlieb, 213-228. Albany: SUNY Press.

_____. *Sustainability: Economics, Ecology, and Justice.* New York: Orbis, 1997.

_____. *Sustaining the Common Good: A Christian Perspective on the Global Economy.* Cleveland: The Pilgrim Press, 1994.

_____, ed. *For the Common Good: Redirecting the Economy Toward Community, the Environment, and a Sustainable Future.* Boston: Beacon Press, 1994.

Coleman, Monica A. "An Exchange of Gifts: Process and Womanist Theologies." In *Handbook of Process Theology,* edited by Jay McDaniel and Donna Bowman, 160-176. St. Louis: Chalice Press, 1989.

Faber, Roland. *God as Poet of the World: Exploring Process Theologies.* Louisville: Westminster John Knox Press, 2004.

_____. "Programmatic Dysfunction in the Chaosmos." In *Deleuze, Whitehead, Bergson: Rhizomatic Connections.* Edited by Keith Robinson, 200-219. New York: Palgrave Macmillan, 2009.

_____ and Andrea M. Stephenson eds. *Secrets of Becoming: Negotiating Whitehead, Deleuze, and Butler.* New York: Fordham University Press, 2011.

_____ and Andrea M. Stephenson eds., *Secrets of Becoming: Negotiating Whitehead, Deleuze, and Butler.* New York: Fordham University Press, 2011.

Fox, Warwick. "The Deep Ecology-Ecofeminism Debate and its Parallels." *Environmental Ethics* 11:1 (1989): 5-25.

_____. *Postmodernism and the Environmental Crisis.* New York: Routledge, 1995.

Kant, Immanuel. *Critique of Pure Reason*. Translated by Paul Guyer and Allen W. Wood. Cambridge University Press, 1999.

Kearns, Laurel and Catherine Keller, eds. *Ecospirit: Religious and Philosophies for the Earth*. New York: Fordham University Press, 2007.

Keller, Catherine. *On the Mystery: Discerning Divinity in Process*. Minneapolis: Fortress Press, 2008.

_____. "Eschatology, Ecology, and a Green Ecumenacy." In *Reconstructing Christian Theology*. Edited by Rebecca S. Chopp and Mark Lewis Taylor, 326-345. Minneapolis: Fortress Press, 1994.

_____. *Face of the Deep; A Theology of Becoming*. New York: Routledge, 2003.

_____. *From a Broken Web: Separation, Sexism, and Self*. Boston: Beacon Press, 1986.

_____. *God and Power: Counter-Apocalyptic Journeys*. Minneapolis: Fortress Press, 2005.

_____, and Anne Daniell, eds. *Process and Difference: Between Cosmological and Poststructuralist Postmodernisms*. (Albany: SUNY Press, 2002).

_____. "Talk about weather." In *Ecofeminism and the Sacred*. Edited by Carol J. Adams, 30-49. New York: Continuum, 1993.

_____. "The Mystery of the Insoluble Evil." In *World without End*. Edited by Joseph A. Bracken, 46-71. Grand Rapids, Michigan: William B. Eerdmans Publishing Company, 2005.

Koller, John M. *Asian Philosophies*, 5th Edition. Upper Saddle River, New Jersey: Pearson, 2007.

Leclerc, Ivor. "Being and Becoming in Whitehead's Philosophy." In *Explorations in Whitehead's Philosophy*. Edited by Lewis S. Ford and George L. Kline, 53-67. New York: Fordham University Press, 1983.

MacKinnon, Mary Heather and Moni McIntyrem, eds. *Reading in Ecology and Feminist Theology.* Kansas City: Sheed & Ward, 1995.

McDaniel, Jay. *Earth, Sky, Gods & Mortals: Developing an Ecological Spirituality.* Mystic, Connecticut: Twenty-Third Publications, 1990.

———. "Elements of Spiritual Glue." *Earth Light* (Spring 1993): 10-11.

———. *Gandhi's Hope: Learning from Other Religions as a Path to Peace.* New York: Orbis Books, 2005.

———. "Green Grace: Four Ways to Find God Through the Earth." *Creative Transformation* 3:1 (1993): 1-2, 6-8.

———, and Donna Bowman, eds. *Handbook of Process Theology.* St. Louis: Chalice Press, 2006.

———. "Land Ethics, Animal Rights, and Process Theology." *Process Studies* 17:2 (1988): 88-102.

———. "Life-Centered Ethics in Christian Perspective." *Church and Society.* [Geneva: World Council of Churches] (September 1987): 82-109.

———. *Of God and Pelicans: A Theology of Reverence for Life.* Louisville: Westminster/John Knox Press, 1989.

———. *With Roots and Wings: Christianity in an Age of Ecology and Dialogue.* Maryknoll: Orbis Books, 1995.

McFague, Sallie. *Life Abundant.* Minneapolis: Fortress Press, 2001.

———. *The Body of God: An Ecological Theology.* Minneapolis: Fortress Press, 1993.

———. *Models of God: Theology for an Ecological, Nuclear Age.* Philadelphia: Fortress Press, 1987.

McGee, Glenn. "The Relevance of Foucault to Whiteheadian Environmental Ethics." *Environmental Ethics* 16 (Winter 1994): 419-424.

Moltmann, Jürgen. *God in Creation: A New Theology of Creation and the Spirit of God.* Minneapolis: Fortress Press, 1993.

Palmer, Clare. *Environmental Ethics and Process Thinking.* Oxford: Clarendon Press, 1998.

_____. "Process Theology as Ecological Theology." *Theology in Green* 1:1 (1992): 243.

Reeves, Gene. "Ecology, Philosophy, and Whitehead." The *Unitarian Universalist Christian* 30:4 (1975-76): 35-43.

Ruether, Rosemary Radford. *Gaia and God: An Ecofeminist Theology of Earth Healing.* San Francisco: Harper, 1992.

_____. *Sexism and Godtalk: Toward A Feminist Theology.* Boston: Beacon Press, 1983.

_____, ed. *Women Healing Earth: Third World Women on Ecology, Feminism, and Religion.* New York: Orbis, 1996.

Schüssler Fiorenza, Elisabeth. *Wisdom Ways: Introducing Feminist Biblical Interpretation.* New York: Orbis Books, 1970.

Sherburne, Donald W., ed. *A Key to Whitehead's Process and Reality.* Chicago: The University of Chicago Press, 1966.

Shiva, Vandana. *Earth Democracy: Justice, Sustainability, and Peace.* Cambridge: South End Press, 2005.

Sia, Santiago. *God in Process Thought.* Dordrecht: Martinus Nijhoff Publishers, 1985.

Taylor, Bron. *Dark Green Religion: Nature, Spirituality, and the Planetary Future.* Berkeley/Los Angeles/London: University of California Press, 2010.

Tucker, Mary Evelyn and John A. Grim, eds. *Worldviews and Ecology: Religion, Philosophy, and the Environment.* New York: Orbis, 1999.

Whitehead, Alfred North. *Adventures of Ideas.* New York: The Macmillan Company, 1933.

_____, and David Griffin, eds. *Process and Reality.* New York: The Free Press, 1978.

_____. *Science and the Modern World.* New York: The Free Press, 1953.

_____. *The Function of Reason.* Princeton: Princeton University Press, 1929.

Postcolonial and Poststructural Theory and Theology

Ashcroft, Bill and Gareth Griffiths. *Postcolonial Studies: The Key Concepts.* London: Routledge, 2000.

Bell, Jeffrey A. *Philosophy at the Edge of Chaos: Gilles Deleuze and the Philosophy of Difference.* Toronto: University of Toronto Press, 2006.

Bhabha, Homi K. *Nation and Narration.* New York: Routledge, 1990.

_____. *The Location of Culture.* London: Routledge, 1994.

_____. "In a Spirit of Calm Violence." In *After Colonialism: Imperial Histories and Postcolonial Displacements.* Edited by Gyan Prakash, 326-344. Princeton: Princeton University Press, 1995.

_____. "Unpacking my library...again." In T*he Post-colonial Question: Common Skies, Divided Horizons*, edited by Iain Chambers and Lidia Curti, 199-211. New York: Routledge, 1996.

Das, Veena. "Subaltern as perspective." In *Subaltern Studies*, Vol. 6. Edited by R. Guha. 310-324. New Delhi: Oxford University Press, 1989.

Deleuze, Gilles. *Difference & Repetition*, Translated by Paul Patton. New York: Columbia University Press, 1994.

_____. *The Fold: Leibniz and the Baroque.* Translated by Tom Conley. Minneapolis: University of Minnesota Press, 1993.

_____ and Felix Guattari. *Anti-Oedipus: Capitalism and Schizophrenia.* Translated by Robert Hurtley. Minneapolis: University of Minnesota, 1983.

_____ and Felix Guattari. *A Thousand Plateaus: Capitalism and Schizophrenia*. Minneapolis: University of Minnesota, 1987.

_____ and Felix Guattari. *What is Philosophy?* Translated by Hugh Tomlinson and Graham Burchell. New York: Columbia University Press, 1994.

D'Costa, Gavin. *Sexing the Trinity: Gender, Culture, and the Divine.* London: SCM Press, 2000.

Hunt, Alex, and Bonnie Roos, eds. *Postcolonial Green: Environmental Politics and World Narratives.* Charlottesville & London: University of Virginia Press, 2010.

Donaldson, Laura E., and Kwok Pui-lan, eds. *Postcolonialism, Feminism, and Religious Discourse.* New York: Routledge, 2002.

Foucault, Michel. *The History of Sexuality Vol. I: An Introduction.* Translated by Robert Hurley. New York: Vintage Books, 1978.

Gramsci, Antonio. *Selections from the Prison Notebooks.* Translated by Quintin Hoare. London: Lawrence & Wishart, 1971.

Gandhi, Leela. *Postcolonial Theory: A Critical Introduction.* New York: Columbia University Press: 1998.

Huggan, Graham and Helen Tiffin. *Postcolonial Ecocriticism: Literature, Animals, Environment* (London and New York: Routledge, 2010).

Irigaray, Luce. *Marine Lover of Friedrich Nietzsche.* New York: Columbia University Press, 1991.

_____. *Speculum of the Other Woman.* Translated by Gillian G. Gill. New York: Cornell University, 1985.

_____. *This Sex which is Not One.* Translated by Catherine Porter trans. New York: Cornell University, 1985.

Jaggar, Alison M. "Globalizing Feminist Ethics." In *Decentering the Center: Philosophy for a Multicultural, Postcolonial, and*

> *Feminist World.* Edited by Uma Narayan and Sandra Harding, 1-25. Indianapolis: Indiana University Press, 2000.

Joh, Wonhee Anne. *Heart of the Cross: A Postcolonial Christology.* Louisville: Westminster John Knox Press, 2006.

Johnson, Elizabeth A. *She Who Is: The Mystery of God in Feminist Theological Discourse.* New York: Crossroad, 1996.

Keller, Catherine. *Apocalypse Now and Then: A Feminist Guide to the End of the World.* Boston: Beacon Press, 1996.

_____. *From a Broken Web: Separation, Sexism, and Self.* Boston: Beacon Press, 1986.

_____. "The Love of Postcolonialism." In *Postcolonial Theologies: Divinity and Empire.* Edited by Catherine Keller, Michael Nausner, and Mayra Rivera, 221-242. St. Louis: Chalice, 2004.

_____. "Hybridity and Chaos: Theology on the Face of the Deep." AAR, October, 1999.

_____, Michael Nausner, and Mayra Rivera, eds. *Postcolonial Theologies: Divinity and Empire.* St. Louis: Chalice Press, 2004.

Kim, Seong Hee. *Mark, Women, and Empire: A Korean Postcolonial Perspective.* Sheffield: Sheffield Phoenix Press, 2010.

Kock, Leon. "Interview With Gayatri Chakravorty Spivak: New Nation Conference in South Africa." *A Review of International English Literature,* 23.3 (1992): 29-47.

Kwok Pui-lan. *Introducing Asian Feminist Theology.* Cleveland: The Pilgrim Press, 2000.

_____. *Discovering the Bible in the Non-Biblical World.* Maryknoll: Orbis Books, 1995.

_____. "Jesus the Hybrid: What Do You Say That I Am?" AAR, October, 1999.

_____. *Postcolonial Imagination and Feminist Theology.* Louisville: Westminster John Knox Press, 2005.

_____. "Unbinding Our Feet." In *Postcolonialism, Feminism and Religious Discourse*. Translated by Laura E. Donaldson and Kwok Pui-lan, 62-81. New York: Routledge, 2002.

_____. "What Has Love to Do With It?: Planetarity, Feminism, and Theology," Stephen D. Moore and Mayra Rivera ed. *Planetary Loves: Spivak, Postcoloniality, and Theology*. New York: Fordham University, 2011.

Lacan, Jacques. *Ecrits: A Selection*. Translated by Bruce Fink New York: W. W. Norton & Company, 1999.

Lewis, Reina and Sara Mills. *Feminist Postcolonial Theory: A Reader*. New York: Routledge, 2003.

Loomba, Ania. *Colonialism/Postcolonialism*. New York: Routledge, 1998.

McClintock, Anne, ed. *Dangerous Liaisons: Gender, Nation, and Postcolonial Perspectives*. London: University of Minnesota Press, 1997.

_____. *Imperial Leader: Race, Gender, and Sexuality in the Colonial Contest*. New York: Routledge, 1995.

McFague, Sallie. *The Body of God: An Ecological Theology*. Minneapolis: Fortress Press, 1993.

Minh-ha, Trinh T. "An Acoustic Journey." *Rethinking Borders*. Edited by John C. Welchman, 1-17. Minneapolis: University of Minnesota Press, 1996.

_____. *When the Moon Waxes Red: Representation, Gender, and Cultural Politics*. New York: Routledge, 1991.

_____. *Woman, Native, Other: Writing Postcoloniality and Feminism*. Bloomington: Indiana University Press, 1989.

Monhanty, Chandra T. *Feminism Without Borders: Decolonizing Theory, Practicing Solidarity*. Durham: Duke University Press, 2003.

_____. *Postcolonial Perspectives*. Minneapolis: The University of Minnesota Press, 1997.

Moore, Stephen D. *Empire and Apocalypse: Postcolonialism and the New Testament* Sheffield: Sheffield Phoenix Press, 2006.

_____. *Poststructuralism and the New Testament.* Minneapolis: Fortress Press, 1994.

_____ and Mayra Rivera eds. *Planetary Loves: Spivak, Postcoloniality, and Theology.* New York: Fordham University, 2011.

Moore-Gilbert, Bart. *Postcolonial Theory: Context, Practices, Politics.* London: Verso, 1997.

Nixon, Rob. "Environmentalism and Postcolonialism," In *Postcolonial Studies and Beyond*, ed. Ania Loomba et al Durham: Duke University Press, 2005.

Russell, Letty M. and J. Shannon Clarkson, eds. *Dictionary of Feminist Theologies.* Louisville: Westminster John Knox Press, 1996.

Said, Edward W. *Culture and Imperialism.* New York: Vintage Books, 1993.

_____. *Orientalism.* New York: Vintage Books, 1979.

Spivak, Gayatri Chakravorty. *A Critique of Postcolonial Reason: Toward a History of the Vanishing Present.* Cambridge: Harvard University Press, 1999.

_____. "Can the Subaltern Speak?" In *Marxism and the Interpretation of Culture.* Edited by Cary Nelson and Lawrence Grossberg, 271-316. Urbana: University of Illinois Press, 1988.

_____. *Death of A Discipline.* New York: Columbia University Press, 2003.

_____. "Identity and Alterity: An Interview" (with Nikos Papastergiadis). *Arena* (1997): 70.

_____. *In Other Words: Essays in Cultural Politics.* New York: Routledge, 1987.

_____. "More on Power/Knowledge." In *The Spivak Reader: Selected Works of Gayatri Spivak*. Edited by Donna Landry and Gerald Maclean, 141-174. London and New York: Routledge, 1996.

_____. *Outside in the Teaching Machine*. New York: Routledge, 1993.

_____. "The New Historicism: Political Commitment and the Postmodern Critic: In *Post-Colonial Critics, Strategies, Dialogues*. Edited by Sarah Harasym, 152-168. London: Routledge, 1990.

_____. "The New Subaltern: A Silent Interview." In *Mapping Subaltern Studies and the Postcolonial*. Edited by Vinayak Chaturvedi, 324-340. London: Verso, 2000.

_____, ed. *The Postcolonial Critic: Interviews, Strategies, Dialogues*. New York: Routledge, 1990.

Sugirtharajah, R. S. *Asian Biblical Hermeneutics and Postcolonialism*. New York: Orbis, 1998.

_____. *Postcolonial Criticism and Biblical Interpretation*. New York: Oxford, 2002.

_____, ed. *The Postcolonial Bible*. Sheffield: Sheffield Academic Press, 1998.

Werbner, Pnina and Tariq Modood ed. *Debating Cultural Hybridity: Multi-Cultural Identities and the Politics of Anti-Racism*. London: Zed Books, 1997.

Young, Robert. *Colonial Desire: Hybridity in Theory, Culture, and Race*. New York: Routledge, 1995.

_____. *White Mythologies Writing History and the West*. London: Routledge, 1990.

Donghak and *Salim*

Ahn, Sang-Jin. *Asian Thought and Culture: Continuity and Transformation*. New York: Peter Lang, 2001.

Beirne, Paul. *Su-Un and His World of Symbols: The Founder of Korea's First Indigenous Religion.* Surrey: Ashgate, 2009.

Cha, Ok-Soong, Kyung-Sook Lee, and Jae-Sun Park, eds. *Hangook Sangmyeong Sasangeui Bburi* [The Root of Korean Philosophy of Life]. Seoul: Ewha Daehakgyo Choolpanboo, 2001.

Choi, Dong-Hui ed. *Saerosseuneun Donghak* [Rewriting *Donghak*]. Seoul: Jjbmoondang, 2003.

Choi Hee An. *Korean Women and God.* New York: Orbis Books, 2005.

Choi, Jae-Woo (Un-Un), Kim Yong-Ok ed. *Donggyeongdaejoen 1.* [Pletharchia] (Seoul: Tongnamoo, 2004).

Choi, Yun-Bae ed. *Sangmyeonggwa Seongryeong* [Life and the Holy Spirit]. Seoul: Daehan Gidokgyo Seowhoe, 2004.

Chung, Hyun-Kyung. *Miraeeseo On Pyeonji: Goddess-spell According to Hyun Kyung* [A Letter from the Future]. Seoul: Yeolimwon, 2001.

_____. *Struggle to be the Sun Again: Introducing Asian Women's Theology.* New York: Orbis Books, 1990.

Chung, Ki-Yeol. *The Donghak Concept of God/Heaven: Religion and Social Transformation.* New York: Peter Lang, 2007.

Cheong, Woo-Seong. *Saram, Sarm, Doisalim* [Human, Life, and *Salim*: An Education for Human Survival]. Seoul: Hanul Academy, 1994.

Duncan, John. "The Emergence of the Tonghak Religion." In *The Sourcebook of Korean Civilization, Vol. 2.* New York: Columbia University Press, 1996.

Hong, Gi-Seong. Gaebyeok gwa Donghak [Re-creation and *Donghak*]. (Chungbook University Minsok Yeonguwhei, 2001).

Kang, Nam-Soon, ed. *Jaesamsaegye Sinhake Natanan Sangmyeongeui BigyoYeongu* [A Comparative Study on the

Philosophy of Life in the Third World]. Seoul: Sankakeui Namu, 2002.

Kang, Won-Don. *Salimeui Gyeongjae* [The Economy of *Salim*: Toward An Ecological Democracy]. Seoul: Hanguk Sinhak Yunguso, 2001.

Kim, Hyeong-Gi. *Hucheon Gaebyeok Sasang Yeongu* [A Study of New Creation]. Seoul: Hanul Academy, 2004.

Kim, Ji-Ha. *Bab* [Rice]. Seoul: Bundo Chulpansa, 1984.

_____. *Donghak Eiyaki* [A Story of *Donghak*]. Seoul: Sol, 1994.

_____. *Kim Ji-Ha Jeonjib I* [Philosophy: *Donghak* and Life]. Seoul: Silcheon Moonhaksa, 2002.

_____. *Kim Ji-Ha Jeonjib II* [Sociology: Life, Environment, Autonomy, Unification]. Seoul: Silcheon Moonhaksa, 2002.

_____. *Salim*. Seoul: Donggwang Chulpansa, 1987.

_____. *Sangmyeong* [Life]. Seoul: Sol, 1999.

_____. *Sangmyeonggwa Jachi* [Life and Autonomy]. Seoul: Silcheon Moonhaksa, 2002.

_____. *Sangmyeonggwa Pyeongwhaeui Gil* [The Way of Life and Peace]. Seoul: Moonhakgwa Jiseongsa, 2005.

_____. *Sangmyeonghak I* [Theory of Life I]. Seoul: Whanam, 2003.

_____. *Sangmyeonghak II* [Theory of Life II]. Seoul: Whanam, 2003.

_____. *Teum* [Interstitial Space]. Seoul: Sol, 1995.

Kim, Kyung-Jae and Kim Sang-Il, eds. *Gwajeong Cheolhakgwa Gwajeong Shinhak* [Process Philosophy and Process Theology]. Seoul: Heemangsa, 1988.

Kim, Sang-Il, *Su-Un gwa Whitehead* [*Su-Un* and Whitehead: A Process Interpretation on Twenty-One Words of *Donghak* Incantation]. Seoul: Jisiksaneopsa, 2004.

_____. *Donghak gwa Jeongtong Sasang* [*Donghak* and Traditional Philosophy]. Seoul: Mosineonsaramdeul, 2004.

Kim, Yung-Hyui. *Woori Hakmooneuiroseo Donghak* [*Donghak* as Our Own Study]. Seoul: Cheksaegye, 2007.

Lee, Eun-Sun. *Postmodern Sidaeui Hanguk Yeoseong Sinhak* [A Korean Feminist Theology in Postmodern Time]. Seoul: Bundo Chulpansa, 1997.

Lee, Hyun-Hui. *Hae-Weol Choi Si-Hyeong eui Sasang gwa Gapjin Gaehyeokundong* [Hae-Weol's Thought and *Gapjin* Reformation Movement]. Seoul: Mosinunsaramdeul, 2003.

Lee, Jung-Bae. *Sinhakeui Sangmyeongwha Sinhakeui Youngseongwha* [Enlivening Theology and Spirituality]. Seoul: Daehan Gidokgyo Seowhoi, 1999.

_____. *Pyeongsindowa Hamkaehaneun Sanmyeong Sinhak* [Theology of Life with People]. (Seoul: Gidokgyo Daehan Gamriwhoi, 2001.

Lee, Jung Young, ed. *Ancestor Worship and Christianity in Korea.* New York: The Edwin Mellen Press, 1989.

Lee, Ki-Baik. *A New History of Korea*. Translated by Edgar W. Wagner. Cambridge: Harvard University Press, 1984.

Masao, Dachenaka. *Haneunimeun Babisida* [God is Rice]. Translated by Kim Ki-Seok. Seoul: Dasan Geulbang, 1991.

Oh, Young-Seop. *Hanguk Geunhyundaisareul Sunoeun Inmooldeul 1* [Remarkable People in Korean Modern History I]. Seoul: Gyeongin Moonwhasa, 2007.

Paek, Andrew Song-Min. "Korean Ancestor Worship." In *East Wind: Taoist and Cosmological Implications of Christian Theology.* Edited by Charles Courtney. 162-177. Lanham: University Press of America, 1997.

Park, Jae-Sun. *Hanguk Sangmyeong Sinhak Mosak* [Searching for a Korean Life Theology]. Seoul: Hanguk Sinhak Yeonkuso, 2000.

_____. *Yaesoo Undonggwa Babsang Kondongche* [Jesus Movement and the Community of Rice]. Seoul: Cheonji, 1988.

Park, Jong-Chun. *Dangunshinwhaeui Sansangiinyumedaehan Shinhakjeok Haeseok: Sangsangeui Shinhak* [Theological Interpretation on the Symbiotic Ideology of the *Dan-Gun* Myth: Theology of Symbiosis]. Seoul: Hanguk Theological Institute, 1991.

Pyo, Young-Sam. *Donghak I: Su-Un eui Salmkwa Saenggak* [Eastern Learning I: Su-Un's Life and Thought]. Seoul: Tongnamoo, 2004.

_____. *Donghak II* [Eastern Learning II]. Seoul: Tongnamoo, 2005.

Seo, Chang-Won. *Salimeui Sinhak* [Theology of *Salim*]. Seoul: Handeul Chulpansa, 2001.

Shin, Il-Cheol. *Donghakgwa Jeontongsasang* [*Donghak* and the Traditional Philosophies]. Seoul: Donghakhakbo, 2003.

Shin, Il-Cheol. *Donghak Sasangeui Eihae* [Understanding *Donghak* Thought]. Seoul: Sahweibipyeongsa, 1995.

Tabuchi, Pumio. *Kim Ji-Ha Ron* [A Theory of Kim Ji-Ha: The Unity of God and Revolution]. Translated by Ji-Ryun Jung. Seoul: Dasan, 1991.

Yoon, Seok-San. *Donghak Gyojo Su-Un Choi Jaewoo.* [Su-Un: The Initiator of *Donghak*] (Seoul: Mosineon Saramdeul, 2004).

Notes

CHAPTER I
INTRODUCTION

1. John B. Cobb Jr. distinguishes "Life," *per se* from life as an abstract noun or collective reference to all living things and indicates that "Life" is the central religious symbol. Therefore, he uses the capital "L." John B. Cobb Jr. and Charles Birch, *The Liberation of Life* (DeLeon Springs: Environmental Ethics Books, 1990), 177.

2. *Salim* is a Korean term that literally means making things alive, restoring, and enlivening. In a narrow and traditional sense, it refers to women's tasks such as cooking, gathering wood, cleaning and washing, raising children, cultivating gardens, and managing household affairs. *Salim* can also include all the activities that make things alive and keep things living. However, *salim* has been gendered and degraded as exclusively women's tasks in Korea.

3. Historically, nature has been alienated from humanity by western culture in its anthropocentric, androcentric worldview. In response to this, John Cobb Jr. raises the issue of western dualism: "The western traditions were monolithically committed to its pervasive dualism and substantialism." John B. Cobb Jr. and David Ray Griffin, *Process Theology: An Introductory Exposition* (Philadelphia: The Westminster Press, 1976), 8.

4. Gayatri Chakravorty Spivak, "The New Subaltern: A Silent Interview," in *Mapping Subaltern Studies and the Postcolonial*, ed. Vinayak Chaturvedi (London: Verso, 2000), 326.

5. Chung Ki-Yeol, *The Donghak Concept of God/Heaven: Religion and Social Transformation* (New York: Peter Lang, 2007), 100.

6. I use Elisabeth Schüssler Fiorenza's way of writing the Divine as G*d instead of "God," except when I use a direct quote. Writing the Divine G*d acknowledges the insufficiency and inability of human language to adequately name the Divine. It seeks to indicate that G*d is ultimately unnamable and ineffable. She is adapting a Jewish orthographic tradition which writes G-d instead of God since G-d is incomplete there is no risk of defacement. Elisabeth Schüssler Fiorenza, *Wisdom Ways: Introducing Feminist Biblical Interpretation* (New York: Orbis Books, 1970), 210.

7. The Whiteheadian idea of G*d is appropriately called Life because the life-giving principle is itself alive. G*d is the supreme and perfect exemplification of the ecological model of life. John B. Cobb Jr. and Charles Birch, *The Liberation of Life*, 195.

8. *Hanulnim* is endlessly creating and recreating in the process of becoming. *Hanulnim* is not a transcendent being beyond the world but is closely embodied in every form of life. *Si-cheon-ju* (侍天主) means that *hanul* dwells in living bodies as well as in non-organic bodies as "life" in which every life-form acquires its dignity and intrinsic value.

9. Cobb defines G*d as Life: "The Spirit of God is God. God is the Spirit. If it is the Spirit that enlivens us, we may equally well say that it is God who makes us alive. If the Spirit is the true Life within us, then God is that Life." Cobb understands that Life as the central religious symbol is G*d. *The Liberation of Life*, 200.

10. McDaniel states, "For me, God is the very Life, immanent within each living being, by which all beings are lured to live, and by which we are lured to care both for ourselves and for other living beings amid our respective struggles to survive with satisfaction relative to the situations at hand." Jay McDaniel, *Of God and Pelicans: A Theology of Reverence for Life* (Westminster: John Knox Press, 1989), 15.

11. Catherine Keller, "The Love of Postcolonialism: Theology in the Interstices of Empire," in *Postcolonial Theologies: Divinity and Empire*, ed. Catherine Keller, Michael Nausner, and Mayra Rivera (St. Louis: Chalice, 2004), 224.

12. Kwok Pui-lan, "Jesus the Hybrid: What Do You Say That I Am?" AAR, October 1999.

13. Catherine Keller, "Hybridity and Chaos: Theology on the Face of the Deep," AAR, October 1999.

14. Gayatri Chakravorty Spivak, *A Critique of Postcolonial Reason* (Cambridge: Harvard University Press, 1999), 381.

15. *Rg Veda* is a Hindu text which contains *Vedic* mythology.

16. Ibid., 382.

17. Catherine Keller, "The Love of Postcolonialism," in *Postcolonial Theologies: Divinity and Empire*, ed. Catherine Keller, Michael Nausner, and Mayra Rivera (St. Louis: Chalice, 2004), 236.

18. Gayatri Chakravorty Spivak, *Death of A Discipline* (New York: Columbia University Press, 2003), 72.

19. Kwok Pui-Lan, "What Has Love to Do With It?: Planetarity, Feminism, and Theology," Stephen D. Moore and Mayra Rivera, ed., *Planetary Loves: Spivak, Postcoloniality, and Theology* (New York: Fordham University, 2011), 33.

20. Rob Nixon, "Environmentalism and Postcolonialism," in *Postcolonial Studies and Beyond*, ed. Ania Loomba et al. (Durham: Duke University Press, 2005), 233.

21. Alex Hunt and Bonnie Roos ed., *Postcolonial Green: Environmental Politics and World Narratives* (Charlottesville & London: University of Virginia Press, 2010), 8-9.

22. Ibid., 255.

23. Graham Huggan and Helen Tiffin, *Postcolonial Ecocriticism: Literature, Animals, Environment* (London and New York: Routledge, 2010), 12.

24. Spivak, *A Critique of Postcolonial Reason*, 114, 200, and 228.

25. Graham Huggan and Helen Tiffin, *Postcolonial Ecocriticism*, 79.

26. William M. Adams, "Nature and Colonial Mind," William M. Adams & Martin Mulligan, ed., *Decolonizing Nature: Strategies for Conservation in a Post-colonial Era* (London: Earthscan, 2004).

27. Graham Huggan and Helen Tiffin, *Postcolonial Ecocriticism*, 7.

28. *Salimist* means a person who is doing *salim*, which means making things alive. It is a Korean-English word that combines *salim* and the English suffix, -ist, for a person who is "doing" something such as an idealist, a novelist, or a specialist. This word has become a term in Korean language. Chung Hyun Kyung names a Korean eco-feminist or anyone who wants to share the vision of a Korean eco-feminist, *salimist* in her book, *Miraeeseo On Pyeonji: Goddess-spell According to Hyun Kyung* [A Letter from the Future] (Seoul: Yeolimwon, 2001), 236.

29. Catherine Keller, "The Love of Postcolonialism," in *Postcolonial Theologies: Divinity and Empire*, eds. Catherine Keller, Michael Nausner, and Mayra Rivera (St. Louis: Chalice, 1993), 224.

30. Comparing the insights of the two theologies does not mean that they are identical but rather, have wisdom which can be important for both to learn from each other. I will not engage the aspect of "identist pluralism." Also, I will strongly reject the Christian imperialistic view toward other religions that considers Christianity as superior and other religions as inferior. Jay McDaniel distinguishes "identist pluralism" from "complementary pluralism." For him, "identist pluralism" is the view that the insights of the many religions are identical, such that any given religion contains all the truth relevant to human flourishing, and one need not turn to the others. *Gandhi's Hope: Learning from Other Religions as a Path to Peace* (New York: Orbis Books, 2005), 9.

31. This negative concept should be applied to nature as a negative golden rule, "Do not hurt nature, if you do not want to get hurt." In this way, non-doing as the principle of *salim* is a practice of "doing non-doing."

Chapter II

Salim as the Korean Metaphor of Life

1. The Naeil News, March 15th, 2010.

2. The Grand Canal Project is an important part of President Lee Myung-Bak's platform. He plans to build one huge long waterway from Busan (the most southern city in South Korea) to Seoul throughout the four major rivers by transforming their own natural streams into a unitary grand flat canal. He asserts that it will generate an economic revival, therefore, it is the *salim* project of four rivers. Not only his political opponents but also the majority of people in Korea criticize that the project is unrealistic and too costly ($120,000,000) to be realized. Most of all, it will cause several negative environmental impacts such as hybridization of all species, killing fishes and plankton through construction, losing nature's self-clarifying function, concretizing the earth with cement and steel reinforcement. Therefore, it is considered a *jugim* project.

3. All translations of Kim Ji-Ha's poems and writings are mine.

4. Kim comments about *Donghak* in his book, *Sangmyeonggwa Pyeongwhaeui Gil* [The Way of Life and Peace] as follows: "*Donghak* created the theme of life [*salim*] which is an ecological cosmology based upon three major Asian religions, Confucianism, Buddhism, and Daoism, and Christianity and goes beyond them by proclaiming a self-constructive evolutionism which is far more advanced than Darwinian evolutionism." 303.

5. Kim Ji-Ha, *Sangmyeonggwa Jachi* [Life and Autonomy] (Seoul: Silcheon Moonhaksa, 2002), 31.

6. Ibid., 32.

7. Kim Ji-Ha, *Sangmyeonggwa Pyeongwhaeui Gil* [The Way of Life and Peace] (Seoul: Moonhakgwa Jiseongsa, 2005), 62.

8. Kim Ji-Ha. *Donghak Eiyagi* [A Story of *Donghak*] (Seoul: Sol, 1994), 9.

9. Kim Ji-Ha, *Sangmyeonggwa Jachi*, 31.

10. Kim Ji-Ha, *Donghak Eiyagi*, 16.

11. Roland Faber calls the creative energy of life, "living vitality," which cannot be captured or enclosed in a form permanently. Roland Faber, *God as Poet of the World: Exploring Process Theologies* (Louisville: Westminster John Knox Press, 2004). 104.

12. Kim Ji-Ha, *Sangmyeonggwa Jachi*, 128.

13. Ibid., 129.

14. Kim Ji-Ha, *Sangmyung* [Life] (Seoul: Sol, 1999), 17.

15. Kim Ji-Ha, *Sangmyunghak I*, 100.

16. Whitehead, *Process and Reality*, 104.

17. Roland Faber, *God as Poet of the World*, 104.

18. For Bhabha, mimicry is constructed around ambivalence rather than a binary. According to Bhabha, mimicry emerges as the representation of a difference that is, itself, a process of disavowal. Thus, mimicry is the sign of double articulation which appropriates the Other as it visualizes power. In this sense, Bhabhan mimicry already rejects the homogenization of power. There cannot be any sameness in two or many. Deleuzian mimicry was used as repetition which is impossible (nonrepeatible) but rhizomatically multiplied. One can refer to the Deleuzian becoming multiple in a Bhabhan way that it is not repeated but is hybridized (multiplied). Homi K. Bhabha, *Location of Culture*, 86.

19. Gilles Deleuze and Felix Guattari, *A Thousand Plateaus: Capitalism and Schizophrenia* (Minneapolis: University of Minnesota, 1987), 11.

20. Ibid., 21.

21. Gilles Deleuze, *The Fold: Leibniz and the Baroque*, trans. Tom Conley (Minneapolis: University of Minnesota Press, 1993), 8.

22. Ibid., 8.

23. Whitehead's hermeneutic reading of the poem of Percy Bysshe Shelley (1792-1822) in his *Science and the Modern World* shows Whitehead's ecological concerns on life. He recognizes the aesthetic values of nature in Shelley's poem and notices six notions of nature through his reading of Shelley: "change, value, eternal objects, endurance, organism, and interfusion." Alfred North Whitehead, *Science and the Modern World* (New York: The Free Press, 1953), 88.

    Shelley's poem, *The Cloud*, is quite aesthetic and ecological in terms of nature which actually contains the six notions about which

Whitehead comments, including also femininity along with the other six. The following appears in the last part of *The Cloud*:

> I am the daughter of Earth and Water,
>
> And the nursling of the Sky;
>
> I pass through the pores of the ocean and shores;
>
> "I change, but I cannot die."
>
> For after the rain when with never a stain
>
> The pavilion of Heaven is bare,
>
> and the winds and sunbeams with their convex gleams
>
> Build up the blue dome of air,
>
> I silently laugh at my own cenotaph,
>
> /And out of the caverns of rain,
>
> Like a child from the womb,
>
> like I arise and unbuild it again.

Albert North Whitehead, *Science and the Modern World* (New York: The Free Press, 1953), 86.

24. Ibid., 87.

25. Sallie McFague, *Life Abundant: Rethinking Theology and Economy for a Planet in Peril* (Minneapolis: Fortress Press, 2001), 182.

26. Ibid., 183.

27. Sallie McFague, *The Body of God: An Ecological Theology* (Minneapolis: Fortress Press, 1993), 56.

28. Bron Taylor, *Dark Green Religion: Nature, Spirituality, and the Planetary Future* (Berkeley/Los Angeles/London: University of California Press, 2010), 203.

29. A Korean term, *whangyeong*, signifies environment. Kim says that "we have to replace the word, environment [*whangyeong*], that indicate nature to life [*salim*]. The first step of the *salim* movement is

to change the name of the environmental movement to the *salim* movement." Kim Ji-Ha, *Sangmyeonghak I* [Theory of Life I], (Seoul: Whanam, 2003), 148.

30. Kim did not use these particular English terms, "microcosm" and "macrocosm." However, he mentioned "*sowooju*" [small *cosmos*] and "*daewooju*" [big *cosmos*] in order to explain the interconnectedness of both bodies as one whole organic unity. Kim Ji-Ha, *Sangmyeonghak I.* [Theory of Life I] (Seoul: Whanam, 2003), 153.

31. Kim distinguishes the Korean term, *jonjae* (存在, 존재), which means being, subsistence, and existence from the term, *saengseong* (生成, 생성) which means coming into being and becoming. He emphasizes that there is no such thing as being but only becoming, as life which, I understand, as *salim*.

32. Kim Ji-Ha, *Sangmyeonghak I*,175.

33. Whitehead, *Process and Reality* (New York: The Free Press, 1978), 22.

34. Ivor Leclerc, "Being and Becoming in Whitehead's Philosophy," in *Explorations in Whitehead's Philosophy*, eds. Lewis S. Ford and George L. Kline (New York: Fordham University Press, 1983), 67.

35. Whitehead, *Process and Reality*, 21.

36. Roland Faber, *God as Poet of the World: Exploring Process Theologies* (Louisville: Westminster John Knox Press, 2004), 23.

37. Whitehead, *Process and Reality*, 7.

38. Roland Faber, *God as Poet of the World*, 23.

39. Kim Ji-Ha, *Sangmyeong* [Life] (Seoul: Sol, 1999), 31.

40. Kim Ji-Ha, *Sangmyeonghak II* [Theory *of Life II*] (Seoul: Whanam, 2003), 227.

41. According to Deleuze and Guattari, puppet strings as a rhizome or multiplicity are tied not to the will of a puppeteer but to a multiplicity of nerve fibers which from another puppet in other

dimensions are connected to the first. Gilles Deleuze and Felix Guattari, *A Thousand Plateaus*, 8.

42. Ibid., 7.

43. Kim Ji-Ha, *Sangmyeonghak II*, 229.

44. Gilles Deleuze and Felix Guattari, *A Thousand Plateaus*, 8.

45. Gilles Deleuze, *The Fold*, 87.

46. This is my English translation of Kim's "*Wooju* [cosmos] *Sangmyeong* [life] *Jilseo* [way]." Kim writes that *ecocracy* should follow the cosmic way of life. Kim Ji-Ha, *Sangmyeonghak II*, 237

47. Kim Ji-Ha, *Sangmyeonggwa Pyeongwhaeui Gil*, 315.

48. Whitehead, *Process and Reality*, 105.

49. Ibid., 103.

50. Gilles Deleuze and Felix Guattari, *A Thousand Plateaus*, 161.

51. Kim Ji-Ha, *Sangmyeonghak II*, 191. Comparative theologian and *Donghak* scholar, Hyo-Dong Lee comments that even though Su-Un's notion of "doing non-doing" shows a Daoist influence, it was not by way of any Daoist school of thought or institution but by a cultural undercurrent.

52. John M. Koller, *Asian Philosophies*, 5th Edition (Upper Saddle River: Pearson, 2007), 247.

53. Kim Ji-Ha, *Sangmyeonghak II*, 191.

54. Kim Ji-Ha adopts this western term, *ecocracy*, in order to explain non-doing (*wuwei*). *Ecocracy* is a form of governance in which all life has participation. It is a concept that recognizes nature as the force regulating the physical universe.

55. Ibid., 193.

56. Kim Ji-Ha, *Sangmyeonggwa Pyeongwhaeui Gil*, 31.

57. Exodus 20:2-17 and Deuteronomy 5:6-21.

58. 1. *Han-Salim* is a cosmological awareness of life.

    2. *Han-Salim* is an ecological awareness of life.

3. *Han-Salim* is a communal awareness of the society.

4. *Han-Salim* is a movement of life and culture which pursues a new conscious, values, and modes.

5. *Han-Salim* is a social practice for establishing a new way of life.

6. *Han-Salim* is a living meditation for self-realization.

7. *Han-Salim* is a communal movement for creating a new world.

Han here means one and unity not suffering. The name *han-salim* symbolizes our symbiotic life as part-whole. *Salim Yeonkuso* [*Salim Institution*], 11/23/2009. http://www.mosim.or.kr/tc/681

59. In Korean, someone who does *salim* is called *salim-kun* which usually refers to housewives traditionally. Kim called ecological activist *salim-kun* regardless of his/her gender. Chung Hyun-Kyung was inspired by Kim's notion of *salim* and *salim-kun*. Later she created the term, *salimist,* for referring to *salimkun*. Through her declaration of "*Salimist* Manifesto," she indicated that her *salimist* ideas were greatly indebted by Kim Ji-Ha in her book, *Goddess-spell According to Hyun Kyung* (2002).

60. It is a new term related to the recycling movement. This term alone has no meaning. However, each syllable is attached as a prefix to verbs as noted above and symbolizes a recycling of syllables or phonemes.

61. Chung Hyun-Kyung, *Goddess-spell According to Hyun Kyung*, 236.

62. Ibid., 236-240.

63. Ibid., 18.

64. Under the influence of Chung Hyun-Kyung, A Korean biblical scholar, Kim Seong Hee, developed a '*salim* hermeneutics' as a form of Korean feminist postcolonial biblical interpretation. Elaborating on Chung's notion of *salim*, Kim claims that the goal of *salim* hermeneutics is making things alive, the mending of broken things, and the opening up of meaning. As Chung refers to *salimist* as Korean ecofeminist that implies the work of women only, Kim refers to Korean women's biblical interpretation as *salim* hermeneutics, reading the Gospel of Mark from a postcolonial feminist perspective.

Kim Seong Hee, *Mark, Women, and Empire: A Korean Postcolonial Perspective* (Sheffield: Sheffield Phoenix Press, 2010). Though Kim quotes Chung's ecofeminist notion of *salim,* she has not developed any ecofeminist readings in her *salim* hermeneutics. Whereas Chung's notion of *salim* focuses on Korean ecofeminist movements (*salim* movement), Kim's *salim* hermeneutics mainly focuses on the postcolonial situation of Korean women in the 19th century.

65. Kim Ji-Ha, *Sangmyeong*, 35.

66. Ibid., 48.

67. Ibid., 49.

68. Ibid., 333.

69. Hae-Weol was the second leader of *Donghak* after Su-Un, the initiator of *Donghak*. Hae-Weol emphasized three principles of *Donghak*, *gyeong-cheon* [reverence toward heaven], *gyeong-in* [reverence toward people], and *gyeong-mool* [reverence toward matter].

70. Kim, Ji-Ha. *Bab* [Rice] (Seoul: Bundo Chulpansa, 1984), 61.

71. John 6:35, NRSV.

72. Kim Ji-Ha, *Sangmyeong*, 334.

73. Kim's notion of *bab* as *hanul* will be further discussed in chapter IV.

74. Ibid., 349.

75. Kim Ji-Ha, *Sangmyeonghak II*, 164.

76. Ibid., 166.

77. Trinh T. Minh-ha, *Women, Native, Other: Writing Postcoloniality and Feminism* (Indianapolis: Indiana University Press, 1989), 67.

78. Ibid., 68.

79. Kim Ji-Ha, *Sangmyeong*, 346.

80. Spivak glosses the term, 'strategic essentialism,' as 'a strategic use of positivist essentialism in a scrupulously visible political interest. Gayatri Spivak, *In Other Worlds: Essays in Cultural Politics* (New York: Routledge, 1987), 205.

81. Gayatri Spivak, *Outside in the Teaching Machine* (New York: Routledge, 1993), 2.

82. Spivak coins the term, "strategic essentialism," which refers to a temporary kind of solidarity for the purpose of social action. For example, the attitude that women's groups have many different agendas makes it difficult for feminists to work for common causes. "Strategic essentialism" is about the need to accept temporarily an "essentialist" position in order to be able to act.

83. Ibid., 10.

84. Gilles Deleuze and Felix Guattari, *A Thousand Plateaus*, 275.

85. Kim Ji-Ha, *Sangmyeonghak II*, 16

86. Ibid., 165.

87. Jacques Lacan, *Écrits: A Selection*, trans. Bruce Fink (New York: W. W. Norton & Company, 1999), 188.

88. Luce Irigaray, *This Sex which is Not One*, trans. Catherine Porter (New York: Cornell University, 1985), 70.

89. Lucy Irigaray, *Speculum of the Other Woman*, trans. Gillian G. Gill (New York: Cornell University, 1985), 26.

90. Catherine Keller, *From a Broken Web: Separation, Sexism, and Self* (Boston: Beacon Press, 1986). 105.

91. Gilles Deleuze and Felix Guattari, *Anti-Oedipus: Capitalism and Schizopherenia*, trans. Robert Hurtley (Minneapolis: University of Minnesota, 1983), 59.

92. Ibid., 80.

93. Keller, *From a Broken Web*, 128.

94. Ibid., 122.

95. Elizabeth A. Johnson, *She Who Is: The Mystery of God in Feminist Theological Discourse* (New York: Crossroad, 1996), 161.

96. Luce Irigaray, *Marine Lover of Friedrich Nietzsche* (New York: Columbia University Press, 1991), 187.

97. Gavin D'Costa, *Sexing the Trinity: Gender, Culture, and the Divine* (London: SCM Press, 2000), 5.

98. For indicating G*d, Irigaray uses the lowercase "g."

99. Irigaray, *Marine Lover of Friedrich Nietzsche*, 138.

100. Ibid., 190.

101. Kim Ji-Ha, *Sangmyeong*, 346.

102. Wonhee Anne Joh, *Heart of the Cross: A Postcolonial Christology* (Louisville and London: Westminster John Knox Press, 2006), 27, 138.

103. Gilles Deleuze and Felix Guattari, *A Thousand Plateaus*, 10.

104. Gayatri C. Spivak, *A Critique of Postcolonial Reason*, 106.

Chapter III

Decolonizing Life: A Postcolonial Reading of *Salim*

1. Ahn Sang-Jin, *Asian Thought and Culture: Continuity and Transformation* (New York: Peter Lang, 2001), 61.

2. Korean Christianity has a two-hundred year history in Catholicism and a one-hundred year history in Protestantism. The Catholic Church mission history begins in 1784 when the first Catholic prayer-house established in Korea. Protestantism was introduced in Korea by Henry Gerhard Appenzeller, a Methodist missionary, in 1885.

3. Kim Ji-Ha, *Sangmyeong*, 13.

4. Ahn Sang-Jin, *Asian Thought and Culture*, 63.

    Han in *Donghak* means oneness and greatness, not suffering (*han*, 囧) though they are pronounced similarly.

5. Shin Il-Cheol, *Donghakgwa Jeongtongsasang* [*Donghak* and the Traditional Philosophies] (Seoul: Donghakhakbo, 2003), 10.

6. Yoon Seok-San, *Donghak Gyojo Su-Un Choi Jaewoo* [Su-Un: The Initiator of *Donghak*] (Seoul: Mosineon Saramdeul, 2004), 197.

7. *Cheondogyo Changgeonsa* [History of Cheondogyo Foundation], ed. Lee Don-Hwa (1933, 1969), 33.

8. Lee Ki-Baik, *A New History of Korea*, trans. Edgar W. Wagner (Cambridge: Harvard University Press, 1984), 254.

9. Era before the Japanese forcibly colonized Korea under Japanese rule for thirty-six years (1910-1945) which is usually described as 'a time of Japanese forced occupation [⬜⬜⬜⬜⬜].'

10. An English merchant ship appeared off the coast of Chungcheong province in 1832. In 1845, an English warship appeared in Korean waters and carried out a survey of the southern coast. In 1854, two armed Russian vessels appeared along the Hamgyeong coast and killed a number of Koreans. Ibid., 263.

11. Ibid., 285.

12. The *Donghak* Peasant Revolution was an anti-government, anti-*yangban* [aristocracy] and anti-foreign uprising in 1894 in Korea which was the catalyst for the first Sino-Japanese War. It was a religious and political movement directed at the *Joseon* dynasty with the intention of establishing social reform and expelling an attempt to expel foreigners. Many Koreans despised the Japanese and their foreign encroachments/influences over their land and the corrupt oppressive rule of the *Joseon* Dynasty. It would also be one of the series of events that would bring the *Joseon* dynasty to an end and to the establishment of Japanese rule over Korea (1910 - 1945).

13. Choi Jae-Woo (Su-Un), Kim Yong-Ok ed., *Donggyeongdaejeon 1* [Pletharchia] (Seoul: Tongnamoo, 2004), 8.

14. Ibid., 9.

15. Ibid., 287.

16. Ibid., 10.

17. Kim Ji-Ha. *Donghak Eiyaki.* [A Story of *Donghak*] (Seoul: Sol, 1994), 12.
18. Ibid., 11.
19. Homi K. Bhabha, *The Location of Culture*, 112.
20. Paul Beirne, *Su-Un and His World of Symbols: The Founder of Korea's First Indigenous Religion* (Surrey: Ashgate, 2009), 24
21. Ibid., 26.
22. Su-Un's notion of *hanul* [the divine] and *si-cheon-ju* [embodiment of the divine] are further discussed in chapter IV.
23. Susan Stanford Friedman, *Mapping: Feminism and the Cultural Geographies of Encounter* (Princeton: Princeton University Press, 1998), 87.
24. Ibid., 88.
25. Joh summarizes the three trajectories of hybridity according to Susan Stanford Friedman's *Mappings*. Ibid. 63-66. Wonhee Ann Joh, *Heart of the Cross: A Postcolonial Christianity* (Louisville: Westminster John Knox Press, 2006), 53.
26. Ibid.
27. Homi K. Bhabha, *The Location of Culture*, 86.
28. Joh, *Heart of the Cross*, 55.
29. Bhabha, *The Location of Culture*, 90.
30. Catherine Keller, "Eschatology, Ecology, and a Green Ecumenacy," *Reconstructing Christian Theology*, eds. Rebecca S. Chopp and Mark Lewis Taylor (Minneapolis: Fortress Press, 1994), 345.
31. In Confucian thought, filial piety [Chinese: 孝; pinyin: *xiào* in Chinese and *hyo* in Korean] is one of the virtues to be cultivated: a love and respect for one's parents and ancestors. The Confucian classic, *Xiao Jing* or Classic of *Xiào*, thought to be written around 470 B.C.E., has historically been the authoritative source of the Confucian tenet of *xiào* / "filial piety." The book, a conversation between Confucius and his student, *Zeng Shen* (Zengzi 曾子), focused on how to set up a moral society using the principle of *xiào*

/ "filial piety." Thus for more than two thousand years, it has been one of the basic texts to be examined in the Chinese Imperial Civil Service Exams.

32. This is the teaching by Hae-Weol. This verse illustrates well his notion of *gyeong* (敬, reverence) toward heaven, human, and matter. Pyo Youngsam, *Donghak II* [Eastern Learning II] (Seoul: Tongnamoo, 2005), 163.

33. Hae-Weol was born in 1827. Hae-Weol received Su-Un's leadership of *Donghak* in 1863 and was martyred in 1864. Cheongju is a city in the southern part of Korea which is one of the towns Hae-Weol in which Hae-Weol frequently preached.

34. Cha Ok-Soong, Lee Kyung-Sook, and Park Jae-Sun, *Hangook Sangmyeong Sasangeui Bburi* [The Root of Korean Philosophy of Life] (Seoul: Ewha Daehakkyo Choolpanboo, 2001], 90.

35. Kim Ji-Ha, *Donghak Eiyagi*, 19.

36. Lee Kyungsook, *Hankook Sangmyung Sasangeui Bburi*, 86.

37. Korean feminist theologians refer to Korean oppressed women as the *minjung* of *minjung*. There are two categories of oppressed women in Korea. In the first category are *minjung* women, those doubly oppressed as both *minjung* and as women, due to their political, economic, and social situations. In the other category are women *minjung,* those discriminated against under the power of male domination solely because they are women. Letty M. Russell and J. Shannon Clarkson ed., *Dictionary of Feminist Theologies* (Louisville: Westminster John Knox Press, 1996), 184.

38. Bill Ashcroft and Gareth Griffiths, eds., *Post-Colonial Studies: The Key Concepts* (London and New York: Routledge, 2000), 215.

39. Antonio Gramsci, *Selections from the Prison Notebooks*, trans. Quintin Hoare (London: Lawrence and Wishart, 1971), 52.

40. See Karl Marx, *The Communist Manifesto*, part I, Bourgeois and Proletarians.

Notes

41. Homi K. Bhabha, "Unpacking my library...again," in *The Postcolonial Question: Common Skies, Divided Horizons*, eds. Iain Chambers and Lidia Curti (New York: Routledge, 1996), 209.

42. Ibid., 210.

43. Bill Ashcroft, *Post-Colonial Studies*, 217.

44. Joh, *Heart of the Cross*, 12.

45. Veena Das, "Subaltern as Perspective," *Subaltern Studies*, vol. 6 (New Delhi: Oxford University Press, 1989), 313.

46. Bhabha, *The Location of Culture*, 193.

47. Ibid., 197.

48. Gayatri Chakravorty Spivak, " Can the Subaltern Speak?" in *Marxism and the Interpretation of Culture*, eds. Cary Nelson and Lawrence Grossberg (Urbana: University of Illinois Press, 1988), 278.

49. Leon Kock, "Interview With Gayatri Chakravorty Spivak: New Nation Writers Conference in South Africa," *A Review of International English Literature*, 23.3 (1992): 47.

50. Spivak, " Can the Subaltern Speak?," 288.

51. Ibid., 285.

52. Ibid., 287.

53. Ibid., 308.

54. *Minjung* theology considers *minjung* as the subject who lead and create history not simply victims who are objectified by the dominant group. In this sense, even though it could be awkward to use the subject of the subject in English, the term, subject, means the main body of the history or the historical agent in *minjung* theology.

55. Choi Hee-An, *Korean Women and God* (New York: Orbis Books, 2005), 38.

56. Kwok Pui-lan, *Postcolonial Imagination & Feminist Theology* (Louisville: Westminster John Knox Press, 2005), 57.

57. *Chapati* is unleavened flatbread in India. *Chapatis* are one of the most common forms in which wheat, the staple of northern south Asia, is consumed.

58. Flatbread entered the human diet around 6,000 B.C.E. Flatbreads have long been integral to Middle Eastern and Mediterranean cuisines. Other types of flatbread similar to *chapati* are *lahvosh* from the Mediterranean and *yufka* from Turkey. Spanish explorers discovered *tortilla* which is popular throughout many parts of the Spanish speaking world, especially Spain and Mexico, and the Jewish people also eat *metzo*. Italians cook *pizza* and the French eat *crêpes*. *Injera* is African (Ethiopian) crêpe-like sourdough flatbread usually made from *tef,* a hardy Ethiopian grain, can be easily replicated at home with all-purpose flour, yeast, and a nonstick skillet. China and Korea have more rice-based flat bread. Korean *boochimgae* is a type of flatbread which can be comparable to the French *crêpe* and the American pancake since it needs to be cooked on a greased frying pan.

59. Bhabha, *The Location of Culture*, 200.

60. Ibid., 204.

61. Ibid., 202.

62. Ibid., 205.

63. Gilles Deleuze, *Difference & Repetition*, trans. Paul Patton (New York: Columbia University Press, 1994), 1.

64. Bhabha, *The Location of Culture*, 207.

65. Bhabha, "In a Spirit of Calm Violence," in *After Colonialism: Imperial Histories and Postcolonial Displacements*, ed. Gyan Prakash (Princeton: Princeton University Press, 1995), 333.

66. Ibid., 208.

67. Alison M. Jaggar, "Globalizing Feminist Ethics," in *Decentering the Center: Philosophy for a Multicultural, Postcolonial, and Feminist World*, eds. Uma Narayan and Sandra Harding (Indianapolis: Indiana University Press, 2000), 7.

68. Lee Eun-Sun, *Postmodern Sidaeui Hankuk Yoesung Sinhak* [A Korean Feminist Theology in Postmodern Times] (Seoul: Bundo Chulpansa, 1997), 188.

69. Michel Foucault, *The History of Sexuality Vol. I: An Introduction*, trans. Robert Hurley (New York: Vintage Books, 1978), 94-95.

70. Ibid., 94.

71. Ibid.

72. bid.,145.

73. Bhabha, *The Location of Culture*, 14.

74. Joh, 54.

75. Ibid., 334.

76. Gayatri Chakravorty Spivak, "The New Historicism: Political Commitment and the Postmodern Critic" *in Post-Colonial Critics, Strategies, Dialogues*, ed. Sarah Harasym (London: Routledge, 1990), 158.

77. Kwok Pui-lan, "Unbinding Our Feet," in *Postcolonialism, Feminism and Religious Discourse,* Laura E. Donaldson and Kwok Pui-lan eds. (New York: Routledge, 2002), 68.

78. Spivak, *A Critique of Postcolonial Reason*, 308.

79. Gayatri Spivak, "Can the Subaltern Speak?," in *Marxism and the Interpretation of Culture*, 303.

80. Ibid., 302.

81. Ibid., 306.

82. Ibid., 309.

83. Ibid., 285.

84. Ibid., 305.

85. Ibid., 284.

86. Ibid., 274.

87. Gayatri Chakravorty Spivak, "The New Subaltern: A Silent Interview," 334.

88. Ibid., 334.

89. *Sati* is a funeral practice in the Hindu communities in which a widowed woman immolates herself on her husband's funeral pyre either voluntarily or by force.

90. Stephen D. Moore and Mayra Rivera eds., *Planetary Loves: Spivak, Postcoloniality, and Theology* (New York: Fordham University Press, 2011), 146.

91. Spivak, "Can the Subaltern Speak?," 287.

92. Ibid., 284.

93. Joh, *Heart of the Cross*, 109.

94. *Dharmasastra* is Hindu *Dharma* in two volumes. *Tat Tvam Asi* is the famous expression of the relationship between the individual and the absolute [*Brahman*] in the nondualistic Vedantic tradition in Hinduism. Uddalaka teaches his son, Shvetaketu, that in his deepest being he is, indeed, the immortal unchanging Atman. *Tat Tvam Asi* symbolizes the realization of the True Self [*Atman*] which is the Ultimate [*Brahman*] in all things. John M. Koller, *Asian Philosophies* 5th edition (Upper Saddle River: Pearson, 2002), 27.

95. Spivak, "Can the Subaltern Speak?," 299.

96. Sallie McFague, *The Body of God: An Ecological Theology* (Minneapolis: Fortress Press, 1993), 165.

97. Spivak, *A Critique of Postcolonial Reason*, 380.

98. Gayatri Chakravorty Spivak, *Death of a Discipline* (New York: Columbia University Press, 2003), 72.

99. Ibid., 73.

100. Spivak, *A Critique of Postcolonial Reason*, 383.

101. Spivak, *Death of a Discipline*, 95.

102. Stephen D. Moore and Mayra Rivera, *Planetary Loves*, 61.

103. Spivak, *Death of a Discipline*, 6.

Notes

104. Spivak, *A Critique of Postcolonial Reason,*, 383.

105. Stephen D. Moore and Mayra Rivera, *Planetary Loves*, 67.

106. Catherine Keller, "The Love of Postcolonialism," in *Postcolonial Theologies: Divinity and Empire*, eds. Catherine Keller, Michael Nausner, and Mayra Rivera (St. Louis: Chalice, 2004), 224.

107. Kim Ji-Ha, *"Teum," Jungsimeui Geuiroum* [Sorrow of the Ground] (Seoul: Sol, 1997).

108. Kim Ji-Ha, *Sangmyeonghak I*, 222.

109. Ibid., 224.

110. 無, *moo*, means a state or condition of nothingness. In order to avoid confusion with the Augustinian notion of nothingness which has no continuity with any past, I intentionally translate *moo* to mean non-being. I understand Kim Ji-Ha's 無 [non-being] as both pre- and post- state of being as *Daodejing* teaches, that is, being is continually becoming passing non-being which is a source of being.

111. Kim Ji-Ha, *Sangmyeonggwa Peoungwhaeui Gil*, 318.

112. Catherine Keller, "The Mystery of the Insoluble Evil," in *World without End*, ed. Joseph A. Bracken (Grand Rapids: William B. Eerdmans Publishing Company, 2005), 69.

113. Kim Ji-Ha, *Bab*, 87.

114. Ibid., 88.

115. Kim Ji-Ha, *Sangmyeonggwa Peoungwhaeui Gil*, 314.

116. Ibid., 315.

117. Ibid., 314.

118. Gilles Deleuze, *Difference & Repetition*, trans. Paul Patton (New York: Columbia University Press, 1994), 299.

119. *Kim Ji-Ha, Sangmyeonggwa Peoungwhaeui Gil*, 315.

120. Tim Clark, "A Whiteheadian Chaosmos?: Process Philosophy from a Deleuzian Perspective," in *Process and Difference: Between Cosmological and Poststructuralist Postmodernisms*, edited by

Catherine Keller and Anne Daniel (Albany: State University of New York Press, 2002), 192.

121. Gilles Deleuze, *The Fold: Leibniz and the Baroque,* trans. Tom Conley (Minneapolis: The University of Minnesota Press, 1993), 81.

122. Ibid., 137.

123. Deleuze, *Difference & Repetition*, 123.

124. Gilles Deleuze and Felix Guattari, *What is Philosophy?,* trans. Hugh Tomlinson and Graham Burchell (New York: Columbia University Press, 1994), 205.

125. Ibid., 121.

126. Ibid., 281.

127. Gilles Deleuze, *Difference & Repetition*, 229.

128. Gilles Deleuze and Felix Guattari, *What is Philosophy?*, 229.

129. Catherine Keller, *Face of the Deep: A Theology of Becoming* (New York: Routledge, 2003), xviii.

130. Jeffrey A. Bell, *Philosophy at the Edge of Chaos: Gilles Deleuze and the Philosophy of Difference* (Toronto: University of Toronto Press, 2006), 36.

131. According to Catherine Keller, Christianity was established as the unquestionable truth that everything is created not from some formless and bottomless something but from nothing: an omnipotent G*d could have created the world *ex nihilo*. Catherine Keller, *Face of the Deep*, xvi.

132. Ibid., i.

133. Ibid., xv.

134. Ibid., xvi.

135. Deleuze and Guattari, *What is Philosophy?*, 205.

136. Kim Ji-Ha, *Sangmyeonggwa Pyeongwhaeui Gil*, 317.

137. Roland Faber, *God as Poet of the World: Exploring Process Theologies* (Louisville: Westminster John Knox Press, 2004), 70.

138. Ibid., 71.

139. Trinh Minh-ha writes, "When stillness culminates, there is movement. The living potential returns afresh, the cycles of the moon go on regularly, again and again the light will wane. In the process of infinite beginnings, even immortality is mortal. Politics waxes and wanes like a lunar eclipse, naming critically is to dive headlong into *the abyss of un-naming.*" Trinh T. Minh-ha, *When the Moon Waxes Red: Representation, Gender, and Cultural Politics* (New York: Routledge, 1991), 1-2.

140. Keller, *Face of the Deep*, 13.

141. Ibid., 14.

142. Bhabha, Homi K. *The Location of Culture*, 114.

143. Ibid., 36.

144. Ibid., 7.

145. Keller, *Face of the Deep*, 103.

146. Ibid., 13.

147. Ibid., 14.

148. Bhabha, *The Location of Culture*, 37.

149. Ibid., 38.

150. Bill Ashcroft, Gareth Griffiths, and Helen Tiffin, eds. *Post-Colonial Studies: The Key Concepts* (New York: Routledge, 2000), 119.

151. Homi K. Bhabha ed. *Nation and Narration* (New York: Routledge, 1990), 211.

152. Ibid., 212.

153. Ibid., 219.

154. Ashcroft, Griffiths, and Tiffin, *Post-Colonial Studies*, 119.

155. Roland Faber, *God as Poet of the World*, 71.

156. Ibid., 72.

157. Deleuze and Guattari use the term, rhizome, to describe a theory that allows for multiple and nonhierarchical entry and exit points in its interpretation in *A Thousand Plateaus*. Through rhizome, Deleuze and Guattari oppose the binary structure of knowledge. Deleuze and Guattari present "rhizome" as a nomadic and fluid movement that rejects a pivotal center. In their notion of rhizome, they envision structure-free movements of becoming that spread towards the multiple exteriors and become unpredictably permutated by coming into contact with whatever lies in their exterior. See Gilles Deleuze and Felix Guattari, *A Thousand Plateaus: Capitalism and Schizophrenia*, (Minneapolis: University of Minnesota, 1987).

158. Roland Faber, "Programmatic Dysfunction in the *Chaosmos*," in *Deleuze, Whitehead, Bergson: Rhizomatic Connections*, ed. Keith Robinson (New York: Palgrave Macmillan, 2009), 206.

Chapter IV
A Process Ecotheological Reading of *Salim*

1. Pantheism (Greek: πάν (*'pan'*) = all and θεός (*'theos'*) = G*d; it literally means "G*d is All" and "All is G*d") is the view that everything is part of an all-encompassing immanent abstract G*d; or that the Universe, or nature, and G*d are equivalent. More detailed definitions tend to emphasize the idea that natural law, existence, and the Universe (the sum total of all that is, was, and shall be) is represented in the theological principle of an abstract 'G*d' rather than a personal, creative deity or deities of any kind. "Pantheism, historically considered G*d with the world; G*d and the world are one." Santiago Sia, *God in Process Thought* (Dordrecht: Martinus Nijhoff Publishers, 1985), 13.

2. Paul Beirne, *Su-Un and His World of Symbols: The Founder of Korea's First Indigenous Religion* (Surrey: Ashgate, 2009), 39.

3. Exodus 3, Isaiah 6, Hosea 4, etc.

Notes

4. John B. Duncan, "The Emergence of the Tonghak Religion," Peter H. Lee ed., *The Sourcebook of Korean Civilization, vol. 2* (New York: Columbia University Press, 1996) 314.

5. Pyo Young-Sam, *Donghak I: Su-Un eui Salmkwa Sangkak* [Su-Un's Life and Thought] (Seoul: Tongnamoo, 2004), 112.

6. Panentheism (from Greek πάν (pân) "all"; εν (en) "in"; and θεός (theós) "G*d"; "all-in-G*d") is a belief system which posits that G*d exists and interpenetrates every part of nature, and timelessly extends beyond as well. Panentheism is distinguished from pantheism, which holds that G*d is synonymous with the material. Santiago Sia summarizes Hartshorne's panentheism as follows: Panentheism holds that G*d includes the world. But it sets itself apart from pantheism in that it does not maintain that G*d and the world are identical. Hartshorne explains that G*d is a whole whose whole-properties are distinct from the properties of the constituents. While this is true of every whole, it is more so of G*d as the supreme whole. The part is distinguishable from the whole although within it. The power of the parts is something suffered by the whole, not enacted by it. The whole has properties too which are not shared by the parts. Similarly, G*d *as whole* possesses attributes which are not shared by his creatures. We perpetually create content not only in ourselves but also in G*d. And this gives significance to our presence in this world. Santiago Sia, *God in Process Thought*, 85-86.

7. Kim Kyung-Jae and Kim Sang-Il ed. *Gwajeong Cheolhakgwa Gewajong Shinhak* [Process Philosophy and Process Theology] (Seoul: Heemangsa, 1988), 117.

8. Ibid., 115.

9. Ibid., 117.

10. Ibid., 114.

11. Ibid., 115.

12. 侍 (*si*) can be interpreted in English as inviting, embracing, and embodying.

13. Pyo Young-Sam, *Donghak I*, 156. Su-Un's notion of *Hanul* in this phrase is similar to Whitehead's notion of G*d as the "universal agency."

Within the concrete process, G*d's grace is manifested everywhere and in everyone (*Process and Reality*, 31, 93, 111).

14. Kim Kyung-Jae, *Gwajeong Cheolhakgwa Gewajong Shinhak*, 5.
15. *Joseon* was the last kingdom in Korea which was known as *Yi* Dynasty before Japanese colonial rule (1910-1945).
16. Cha Ok-Soong, *Hangook Sangmyeong Sasangeui Bburi* , 86.
17. Chung Ki-Yeol, *The Donghak Concept of God/Heaven: Religion and Social Transformation* (New York: Peter Lang, 2007), 57.
18. Yoon Seok-San, *Donghak Gyojo Choi Jae-Woo* [The Initiator of Donghak, Choi Jae-Woo] (Seoul: Mosineunsaramdeul, 2004), 367.
19. Ibid., 199.
20. *Yongdamka* is Su-Un's poem of *Yongdam* [龍㴭, Dragon Pond] which is located in Gyeongju where he was born, raised, and enlightened. He praised the beauty of the place and his joy of enlightenment in the poem.
21. Ibid., 113.
22. Ibid., 114.
23. Kim Ji-Ha. *Donghak Eiyagi*, 16.
24. Ibid., 19.
25. Whitehead, *Process and Reality*, 22.
26. Ibid., 8.
27. Ibid., 23.
28. Monica A. Coleman, "An Exchange of Gifts: Process and Womanist Theologies," *Handbook of Process Theology*, eds. Jay McDaniel and Donna Bowman (Danvers: Chalice Press, 1989), 161.
29. Whitehead, *Process and Reality*, 344.
30. Ibid., 345.
31. Donald W. Sherburne ed., *A Key to Whitehead's Process and Reality* (Chicago: The University of Chicago Press, 1966), 181.

32. Cha Ok-Soong and Lee Kyungsook, *Hangook Sangmyeong Sasangeui Bburi*, 90.

33. Kim Sang-Il, *Su-Un gwa Whitehead: Donghak Jumoon 21gaeuidaehan Gwaeoungshinhakjuk Pooli* [Su-Un and Whitehead: A Process Rendition of the Twenty-One Incantations of *Donghak*] (Seoul: Jisiksanupsa, 2004), 33.

34. Whitehead, *Process and Reality*, 21.

35. Ibid.

36. Pyo Young-Sam, *Donghak I*, 117.

37. Roland Faber, *God as Poet of the World: Exploring Process Theologies*, 24.

38. Ibid., 88.

39. Ibid., 225.

40. David Ray Griffin, "Religious Pluralism," in *Handbook of Process Theology*, eds. Jay McDaniel and Donna Bowman (St. Louis: Chalice Press, 1989), 55.

41. Kim Kyung-Jae and Kim Sang-Il, *Su-Un gwa Whitehead*, 105.

42. Jay McDaniel, "A Process Approach to Ecology," in *Handbook of Process Theology*, eds. Jay McDaniel and Donna Bowman (St. Louis: Chalice Press, 2006), 232.

43. Ibid., 236.

44. John B. Cobb, Jr. *A Christian Natural Theology: Based on the Thought of Alfred North Whitehead* 2nd edition (Louisville: Westminster John Knox Press, 2007), 120.

45. John B. Cobb, Jr. and David Ray Griffin, *Process Theology: An Introductory Exposition* (Philadelphia: Westminster Press, 1976), 98.

46. Ibid., 99.

47. As I mentioned above, *heoryeong* [the empty Spirit, 虛靈] *changchang* [creating and creating, 蒼蒼] means the endless becoming and creating, through an endless openness.

48. Ibid., 100.

49. Park Jong-Cheon, *Dankunshinwhaeui Sansangiinyumedaehan Shinhakjeok Haeseok: Sangsangeui Shinhak* [Theological Interpretation on the Symbiotic Ideology of the *Dan-Gun* Myth: Theology of Symbiosis] (Seoul: Hanguk Theological Institute, 1991), 268.

50. Kim Ji-Ha, *Bab*, 14.

51. The thirteen words of incantation which Su-Un taught are 侍天主 造化定 永世不忘萬事知 (*shi-cheon-joo-jo-wha-jeong-young-sae-bul-mang-man-sa-ji*). An English translation reads, "if you embrace *hanul*, everything will be transformatively creating with peace and harmony. If you remember these words, you will be knowing everything."

52. John B. Cobb, Jr. and David Ray Griffin, *Process Theology*, 106.

53. Charles Birch and John B. Cobb, Jr., *The Liberation of Life* (Denton: Cambridge University Press, 1990), 200.

54. Ibid., 195.

55. Lee Hyo-Dong, a *Donghak* Scholar and a comparative theologian, comments that this "paradox" is an intrinsic feature of panentheism with a ground-contingency asymmetry. If G*d and the world are purely interdependent, G*d becomes part of the world that encompasses the G*d-world polarity.

56. Ibid., 197.

57. Ibid., 198.

58. Charles Birch and John B. Cobb, Jr., *The Liberation of Life*, 198.

59. Alfred North Whitehead, *The Function of Reason* (Princeton: Princeton University Press, 1929), 5.

60. Jay McDaniel, *Gandhi's Hope: Learning from Other Religions as a Path to Peace* (New York: Orbis Books, 1995), 63.

61. McDaniel, *Handbook of Process Theology*, 234.

62. McDaniel, *Gandhi's Hope*, 13.

63. Roland Faber, *God as Poet of the World: Exploring Process Theologies*, 25.

64. "God does not create the world, he saves it: he is the poet of the world, with tender patience leading it by his vision of truth, beauty, and goodness." Alfred North Whitehead and David Griffin, eds. *Process and Reality*. (New York: The Free Press, 1978), 346.

65. Kim Ji-Ha's poems are classified into two periods, the *minjung*-period and the eco-period. His poem, *Reverence* [恭敬], was written in the second period (eco-period), and belongs to his corpus of eco-poems. Writing as a *minjung* poet in his first period (1970s and early 1980s), his poems belongs in his corpus of *minjung* poems which demonstrate his strong intention and commitment to fight against the Korean dictatorship with hope for the liberation of the *minjung* while his poems written during the second period focus on the ecological hope of transformation to eco-centered life issues (symbiotic life of all, not only human beings). The poem written, *Reverence*, was written from his deep ecological concern for the symbiotic life of the planet and influenced by Hae-Weol's notion of reverence.

66. *Si-Cheon-ju* means embracing the divine.

67. Pyo Young-Sam, *Donghak I*, 120.

68. Kim Ji-Ha, *Sangmyeonghak I*, 86.

69. Ibid., 87.

70. According to Kant's view in *Critique of Pure Reason*, humans can make sense out of phenomena in these various ways, but can never directly know the "things-in-themselves" which is the *noumena*. According to Kant, our minds may attempt to correlate it in useful ways, perhaps even closely accurate ways, with the structure and order of the various aspects of the universe, but cannot know these "things-in-themselves." For Kant, we are therefore never able to fully know the "thing-in-itself [*Ding an sich*]."

71. "...though we cannot know these objects as things in themselves, we must yet be in a position at least to think of them as things in themselves; otherwise we should find ourselves in the absurd conclusion that there can be appearance without anything that appears." Immanuel Kant, *Critique of Pure Reason,* trans. Paul Guyer and Allen W. Wood (Cambridge: Cambridge University Press, 1999), xxvi-xxvii.

72. I would refer to it as *hanul*.
73. Kim Ji-Ha, *Sangmyeonghak I*, 88.
74. Alfred North Whitehead, *The Function of Reason*, 3.
75. I borrow McDaniel's words from his book, *Of God and Pelicans: A Theology of Reverence for Life*. McDaniel names this beautiful harmony of harmonies of the universe as "cosmological hybridization" of G*d's indwelling.
76. McDaniel, *Gandhi's Hope*, 38.
77. "*Hanul* is weaving cloth." *Cheon-ju-jik-po-seol* was preached in 1885 by Hae-Weol.
78. Lee Hyeon-Hui, *Hae-Weol Choi Si-Hyeong eui Sasang gwa Gapjin Gaehyeokundong* [Hae-Weol's Thought and *Gapjin* Reformation Movement] (Seoul: Mosineunsaramdeul, 2003), 331.
79. Choi Dong-Hui, *Saeroseunun Donghak*, 133.
80. McDaniel, *Gandhi's Hope*, 70.
81. McDaniel, *Earth, Sky, Gods & Mortals*, 170.
82. Ibid., 171.
83. Deleuze and Guattari, *A Thousand Plateaus*, 275.
84. Ibid., 280.
85. Ibid.
86. Spivak, *A Critique of Postcolonial Reason*, 426.
87. Ibid., 427.
88. McDaniel, *Earth, Sky, Gods & Mortals*, 170.
89. Pyo Young-Sam, *Donghak II*, 299.
90. McDaniel, *Earth, Sky, Gods & Mortals*, 173.
91. McDaniel, *Gandhi's Hope*, 83.
92. McDaniel, *Earth, Sky, Gods & Mortals*, 104.
93. Kim Hyeog-Ki. *Hucheon Gaebyeok Sasang Yeongu* [A Study of New Creation] (Seoul: Hanul Academy, 2004), 95.

94. Jay B. McDaniel, *Of God and Pelicans: A Theology of Reverence for Life* (Eugene: Wipf and Stock Publishers, 1999), 112.

95. Keller, *Face of the Deep*, 223.

96. McDaniel, *Of God and Pelicans*, 126.

97. Ibid., 106.

98. Ibid., 109.

99. McDaniel, *Earth, Sky, Gods & Mortals*, 104.

100. Jay B. McDaniel, *With Roots and Wings: Christianity in an Age of Ecology and Dialogue* (New York: Orbis Books, 1995), 97.

101. Ibid., 97.

102. Ibid., 98.

103. Pyo Youngsam, *Donghak 1*, 130.

104. Deleuze and Guattari, *A Thousand Plateaus*, 11.

105. Ibid., 254.

106. Pyo Youngsam, *Donghak 1*, 121.

107. This poem, *Bab* [Rice], was written in 1975 by Kim Ji-Ha when he was in prison for his involvement with the *Minjung* movement.

108. Hae-Weol's preaching in 1890 in *Saeroeseuneun Donghak* [Rewriting *Donghak*: Thoughts and Texts], Choi Dong-Hee and Lee Won-Won (Seoul: Jipmoondang, 2003), 132.

109. Hae-Weol's preaching in 1898 in *Cheondogyoseo* [Books of *Donghak*] (Seoul: Goryeo University), 1962.

110. Pyo Youngsam, *Donghak II*, 134

111. Kim Ji-Ha, *Bab*, 81.

112. For Jay McDaniel, hybridity is like a loaf of multigrain bread which contains all different grains and seeds. When we eat the bread, we taste and feel the difference of each grain and it is hybridized in us, finally the hybridity of the bread becomes a part of us as hybridity of hybridities. [Comment of Jay McDaniel made at Drew University, December, 2009]

113. In chapter III, I mentioned *bab* as hybridity briefly by analyzing Homi Bhabha's *chapati* tales. Through the sharing of the recipes, the subaltern share and transmit their stories. Therefore, the history of the subaltern finds its agency as subaltern consciousness. In doing so, all of the different flatbreads represent the hybridity of hybridities.

114. Whitehead, *Process and Reality*, 105.

115. Ibid., 104.

116. Ibid., 107.

117. Ibid., 339.

118. Kim Ji-Ha, *Teum* [Interstitial Space] (Seoul: Sol, 1995), 189.

119. Ibid., 190.

120. Ibid., 191.

121. Jay B. McDaniel, *Earth, Sky, Gods & Mortals*, 66.

122. Alfred North Whitehead, *Process and Reality*, 167.

123. Ibid.,106.

124. Ibid., 105.

125. Jay B. McDaniel, *Earth, Sky, Gods & Mortals*, 88.

126. Kim Ji-Ha, *Bab*, 55.

127. Kim Ji-Ha, *Sangmyeonggwa Pyeongwhaeui Gil*, 83.

128. Ro Young-Chan, "Ancestor Worship: From the Perspective of Korean Tradition," in *Ancestor Worship and Christianity in Korea*, ed. Jung Y. Lee (Lewiston: The Edwin Mellen Press, 1988), 12.

129. Andrew Song-Min Paek, "Korean Ancestor Worship," *East Wind: Taoist and Cosmological Implications of Christian Theology*, ed. Charles Courtney (Lanham: University Press of America, 1997), 170.

130. Kim Ji-Ha, *Donghak Eiyagi*, 253.

131. Paek, "Korean Ancestor Worship," 172.

132. Hae-Weol's preaching in chapter 9, in Hong Gi-Seong, "Gaebyeok gwa *Donghak*" [Re-creation and *Donghak*] (Chungju: Chungbook University Minsok Yeonguwhei, 2001), 141.

133. Ibid., 142.

134. Kim Ji-Ha, *Bab*, 57.

135. Ibid., 58.

136. Lee Hyo-Dong comments that, "It could be the beginning of a new relationship. However, the *hyang-ah-seol-wi* means simply placing *bab* toward the male descendants who are participants of *jaesa*. Then, there should be another step, which is to let the women in the kitchen come into the room before the altar." Lee's comment is very crucial to point out a very important and necessary step for a feminist view in terms of Hae-Weol's notion of *hyang-ah-seol-wi* which other *Donghak* scholars never have mentioned. Of course the literal meaning of *hyang-ah-seol-wi* is only switching the position of *bab*. There is also no evidence that Hae-Weol blocked women as *hanul* for joining in the *bab* table. Nonetheless, Hae-Weol referred to women as *hanul* by which the invitation of Hae-Weol's *bab* table must be open to everybody and probably so.

137. Ibid., 54.

138. Ibid., 55.

139. Chung Hyun Kyung quotes this poem from "Jami Bi – With Love," in *O'Grady*, 11. Chung Hyun Kyung, *Struggle to be the Sun Again: Introducing Asian Women's Theology* (New York: Orbis Books, 1990), 72.

140. Park, Jae-Sun, *Yaesoo Undong gwa Babsang Gongdongche* [Jesus' Movement and the Community of *Rice*] (Seoul: Cheonji, 1988), 240.

141. Ibid., 43.

142. Ibid., 49.

143. Kim Ji-Ha, *Sangmyeong*, 145.

144. Ibid.,144.

145. Jay McDaniel offered his insight on hybridity for my *salim* project in relation to *bab*.

146. Whitehead, *Process and Reality*, 107.

147. Ibid., 21.

Chapter V

Salim for All: Toward a Postcolonial Ecofeminist Theology

1. Lee Hyo-Dong comments that harmony and balance are also included in *jo-hwa-jeong* [造化定] in its colloquial meaning though the usual translation for 造化定 is "Creative Transformation." In the previous chapter, I mentioned that *salim* can be understood as creative transformation. According to Lee's comments, *jo-hwa* can be understood to mean "wondrous becoming" which *jeong* implies harmony which ultimately brings "peace." His translation of *jo-hwa* as "wondrous becoming" is crucial for the process reading of Su-Un. I can then understand *jo-hwa-jeong* [造化定] in relation to *salim* as *shalom*, creative transformation with peace.

2. McDaniel, *Gandhi's Hope*, 8.

3. Ibid., 8.

4. http://www.jesusjazzbuddhism.org/between-two-strings.html

5. Kim Ji-Ha, *Sangmyeonglon II*, 193.

6. Ibid., 196.

7. McDaniel, *Gandhi's Hope*, 64.

8. Ibid., 78.

9. Ibid., 79.

10. McDaniel, *Earth, Sky, Gods & Mortals*, 18.

11. The Korean term "*an-nyeong* (안녕)" is used to greet a person, saying hello and good bye, meaning peace and well-being.
12. Catherine Keller, "Talk about the weather," in *Ecofeminism and the Sacred*, ed. Carol J. Adams (New York: Continuum, 1993), 43.
13. McDaniel, *Gandhi's Hope*, 81.
14. Bhabha, *The Location of Culture*, 219.
15. Ibid., 219.
16. Alfred North Whitehead, *Adventures f Ideas* (New York: The Macmillan Company, 1933), 367.
17. Whitehead, *Process and Reality*, 340.
18. Whitehead, *Adventures f Ideas*, 368.
19. Ibid., 368.
20. Ibid., 369.
21. "For we know that the whole creation has been groaning together in the pains of childbirth until now. And not only the creation, but we ourselves, who have the firstfruits of the Spirit, groan inwardly as we wait eagerly for adoption as sons, the redemption of our bodies. For in this hope we were saved. Now *hope that is seen is not hope.* For who hopes for what he sees? But if *we hope for what we do not see*, we wait for it with patience." (Romans 8:22-25)
22. Ibid., 381.
23. Ibid., 368.
24. Kim Ji-Ha believes that by practicing doing non-doing through a specific way of life, we can change the contemporary *jugim* [violence] culture to a *salim* [enlivening] culture which he refers to as *ecocracy*.
25. Ibid., 65.
26. Ibid., 66.
27. I introduced this project briefly in the beginning of chapter II.
28. *Yeon-hap* News, December 29th.

29. Along the riverside of the Nak-dong River, about 120 apple trees which are 40-50 years old (diameter 30-40cm) were cut and the beautiful white sand was replaced with dirt. In addition, the water of the river has been contaminated by metallic and oxide, is no longer drinkable (reported by *Oh My News* March 3rd, 2010).

30. Jay McDaniel, "A Process Approach to Ecology," in *Handbook of Process Theology*, eds. Jay McDaniel and Donna Bowman (Danvers: Chalicpress, 2006), 229.

31. The Grand Canal Project is one of the presidential manifestos as "a *salim* campaign for the Korean economy." His so-called *salim* campaign is recognized as a "market-friendly" campaign rather than an eco-friendly campaign among the Korean ecological activists. (*Saesangsaneun Yiyagi* [Stories of Living], January 2010)

32. Gayatri Spivak, *A Critique of Postcolonial Reason*, 380.

33. Ibid., 381.

34. Stephen D. Moore, *Empire and Apocalypse: Postcolonialism and the New Testament* (Sheffield: Sheffield Phoenix Press, 2006), 98.

35. Edward W. Said, *Culture and Imperialism* (New York: Vintage Books, 1993), 20.

36. McDaniel, *Earth, Sky, Gods & Mortals*, 19.

37. http://www.jesusjazzbuddhism.org/the-mind-of-jazz.html

38. Kim Ji-Ha, *Sangmyeonggwa Jachi*, 403.

39. A. David Moody, *Thomas Stearns Eliot* (New York: Cambridge University Press, 1994), 332.

40. Kim Hyeong-Gi, *Hucheon Gaebyeok Sasang Yeongu* [A Study of New Creation] (Seoul: Hanul Academy, 2004), 160.

41. Shin Ill-Cheol, *Donghak Sasangeui Eiihae* [Understanding *Donghak* Thought] (Seoul: Sahweibipyeongsa, 1995), 21.

42. This event was known as *Gao-o-gyeong-jang* [甲午更張] at the time. Later historians named the event, *Gab-o-gae-hyeok* [甲午改革]. *Gyeong-jang* [更張] means "to change." Both refer to a modern reformation of

Korea by the Korean government in the year of *Gab-o* [a year of horse] (1894).

43. Oh Young-Seop, *Hanguk Geunhyeondaisareul Sunoeun Inmooldeul 1* [Remarkable People in Korean Modern History I] (Seoul: Kyeongin Moonwhasa, 2007), 316.

44. Bill Ashcroft and Gareth Griffiths, *Post-Colonial Studies: The Key Concepts* (London and New York: Routledge, 2000), 34.

45. Gayatri Spivak, "More on Power/Knowledge," in *The Spivak Reader: Selected Works of Gayatri Spivak*, eds. Donna Landry and Gerald Maclean (London and New York: Routledge, 1996), 143.

46. Gayatri Spivak, "Identity and Alterity: An Interview" (with Nikos Papastergiadis) *Arena* (1997): 70.

47. Stephen D. Moore, *Empire and Apocalypse: Postcolonialism and the New Testament*, 106.

48. Ibid., 106.

49. Shin Ill-Cheol, *Donghak Sasangeui Eiihae*, 21.

50. "*Cha-cha-cha-cha*" is an adverb in Korean which means a gradual change through time.

51. *Gyohoonga*, 敎訓歌, "A Song for Teaching," is included in *Yondamyusa* (1860), one of the famous writings by Su-Un. *Saerosseuneun Donghak* [Rewriting *Donghak*], ed. Choi Dong-Hui (Seoul: Jjbmoondang, 2003) 349.

52. McDaniel, *Of God and Pelicans*, 33.

53. *Joseon* is the name of Korea during the period of the *Yi* Dynasty (1392–1910).

54. Shin Il-Cheol, *Donghak Sasangeui Ieehae*, 92.

55. Ibid., 93.

56. 'Convolution' is a mathematical term which indicates the integrity of all the values and functions of a group as a set. I use this word to describe how entities evolve together as a macro-cosmic body through all the tiny movements of the microcosm. By working together (synergy), all

different entities cooperate with one another and create a co-relational outcome.

57. Catherine Keller, "Talk about weather," 36.

58. Ibid., 37.

59. Catherine Keller, "Eschatology, Ecology, and a Green Ecumenacy," in *Reconstructing Christian Theology*, ed. Rebecca S. Chopp and Mark Lewis Taylor (Minneapolis: Fortress Press, 1994), 328.

60. The term, *creatio continua*, refers to G*d's continuing creative activity throughout the history of the universe.

61. Ibid., 339.

62. Ibid., 341.

63. Stephen D. Moore, *Empire and Apocalypse*, 37.

64. Ibid., 38.

65. Ibid., 99.

66. Catherine Keller, *Apocalypse Now and Then: A Feminist Guide to the End of the World* (Boston: Beacon Press, 1996), 62.

67. Ibid., 63.

68. Roland Faber and Andrea M. Stephenson, eds., *Secrets of Becoming: Negotiating Whitehead, Deleuze, and Butler* (New York: Fordham University Press, 2011), 4.

69. Rosemary Radford Ruether, *Sexism and Godtalk: Toward A Feminist Theology* (Boston: Beacon Press, 1983), 254.

70. Catherine Keller writes 'abandoning home' in "Eschatology, Ecology, and a Green Ecumenacy," 332: "Apocalypse means homelessness, abandoning out home."

71. Ibid., 342.

72. John B. Cobb Jr., *Is It Too Late?: A Theology of Ecology* (Denton: Environmental Ethics Books, 1995), 82.

73. Through this passage I read that Su-Un strongly believes that spring (a new world) will and should come. This is his hope, faith and volition of

life. It is not mere passivity yet, it demonstrates the conviction of nature's way to reflect change and endurance. In addition, Su-Un's analogy of "sunshine" is like Whitehead's "color "of nature in terms of eternality of life when he interprets Shelley's poem, *The Cloud*, "A color is eternal. It haunts time like a spirit. It comes and it goes. But where it comes, it is the same color. It neither survives nor does it live. It appears when it is wanted." Alfred North Whitehead, *Science and the Modern World* (New York: The Free Press, 1953), 87. Therefore, what Su-Un suggests here is "hope" for a new world which will and should come like the color of nature and sunshine.

74. Choi Dong-Hui and Lee Kyeong-Won, eds. *Saeroseuneun Donghak* [Rewriting *Donghak*] (Seoul: Jibmoondang, 2003), 312.

www.ingramcontent.com/pod-product-compliance
Lightning Source LLC
Chambersburg PA
CBHW020331240426

43665CB00043B/371